Family Business

Family businesses are the most common business form in the world, ranging from the millions of small local businesses to giants such as Walmart. This book showcases the crucial contribution that family businesses make to the world economy and informs students of the existing and potential research in this area.

Drawing upon global academic research and case studies, theories of family businesses are explained and prevailing myths and assumptions are tested. Features including exercises linked to case studies develop skills in applying theories in practice.

This concise textbook is essential reading for students of family business and useful additional reading for those interested in entrepreneurship more broadly.

Carole Howorth is Professor of Family Business and Entrepreneurship at the University of York, UK.

Nick Robinson is a writer and editor with over 30 years' experience as an entrepreneur, including founding and running family and non-family businesses.

Routledge Masters in Entrepreneurship
Edited by Janine Swail and Robert Wapshott

The **Routledge Masters in Entrepreneurship** series offers postgraduate students specialist but accessible textbooks on a range of entrepreneurship topics. Collectively, these texts form a significant resource base for those studying entrepreneurship, whether as part of an entrepreneurship-related programme of study, or as a new, non-cognate area for students in disciplines such as science and engineering, helping them to gain an in-depth understanding of contemporary entrepreneurial concepts.

The volumes in this series are authored by leading specialists in their field, and although they are discrete texts in their treatment of individual topics, all are united by a common structure and pedagogical approach. Key features of each volume include:

- a critical approach to combining theory with practice, which educates its reader rather than solely teaching a set of skills
- clear learning objectives for each chapter
- the use of figures, tables and boxes to highlight key ideas, concepts and skills
- an annotated bibliography, guiding students in their further reading, and
- discussion questions for each chapter to aid learning and put key concepts into practice.

Resourcing the Start-Up Business
Creating Dynamic Entrepreneurial Learning Capabilities
Oswald Jones, Allan Macpherson and Dilani Jayawarna

Entrepreneurship, Small Business and Public Policy
Evolution and Revolution
Robert J. Bennett

Finance for Small and Entrepreneurial Businesses
Richard Roberts

Managing Human Resources in Small and Medium-Sized Enterprises
Entrepreneurship and the Employment Relationship
Robert Wapshott and Oliver Mallett

Building an Entrepreneurial Organisation
Simon Mosey, Hannah Noke and Paul Kirkham

Family Business
Carole Howorth and Nick Robinson

Family Business

Carole Howorth and Nick Robinson

LONDON AND NEW YORK

First published 2021
by Routledge
2 Park Square, Milton Park, Abingdon, Oxon OX14 4RN

and by Routledge
52 Vanderbilt Avenue, New York, NY 10017

Routledge is an imprint of the Taylor & Francis Group, an informa business

© 2021 Carole Howorth and Nick Robinson

The right of Carole Howorth and Nick Robinson to be identified as authors of this work has been asserted by them in accordance with sections 77 and 78 of the Copyright, Designs and Patents Act 1988.

All rights reserved. No part of this book may be reprinted or reproduced or utilised in any form or by any electronic, mechanical, or other means, now known or hereafter invented, including photocopying and recording, or in any information storage or retrieval system, without permission in writing from the publishers.

Trademark notice: Product or corporate names may be trademarks or registered trademarks, and are used only for identification and explanation without intent to infringe.

British Library Cataloguing-in-Publication Data
A catalogue record for this book is available from the British Library

Library of Congress Cataloging-in-Publication Data
Names: Howorth, Carole, author. | Robinson, Nick (Editor), author.
Title: Family business / Carole Howorth and Nick Robinson.
Description: Abingdon, Oxon ; New York, NY : Routledge, 2020. | Series: Routledge masters in entrepreneurship | Includes bibliographical references and index.
Identifiers: LCCN 2020009751 (print) | LCCN 2020009752 (ebook) | ISBN 9781138217461 (hardback) | ISBN 9781138217478 (paperback) | ISBN 9781315440323 (ebook)
Subjects: LCSH: Family-owned business enterprises.
Classification: LCC HD62.25 .H688 2020 (print) | LCC HD62.25 (ebook) | DDC 338.7–dc23
LC record available at https://lccn.loc.gov/2020009751
LC ebook record available at https://lccn.loc.gov/2020009752

ISBN: 978-1-138-21746-1 (hbk)
ISBN: 978-1-138-21747-8 (pbk)
ISBN: 978-1-315-44032-3 (ebk)

Typeset in Bembo
by Swales & Willis, Exeter, Devon, UK

Contents

List of figures x
List of boxes xi

1 What's so special about family business? 1
Learning objectives 2
A day in the life: family business in Anytown 2
Exemplifying family business issues 4
Why study family businesses? 8
Structure of the book 9
Key learning points 10
Summary 10
Discussion questions 11

2 Nothing so practical as a good theory 12
Learning objectives 12
Families and businesses 12
Three-Circle Model 14
Three-Dimensional Development Model 18
Analysing the family: genograms 20
Analysing ownership 23
Analysing the business 25
Key learning point 26
Summary 26
Discussion questions 27
Case study 2.1: The prodigal daughter 27

3 Family firms: same or different? 29
Learning objectives 30
Definitions of family business 30
    Importance of family business definitions 31

Variety of definitions 32
Scales of familiness 33
Different types of family firms 34
Warm hearts, deep pockets 35
Agency theory and stewardship theory 36
Six conceptual types of family firms 37
Variation within types 39
Key learning points 40
Summary 40
Discussion questions 41
Case study 3.1: When blood boils over 41

4 Professionalisation and governance   44
Learning objectives 45
What are the relevant issues for governance? 45
Family governance 48
Family charter 49
Why would you need a family charter? 50
Family meetings 51
Family assembly 51
Family council 51
Family office 52
Corporate governance 53
Boards of directors 54
Professionalisation process 57
Key learning points 58
Summary 59
Discussion questions 60
Case study 4.1: Succession and governance in the Guinness family 60
Case study 4.2: Professionalisation for long-term sustainability in the Dennis family 61

5 Families in business: expansion and entrepreneurship   63
Learning objectives 64
From family business to families in business 64
Social capital 65
Social capital and familiness 67
Stewardship influence on entrepreneurship 69
Trust 70
Portfolio entrepreneurship 72
Family business groups 74

Contents vii

    Family entrepreneurial teams 75
Putting entrepreneurship into context 77
Key learning point 78
Summary 78
Discussion questions 79
Case study 5.1: Families across borders, across boundaries 79
Case study 5.2: La Empalizada – power of networks versus power of land 80

6 Succession issues and alternatives 82

Learning objectives 83
What are the issues for succession? 83
    Incumbents not letting go 83
    Successor selection 85
    Limitations of the gene pool 85
    Commitment 86
    Divorce, cohabitation, and stepchildren 86
    Motivation of successors 87
Typology of post-succession retirement styles 88
Succession alternatives 90
Management succession 90
    Non-family management 92
    Stop-gap manager 93
    Joint CEOs 93
Ownership succession 95
    Alternatives to family ownership succession 96
    Selling the family business 96
    Management buyout 97
    Trade sale 97
    Liquidation 98
Key learning points 98
Summary 98
Discussion questions 99
Case study 6.1: LVMH Moët Hennessy Louis Vuitton 99
Case study 6.2: Forced succession at Brown Brothers wine estate 100

7 Succession processes and the next generation 102

Learning objectives 102
Why many family businesses avoid succession planning 103
    Resistance to change 103
    Sibling rivalry 104
    Power 104

      Sensitivity 105
      Too busy 106
      Summary of reasons 106
  The succession process 107
      Succession as a relay race 108
      Succession as a dance 109
      Correlates of success 110
  Fairness and procedural justice 110
  Tax considerations 111
  The succession process and learning 112
  Succession process and education 113
  Next generation and gender 114
  Next generation perspective 115
  Key learning points 116
  Summary 116
  Discussion questions 117
  Case study 7.1: Fair shares and Gucci 117
  Case study 7.2: Socialisation and a change of heart 119

8 Finance, investment, and shareholding   121

  Learning objectives 122
  Are finance issues different for family businesses? 122
      Illiquid shares 122
      Agency issues 123
      Contextual factors 123
  Rights and responsibilities of family business shareholders 123
  Supply of finance 125
      Information asymmetries and agency theory 125
  Demand for finance 127
      The pecking order hypothesis 127
  Financial strategies 128
      Private equity 128
      Public listing of family businesses 130
      Classes of shares 130
  Pruning the family tree 131
  Exit strategies 132
      Negotiating a value for the family business 132
  Key learning point 134
  Summary 134
  Discussion questions 135
  Case study 8.1: The Stronach succession 135

9 Community, philanthropy, and social responsibility 138

Learning objectives 139
Distinguishing between different concepts 140
    Philanthropy 140
    Corporate social responsibility 141
    Charitable giving 142
    Community engagement 143
Theoretical insights 144
    Embeddedness 145
    Altruism, reciprocity, and giving 145
Cultural, contextual, and business drivers of philanthropy 147
Faith and family business philanthropy 148
Practicalities of philanthropy 150
Key learning point 150
Summary 150
Discussion questions 151
Case study 9.1: Tata Sons philanthropy in India 151
Case study 9.2: Wilsden Equestrian Centre 153

10 Longevity and the future for family firms 155

Learning objectives 156
Looking back to look forward 156
The oldest family businesses in the world 156
A historical perspective on longevity 157
Continuity and change: an insight into innovation 160
    Theories of innovation 161
How might family businesses help or hinder innovation? 162
Long-term orientation 165
Industry and technology 166
What does the future hold for family businesses? 167
Key learning points 168
Summary 169
Discussion questions 169
Case study 10.1: J. W. Lees continuity and discontinuity 169

References 171
Index 177

Figures

2.1	Three-Circle Model (based on Tagiuri and Davis, 1982, 1996)	15
2.2	A Three-Dimensional Development Model (adapted from Gersick et al., 1997)	19
2.3	Genogram: five generations of the Moore Family in 2017	21
2.4	Ownership structure chart for Agarwal Merchants	24
2.5	Portfolio ownership structure, Agarwal Group	24
3.1	Different types of family firms (adapted from Westhead and Howorth, 2007)	38
4.1	Waves of Professionalisation (adapted from: Howorth et al., 2016b)	58

Boxes

4.1	Reasons for family governance	49
4.2	A family charter might include processes and policies relating to the following	50
4.3	The Wates Principles (2018)	54
7.1	Recommendations for successful succession	108
7.2	Engaging the next generation: Sir Michael Bibby	113
10.1	Some of the oldest family businesses in the world	158
10.2	Elements of family culture that can stifle creativity	164

1 What's so special about family business?

Family businesses are the most prevalent form of business and in many countries they represent at least two thirds of all businesses. As you join us in learning about family businesses, we would like you to stop and think about whether you have any preconceptions. Some people believe that family businesses are all traditional 'mom and pop' type businesses, or they are all small firms; some may believe that family businesses are always embroiled in conflict whereas others perceive them to be havens of harmony. The reality is that family businesses vary and include some of the biggest companies in the world as well as the local corner shop; you will always be able to find one that matches your own stereotype but there will be many more that do not. Your preconceptions will probably be based on your own experience or stories that are more newsworthy because they present extreme cases. We would ask you to put aside any preconceptions that you might have and learn with us as we review the evidence and research on family businesses to provide you with new insights, understanding and recommendations.

In this introductory chapter, we will look at the prevalence of family businesses and introduce some of the issues that will be examined in later chapters. We will be considering some thorny questions. Are family businesses better or worse than non-family businesses? Do family owners care more about their business? Are families in business a hotbed for entrepreneurship? Or are they a hotbed for conflict? Do non-family employees have as good career prospects as in an enterprise with no blood ties? Is the image of family business as positive as other types of firms? Do they have the same capacity to innovate? Are their prospects hampered by having to involve less able workers simply because they are family?

Each chapter will introduce two or three relevant theories and provide explanations of how they can be applied to provide a better understanding of real issues. In Chapter 2, we explain why we agree that there is 'nothing so practical as a good theory' (Lewin, 1943). Overall, our interest is in understanding how we can manage family businesses better to ensure that this significant sector of the economy makes a positive contribution to society. In this first chapter, we have the following learning objectives.

Learning objectives

Knowledge of the prevalence and variation of family businesses
Understanding the value and breadth of insights from family business research
Introduction to key terms and concepts in family business

A day in the life: family business in Anytown[1]

Have you ever considered how many family businesses you engage with in your daily life? Let me tell you about my morning in Anytown, which for me is a small town in the north of England.

As I open my eyes first thing in the morning, it feels very cosy in my Harrison Spinks bed. Harrison Spinks is a fifth-generation family business that has been making mattresses for over 170 years. I have some lovely new sheets and pillowcases that I bought from Boundary Mill, a factory outlet founded by the Bannister family 30 years ago who have now expanded to four stores, a hotel, golf course, and outdoor pursuits centre. I am looking forward to the day I have booked at their spa next week. I go outside to collect my pint of milk, which has been delivered by James, our local milkman. James is part of a family who have been farming in the area for over 200 years. His brother runs the dairy herd while his sister has developed a very successful cheese-making business. His parents have branched out into local property and they own a couple of petrol stations and rent out some cottages in the village. They also own the town's cinema, which they rent out to a community management company for a peppercorn rent. I pour the milk onto my Jordans breakfast cereal. Jordans was founded in 1855 and the family continue to own nearly 40% of the company, as well as heading up the board of directors. In 2003 Bill and Deb Jordan bought Pensthorpe Natural Park, which became the home of BBC's *Springwatch* programme for three years from 2008.

A cup of Yorkshire tea from Taylors does the trick in waking me up. Bettys and Taylors was founded in 1919 when a Swiss confectioner arrived in Yorkshire, married a local girl and opened his first Bettys tea room in the spa town of Harrogate. Fourth generation descendants, the Wild family, ensure that Bettys and Taylors teas and coffees are all ethically sourced, and they work closely with tea and coffee producers overseas. I was impressed to discover that a recent project working with tea growers aimed to plant one million trees in Kenya. Popping a slice of bread into the toaster, I notice that it is from Roberts Bakery, who have introduced new packaging and a new logo: their strapline is that they are 'the next generation family bakery'. The packaging states 'As a family business we've been challenging traditions and shaking up baking since 1887'. I like the creative mix of tradition and innovation that they manage to achieve in their branding. Sometimes it is assumed that family food businesses are more about tradition than innovation.

I get my news online these days, long gone are the days when I would call in at the local newsagent to pick up a newspaper. Sadly, the shop has closed down; the couple who ran it have retired to the seaside. However, the Murdoch family and NewsCorp seem to have survived the shift to digital news. While I am eating breakfast, I do a little online shopping. I check out H&M, Zara, and Uniqlo. Interesting that some of the world's largest fashion brands are family-owned companies but, unlike the food companies, they rarely use their family ownership in their branding.

Much as I would like to use public transport, my office is out of town and so it is easier to drive. I got a new car last month from JCT600. The car dealership was founded in 1946 by Edward Tordoff. His son Jack Tordoff took over the business and renamed it after his Mercedes 600 car, which had the registration plate JCT600. Now run by the fourth generation of the Tordoff family, with 2000 employees it is one of the largest car retailers in the UK. I put on my old Berghaus jacket as it looks like rain. Interesting that the Rubin family who own Pentland Brands and therefore Berghaus are relatively unknown compared with all their brands.

As I round a corner on the drive to work, I get stuck behind a queue of cars, all crawling along behind a JCB digger. Whilst I admire the Bamford family and their iconic diggers, I really do not want to meet one on the way to work. In frustration, I turn off into the local supermarket to fill up with petrol and buy something for lunch. ASDA is one of the big four supermarket chains in the UK; until recently, it was owned by Walmart. Walmart is one of the biggest companies in the world, and although its shares are publicly traded, it is believed that the Walton family own about half of the shares, making them one of the wealthiest families in the USA and the world.

As I browse the supermarket shelves, I note many family business brands. I select some bread from Warburtons and some cheese from Butlers Farmhouse Cheeses, with a Mars bar for an extra boost of energy. Warburtons was founded in the 1870s when Ellen Warburton started baking bread to sell in their family's grocer's shop in Lancashire. The company has grown to employ 4,500 people, and is managed by fifth generation cousins Jonathan, Brett, and Ross Warburton. Butlers is headed up by Gillian Hall, but her sons are taking on increasing responsibility in preparation for succession, allowing her to develop other interests outside the business. The Mars family are another of the world's wealthiest families. I used to think the Mars bar had something to do with space travel and didn't realise that there was actually a family called Mars. This is probably because in the past the Mars family were famous for being extremely secretive, avoiding any media and tightly controlling the release of any company information.

I'm looking forward to dinner tonight, when we will be treating ourselves to a meal at a local pub. It used to be part of a family business that started out as a brewery 200 years ago and shifted to just owning and managing pubs and hotels about 10 years ago, following a succession. There was a period of buying back shares to consolidate the family ownership and ambitious expansion plans, but, sadly, the decline in the industry meant that high levels of debt were unaffordable and the family business went into administration last year. The portfolio was broken up and sold off by the receivers. Our local pub is now part of a national chain.

Exemplifying family business issues

Throughout our day, we engage with many family businesses whether we realise it or not. The examples in the short piece above are all family businesses and highlight some of the issues that we will explore in this book. As we see in Anytown, family businesses come in all shapes and sizes, and include enormous multi-national companies, portfolios of interconnected firms, and small local businesses. Family businesses occur in all industries, including high technology, manufacturing, extractive and heavy industries, but they are more prevalent in agriculture, food, and retail sectors. They include some iconic brands, but we do not always know that they are family owned, as family businesses vary in whether they emphasise family ownership in their marketing. For some, family ownership is believed to enhance their brand, as family businesses are perceived to be trustworthy and reliable. Others play down their family ownership because it might be seen as too traditional and not fitting their product or service image. Pentland Brands own a portfolio of high street brands, including Berghaus, Speedo, Ellesse, and others, but it is rarely noticed that the Rubin family are the ultimate owners of the companies through the Pentland Group structure. Others hide their family ownership due to concerns about not displaying their wealth. Not all family businesses carry the name of the owning family. Marketing is just one issue that highlights why we should not generalise to family businesses and assume they are all alike; this will be a recurring theme in our book.

Family business is not a new phenomenon. The origins of entrepreneurship are in the family. As far back as the hunter-gatherer period, individual family members would trade the products of their particular skills with other families. The need to provide for your family resulted in innovative and inventive ways of making goods and services to make money. As towns and communities grew, businesses expanded, and family firms started to sell their products or services further afield. Entrepreneurship is at the heart of family business and family firms appear extremely resilient in developed economies. An important question is whether this resilience is due to the backwardness of entrepreneurial models, or an intrinsic efficiency. Business historians up until the late 20th century viewed family business negatively, as stifling innovation. Pulitzer Prize-winning historian Alfred Chandler argued strongly that family business – or 'personal capitalism' – acted as a barrier to innovation (Handler, 1990). This view still persists in some quarters, but is heavily critiqued in more recent historical studies of family businesses (see Colli, Howorth and Rose, 2013).

The key characteristic that makes family businesses distinct from non-family businesses is the intertwining and influence of family relationships. Gordon and Nicholson (2008: 2) suggest that 'family firms have the capacity to outperform non-family comparators, but at the same time they are at risk to family hazards that can overspill or engulf them'. Family businesses are owned by husbands, wives, mothers, fathers, brothers, sisters, cousins, aunts, uncles, and grandparents. In some cases, shares are owned by all these at the same time, bringing a huge complexity of relationships. Families are all about relationships, characterised by emotional ties, attachments, and beliefs. Businesses, however, are expected to be rational economic systems that emphasise efficiency. For families, love, nurture, forgiveness, and protection of the vulnerable are the norm. Also common in families are sibling rivalries, generational conflicts, hurts, arguments, and factions. Families might argue amongst themselves but stand together against any outsiders. Where love and attachments are brought into the family business, they can engender commitment, strong value systems and positive attitudes. Protection of the vulnerable might entail providing a job for a family member who is unable to get one elsewhere. The family might be a powerful force, within the business and in the community. However, conflict and nepotism might be damaging for the business. As we explore the fascinating world of family businesses, it is important to recognise that family ownership can have both positive and negative implications. This is known as the bivalent nature of family business characteristics, and will be explored more in Chapter 2.

The family businesses in Anytown were of many different sizes, and some of them have shares that are publicly traded. If the Jordans family own 40% of the shares, can they still be defined as a family business? What about Walmart, which is one of the world's largest companies? In Chapter 3 we will examine what defines a family business, and discover that there are differences of opinion. Some would argue that a family business is any business where the family has significant influence; others argue that family businesses have to be majority owned by members of the same family. As we explore the variation in definitions in Chapter 3, we will build your skills in critically analysing research studies, looking behind the headline results to understand what is really going on. Chapter 3 also highlights that family businesses vary in their ownership and management structures, with degrees of family and non-family ownership and management, as well as variation in the extent to which they emphasise family or business objectives.

Like any business, family businesses need good governance, but the intertwining of family and business systems brings added complexity relative to non-family businesses. Warburtons is managed by three fifth-generation cousins (i.e., a cousin consortium) but ownership extends to other cousins and siblings. The cousins have partners and children, some of whom are adults. The business has a board of directors that includes family and non-family members. Is the employment of a junior family member an issue for the family or the business? Whose responsibility is it to select the next CEO?

Is it better if the CEO is a family member or not? Chapter 4 provides insight into the tricky issue of governing the family business. We identify structures and processes for corporate and family governance. We highlight that professionalisation is not a once-and-for-all threshold but a process that occurs in waves over many years.

Anytown provides examples illuminating the outstanding longevity of some family businesses. Continuity and succession are often as important to a family firm as profitability. While some families sell up and cash in on their parents' efforts, many others strive to maintain and grow the family business for generation after generation. It is not unusual for family businesses to be more than 100 years old, and in various countries there are family businesses that can trace their roots back over 1,000 years. It has been suggested that a long-term view is a particular feature of family businesses compared with other types of organisations. We will examine how longstanding family businesses ensure their continuity through generations, the values they bring to the business, their attitudes, and their ability to survive through good and bad times. Longevity requires entrepreneurial renewal, balancing continuity and discontinuity by building on relevant traditions and strengths, while investing in innovation. Some families develop portfolios of firms that allow a wide range of entrepreneurial activities and opportunities to be pursued. Family members might share their resources, networks, and knowledge to enhance the family's businesses. Often, we also see collaborations between business families who seem to share a bond or cognitive understanding. The businesses in Anytown have taken different approaches to expansion. Walmart, Jordans, and the retail businesses have expanded internationally. When the Warburton cousins took over the family business, they divested a random portfolio of non-core businesses to focus on building a strong bakery business nationally. The Bannister family have adopted a portfolio approach. Families might expand their businesses locally, nationally, or internationally. They might grow the core business or develop a portfolio of businesses. In Chapter 5 we examine entrepreneurship and expansion in family businesses and see that through history, international trade has flourished through families drawing on their resources and expanding their interests.

A particular characteristic of family businesses is the involvement and influence of family members who do not have a formal role as an employee or owner of the business. In Chapter 2, the three-circle model provides a simple theoretical model that captures the influence of this invisible group, which can have both positive and negative influences. However, it is in entrepreneurship that family members who are external to the business can be particularly valuable, providing social capital, resources, mentoring, idea development, and sometimes funding for new ventures. It is suggested that, in many countries, the 'invisible' family group contains more women. In Anytown we see an interesting example: the Jordans website states that the nature reserve was bought by Bill Jordan, but it was spouse Deb Jordan who wanted to develop the nature reserve in her home county and it was actually the husband and wife team who bought the reserve. The writing out of women in history is a common issue and is brought to light in examining family businesses.

Many of the businesses in Anytown are multi-generation businesses, which means they are owned or controlled by more than the first generation, and they will have gone through at least one succession of ownership, some of them four or five successions. Succession is an important issue for family businesses, and it involves much more than just handing over the baton to an incoming generation. As we will discover, the next generation needs to be educated to take on their role, whether as owners or executives. The early selection of successors can allow family businesses to invest in the development of the next generation, but it can also give rise to sibling rivalries, accusations of nepotism, and conflict. How should family businesses like Butlers Farmhouse Cheeses decide who is the next CEO? Should it be one of the sons already working in the business or should it be a non-family member? Chapters 6 and 7 examine succession, with the former looking at succession issues and the latter examining succession processes, and particularly next generation development and learning. Succession often involves renewal and innovation, but as we see in the pub business above, it can also be a critical juncture, and not all family businesses will survive the changes brought in by succeeding generations. Many of the issues that family businesses face will be due to their context, their size, industry or location, or a combination of factors, as with the pub business. Throughout the book we emphasise that, to avoid inappropriate solutions, it is important to be clear in attributing causality.

A major factor in the failure of the pub business in Anytown was high levels of debt that were incurred to fund expansion plans, but also to restructure the ownership post-succession and buy back shares. Chapter 8 explains that dispersed ownership can be problematic for some family firms, whereupon they decide to 'prune the family tree', which is a strategy adopted to reduce the spread of ownership to a committed and more tightly knit group of family members. Chapter 8 examines financial strategies and highlights that some family businesses' longevity has been attributed to an avoidance of debt. However, other family businesses have grown very successfully, using both debt and external equity. The pros and cons of different financing strategies are considered.

Bettys and Taylors highlight that family businesses are not just seekers of resources, but they may also be involved as providers of resources in community projects, charitable foundations, and other types of philanthropy. Later generations may build up significant wealth and have extensive philanthropic activities. Even very small family businesses are often involved in charitable endeavours. Many family businesses are highly embedded in their local community, and family business leaders may be at the heart of community projects. In Anytown, James' family demonstrate that longevity of the business and contribution to the community may be more important objectives than maximising their wealth opportunities. In Chapter 9 we see that philanthropy is very common among family businesses of all sizes. Family business owners who are less involved in the operations of the business may gain fulfilment from their charitable or community activities, like Bill and Deb Jordan developing a nature reserve. Philanthropy for family businesses goes beyond corporate social responsibility and is often separate from the business, although it may have a knock-on effect in terms of goodwill and social capital. Many leading trusts and foundations arose from wealth created by family businesses. For example, the Leverhulme Trust was created out of the estate of Lord Leverhulme in 1925, deriving its income from the shares he owned in Lever Brothers, now Unilever. The Joseph Rowntree Foundation arose from wealth created by the Rowntree family's chocolate business in York, and along with three other trusts, focusses on poverty alleviation. Similar trusts and foundations are observed throughout the world.

Family business leaders like Joseph Rowntree, Lord Leverhulme, or Henry Ford can have very high profiles, which in their cases continued after their deaths through the foundations and trusts set up in their names. Although some international family business leaders' profiles have a powerful legacy, we should not discount the contribution to their community of smaller family businesses. Chapter 9 shows that many members of family businesses undertake important community roles and it is not unusual for them to become involved in politics. Even when members of the family are not involved in the business, their profile may be such that any good deed or misdemeanour by family members has the potential to influence the brand of the business.

The family businesses in Anytown highlight the potential longevity of family-owned businesses. Chapter 10 examines survival and failure, which are two sides of the same coin. We look at family businesses that have survived for centuries to draw out the lessons for longevity. We consider how family businesses will survive going forward in the digital age. Throughout the book, potential dangers are illuminated and suggestions made to help avoid or alleviate the behaviours and situations that can destroy family businesses.

Why study family businesses?

It is interesting that despite the prevalence of family businesses, mainstream management literature has paid little attention to them. Management theories and prescriptions tend to have been developed to fit the large publicly listed types of business that dominate the headlines. Management and finance textbooks are predicated on notions of growth, efficiency, or maximisation of shareholder wealth. Study of family businesses highlights the legitimacy of alternative objectives, such as business survival, longevity, providing for the next generation, and contributions to society. We note a step change in management schools and in society where the maximisation of wealth for a minority is increasingly questioned and alternative objectives and responsibilities are becoming more talked about, alongside concerns about environmental sustainability.

A more mundane but equally valid reason to study family businesses is that most people who work in the corporate sector will either work in or work with family businesses, as customers or suppliers. In this book we provide insights into the research on family business. By confronting practice with tried and tested theories, as well as recognising less reliable theories and assumptions, those working in or with family businesses are more able to avoid unfounded assumptions, improve their understanding of why things happen the way they do and how to approach the challenges they face.

Family businesses bring the human element into the foreground because families are about people: people who get along and people who fall out; people who influence the business for good or bad. All businesses are dependent on people, as employees, leaders, managers, customers, and suppliers. Family businesses open up the human element of business to provide insight into how relationships influence behaviours and business outcomes. Family business researchers understand the invisible influences of family members, partners, and parents that can impact on approaches to work. Family business studies accept that people may have varying objectives, such as providing for their kids, enjoying family relationships, and contributing to a community, which might be a stronger motivation than financial reward. New enterprises are often part of a network of businesses supported and resourced by a family, but entrepreneurship research that examines firms or entrepreneurs in isolation from their families may miss the importance of such connections to an entrepreneur's success. Family business has provided the opportunity to thoroughly study succession, providing insights that other organisations can learn from. Family business research highlights the positive and negative aspects of nepotism, which could provide insights into the commonly observed but less frequently discussed cronyism that occurs in some boardrooms.

Thus, study of family businesses is important because they are the dominant form of business ownership, and analysis can provide insights for family businesses, but also study of family businesses can provide insights for other types of organisations.

Structure of the book

In each chapter you will read about a particular aspect of family business. You will be introduced to two or three theories in every chapter that help you to apply theory to practice, extending your critical understanding. As Chapter 2 highlights, there is 'nothing so practical as a good theory'. The application of theory to practice will help you to understand alternative scenarios and explanations. Each chapter includes case studies and illustrations drawing on real family businesses to help illuminate issues. Key learning points summarise the most important points you need to understand about that particular aspect of family business. The chapter summary will help to cement learning and provide an aid to your memory.

We will introduce you to lots of family businesses through the book. Some of them will be mini-case studies. Keep your eyes open for other family businesses that you come into contact with. As we highlighted earlier, it is obvious that some firms are family businesses, but not every firm employs the family brand in their marketing, and others keep their family ownership hidden.

There is a logic to the structure of the book, and we recommend that you follow the chapters in order. Chapters 2 and 3 introduce key concepts and theories that will help to deepen understanding of later chapters. An understanding of governance structures (Chapter 4) will help in following chapters on succession and finance. Chapter 6 introduces succession issues and should be read before Chapter 7, which addresses the succession process.

This book is aimed at all those interested in understanding family businesses. It does not shy away from theories and research, because we believe it is important to base practical recommendations on tried and tested theories. However, space limits the depth of our explanation of theories, so references are provided for those who wish to learn more about particular theories or research studies.

Key learning points

Family businesses are the dominant business form around the world, covering all industries and sizes of firms. It is important that we do not generalise and assume that all family businesses are the same.

The key difference for family businesses is the intertwining of family relationships with business imperatives. Whereas families are all about relationships, emotional ties, attachments, and beliefs, businesses are expected to be rational economic systems that emphasise efficiency. Family ownership brings many positive and some negative aspects that need to be managed in a business.

Summary

In many countries, family-controlled businesses represent at least two thirds of all businesses. It would be unusual if that many businesses were all the same. Researchers stress the importance of avoiding myths and assumptions, highlighting the dangers of generalisations that might assume that all family businesses are of a particular type or act in a certain way. All family businesses are affected by the intertwining of family relationships with business imperatives, but the issues they face will be determined by their specific context and circumstances.

Family businesses appear to survive longer than other types of businesses, and the book will explore some of the evidence and reasons for this. A long-term perspective and commitment to future generations introduce alternative ways of perceiving business that might bring into question some of the theories and assumptions we have about business. The love and commitment that a family have for each other can be a powerful source of advantage for family businesses. However, they can also bring behaviours that are damaging and threaten the survival of the business. For some, family ownership is believed to enhance their brand, but, for others, it might be seen as too traditional and not fitting the image they wish to portray. The bivalent nature of family business characteristics will be a recurring theme through the book.

This chapter has identified relevant themes that will be considered in detail in later chapters, including definitions, governance, succession, entrepreneurship, innovation, financial strategies, philanthropy, and the future of family businesses. Key terms have been introduced, including: longevity and the long-term view of business; succession; professionalisation; family governance; cousin consortium; sibling rivalry; multi-generational business; pruning the family tree, and nepotism.

The study of family businesses is important for three reasons: 1) they are the most prevalent ownership form of business; 2) it provides insights for those who work in or with family businesses; 3) it provides insights into management issues and theories in other types of organisations.

Discussion questions

1   What makes family businesses different to non-family businesses?
2   Investigate some of your favourite products and find out who owns the company that makes them. Is it a family or non-family company? Consider how and why family ownership is important to their brand or not.
3   Maximisation of shareholder wealth is a major assumption underpinning finance theory. Consider whether this assumption holds for family businesses. What other objectives might be important for family businesses?

Note

1   All the information on businesses mentioned here was correct at the time of writing. Some of the smaller businesses are combinations of actual businesses. Information is from sources in the public domain. The idea for this piece came from John Pearce' book *Social Enterprise in Anytown* (2003, Calouste Gulbenkian Foundation).

2 Nothing so practical as a good theory

Kurt Lewin is the first person attributed to saying 'There is nothing so practical as a good theory'. In this chapter we will examine some of the theories and theoretical models that help us to understand family businesses and how they can be applied in practice. The Three-Circle Model provides a useful starting point for analysis of family businesses, so the model is described in some detail and its usefulness and limitations are explained. In doing this, critical analysis is demonstrated, as we encourage you to adopt a questioning approach to models, theories, and research findings.

The Three-Circle Model is critiqued for providing only a snapshot, and so the Three-Dimensional Development Model is presented to capture some of the changes that occur in family business. We then look at tools and methods for analysing each of the family, ownership, and business dimensions, starting with how to construct a genogram and introducing some theories along the way that are explained in more detail in later chapters.

It is important that understanding of these models and theories is developed at the start of our journey into family business because they provide the basis for later chapters, where we look at the critical issues that family businesses face.

Learning objectives

Understand how to apply the Three-Circle Model and the Three-Dimensional Development Model to analyse owner, family, and business systems

Understand how to construct and use a genogram in family business analysis

Build understanding of critical analysis, particularly in relation to theories and research studies

Families and businesses

Many of the theories that are employed to help us understand family businesses have their roots in other disciplines, such as economics, psychology, or sociology. More recently, family business researchers have been developing theories from their understanding and analysis of family businesses that can be applied outside the family business context: for example, the development of a theory of socio-emotional wealth by Luis Gomez-Mejia and colleagues (2007).

Whilst theories arise and are superseded as understanding develops, some have stood the test of time. Andrew Van de Ven (1989) edited an issue of *Academy of Management Review* (*AMR*) dedicated to providing a better understanding of what makes a good theory. In a homage to Lewin, the editorial is titled 'Nothing is quite so practical as a good theory' (Lewin, 1943). Contributors to that issue remind us that a good theory should be plausible and interesting (Weick, 1989); theory is defined as 'an ordered set of assertions about a generic behaviour or structure assumed to hold throughout a significantly broad range of specific instances' (Sutherland, 1975, p. 9 in Weick, 1989).

Early theorising about family businesses in the 1960s and 1970s recognised that there were two 'systems' at play, i.e., family and business. The fundamental difference for family businesses compared with non-family businesses is the intertwining of family and business, each with their values, norms, structures, and objectives. The business is viewed as a performance-driven system based on economic objectives, whereas the family is seen to be a relationship-based system, characterised by emotions and attachments. There is a tendency to assume that economic objectives and reasoning are more 'rational', and some will talk about 'rational economic objectives'. However, by recognising the important emotions, values, and attachments within the family system, we can see that behaviour that from an economic perspective may not seem rational, is rational within the values and norms of a family system. For example, within an economic 'system' it would not seem rational to employ young family members with no experience. From a family perspective, it makes sense to develop youngsters within the business, where they can be provided with a range of relevant experiences and learning under the wing of their parents.

The concept of two systems continues to be a useful basis for identifying and understanding some of the issues and behaviours in family businesses. Within a business system, employment decisions are likely to be driven by performance, so that family members may have to demonstrate how they are better than any other candidate. Within a family system, employment might be about providing an opportunity for any family member and supporting their personal development. Thus, in family businesses where such family values are important, we may see greater employment of members of the owning family, but also of multiple members of employees' families. In Chapters 3 and 4 we look in more detail at the intertwining of family and business systems. Chapter 4 discusses governance structures and processes, which may often be derived from the two-systems concept.

In a different context, agency theory (explained in more detail in Chapter 3) developed the concept of separation of ownership and control

(Berle and Means, 1932) to provide an understanding of the behaviour and incentivisation of managers in large publicly listed organisations. Agency theory is based on the premise of owners (in this theory they are called principals) being separate from managers, who act as 'agents' running the company on behalf of the owners. In smaller companies, there may be little or no separation of ownership and control and therefore no principals and agents to speak about. However, family businesses cover the full range of business types and sizes, as we see in Chapter 3. For some family businesses, ownership is distinct from management; for other family businesses, ownership overlaps with management to a greater or lesser extent. Owners or managers may be family members and/or non-family members. Thus, various permutations of ownership and management might exist in family businesses. A model that is able to distinguish between owners, managers, and the family, and identify the overlaps and separation of each, is therefore likely to be useful. This is the basis of the Three-Circle Model, a conceptualisation that has stood the test of time and one that continues to be fundamental to analysing issues for different types of family businesses.

Three-Circle Model

Renato Tagiuri and John Davis first developed the Three-Circle Model of the Family Business System in the 1970s at Harvard Business School. It became part of Davis' doctoral thesis in 1982 and was published in their seminal article 'Bivalent attributes of the family firm' and then in 1996 in *Family Business Review*.[1]

Figure 2.1 reproduces this simple model, which is a basic Venn diagram, instantly recognisable and highly practical. It has since been employed by many family business consultants, researchers, and business professionals, providing an excellent starting point for analysing any family business. It can be used to explain how the family, ownership, and business domains overlap and intersect, which was its original purpose, and it can be used to understand just who is involved or influential in a specific family business. Many family businesses and their advisors find it useful for getting family members to think about communication channels, power relationships, decision making, exclusion, succession, and a host of family business issues. Tagiuri and Davis (1982) suggest that the Three-Circle Model was novel in including the Ownership dimension, separately from, and in addition to, the Family and Business dimensions, which had previously been the chief focus of family business analysts. As mentioned earlier, the separation of ownership and management domains had been identified many years previously as an issue for public firms (Berle and Means, 1932) and had developed into agency theory, which is widely used today. The Three-Circle Model, however, enables identification of overlap – as well as separation – of ownership, management (or business), and family domains.

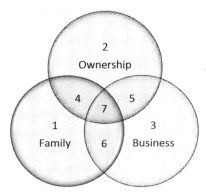

Figure 2.1 Three-Circle Model (based on Tagiuri and Davis, 1982, 1996).

The seven segments in the overlapping circles represent the possible positions that any individual might hold. Only owners can be located somewhere in the upper circle, family in the left-hand circle and employees in the right-hand circle. Each segment is mutually exclusive in that no one can occupy more than one segment at any point in time. Segment 1 contains family members who are not (yet) owners or employees of the business, which might include spouses, next generation and retirees. Those in Segment 4 would be family owners who are not employees of the business and Segment 6 would be family employees who have no ownership. Segment 2 contains owners who are not family members or employees, such as external or institutional investors. Segment 5 contains employees with an ownership stake who are not family members, such as executives who have received shares. Segment 3 contains employees who are not family members and do not have any ownership. Analysis of larger family firms might only include management, rather than all employees, in Segment 3. Individuals at the centre of the diagram (Segment 7) will be family owner managers. Typically (but not always), Segment 7 people are more actively involved, the most well-informed and often the most powerful individuals in the family business.

Each group (segment) is likely to have particular perspectives and issues that impact on the family business. Tagiuri and Davis used the Three-Circle Model to highlight the 'bivalent attributes' of family firms, in other words: the particular characteristics that can bring both advantage and disadvantage to family firms; characteristics arising from the overlap of family, ownership, and management, such as simultaneous roles, shared identity, lifelong common history, emotional involvement, private language, mutual awareness, and privacy. Tagiuri and Davis highlighted that families in business need to understand and manage bivalent attributes to maximise positive effects and minimise negative ones.

This model is very helpful in understanding family businesses because it leads us to consider the issues and perspectives of people in each segment of the diagram. For example, family owners (in Segment 4) hold shares but do not have any involvement in the business. An issue for family owners could be the illiquid nature of their equity holding, as there is no ready market for them to sell their shares. Family owners' chief interest then might be in ensuring that they get as much dividend as possible, which could conflict with business strategies to retain profit for investment. Family owners do not have a role in the operations of the business and two issues could be: a) family owners' lack of understanding of the business; and/or b) family owners trying to be involved (interfering) in operational decision making. Advisors and researchers have employed the Three-Circle Model to analyse and advise on a host of issues that relate to role clarity, communication, priorities, and boundaries in family firms. Problem a) could be helped by improved communications, introducing a family assembly (see Chapter 3) and additional family governance measures. Problem b) could be helped by increased role clarity and agreeing boundaries. Some family businesses have gone to more extreme lengths and removed family owners through 'pruning the family ownership tree'. These are examples of how a theoretical model can guide us to very practical solutions.

It is important that we do not ignore the influence of family members who do not have ownership or employment roles (Segment 1). Family business studies have highlighted that these family members can be quite powerful, indirectly through their influence on other family members and directly by getting involved in the business. The influence of family members provides a powerful example of bivalent attributes: their loyalty to the family business means they might act as ambassadors, recommend the business' products or services, initiate introductions and thus extend the social capital of the business; they might suggest ideas and provide a helpful sounding board or informal advisory role. However, they might also interfere excessively in the operations, undermine decision making, cling on to the way things were done in the past, and carry the shadow of previous generations. In some cultures there is a gender divide, and men are more likely to have executive roles and ownership stakes, whereas women undertake an 'invisible' but sometimes very influential role (Hamilton, 2006). In such circumstances, Segment 1 is more likely to be the domain of the women in the family. Ellie Hamilton (2006, 2013) went behind the façade of family businesses to dig out the fascinating stories of women who were supporting their partners' family businesses physically, financially, emotionally, and entrepreneurially. The support of non-owning family members has been shown to be especially crucial in the start-up stages, and this is the case for many family and non-family businesses. The difference for family businesses is that family members often continue their involvement throughout the lifespan of the business. The emotional attachment that family members have to the businesses of their kin is captured in the concept of psychological ownership. Psychological ownership explains the sense of responsibility and emotional attachment we have for things that we care about, even though we have no financial interest in them. We explain this theory in more detail in Chapter 6, when we look at succession.

The Three-Circle Model provides the basis for a really useful exercise for any individual family business. It is a simple process to draw three overlapping circles and then consider each person in the business and insert their names into the diagram, but when we have conducted this exercise for some families it has been an 'Aha!' moment as they suddenly gain insight into the behaviour of a particular individual or group, particularly when they also map communication channels onto the model.

One family business we worked with was questioning the performance of a non-family manager who had been appointed to relieve some of the pressure from the family CEO. The CEO could not understand why this manager did not seem to understand key decisions and always seemed to be behind the curve. Mapping individuals onto the model identified the family CEO at the centre, her sons – one of whom was a family employee – her husband, who was a family owner, her brother, who had a small ownership stake and was a key supplier for the company, all in various segments of the family circle, and the non-family manager sitting in Segment 3 of the management circle on her own. The 'Aha!' moment came when we asked where they talked most about the business – it was in the car, at the dinner table, at breakfast discussing the day ahead, at family gatherings. The non-family manager was excluded from these conversations because she was not present, which explained why she felt isolated and marginalised. The CEO was previously unaware of the extent of business thinking and strategising that occurred during these family conversations. This is a very common problem for growing family firms who bring in non-family managers, and it is caused by the permeable boundary between business and family. The situation for this firm was improved, first through awareness of the issue, then revisiting communication channels and implementing a combination of regular formal management meetings and frequent informal chats.

Larger family businesses are likely to be quite complex, and it will be more difficult for them to map all the relevant individuals onto the Three-Circle Model. For them, the principle of overlapping circles is the key point alongside understanding the perspectives, issues, and implications for groups in each of the segments. Many larger family businesses might have complex shareholdings, and the family could hold shares in trusts and holding companies as well as, or instead of, directly as individuals. The basic Venn diagram may be too simplistic in these cases and might need to be adapted if such families wish to make it representative of their variety of types of stakeholders.

The Three-Circle Model is an example of a model that has immediate face validity and is easy to employ, whilst also providing insight into quite complex overlapping systems. Earlier analysis of family businesses focussed only on the family and business systems. The Three-Circle Model enables insights into important factors arising from the ownership system. Davis (2019) suggests that linking the three sub-systems of business, family, and ownership fully captures the family business system.

While the Three-Circle Model is a useful starting point for analysis of family businesses, one of the limitations of the model is that it only provides a snapshot or static representation, whereas, in reality, individuals may move from one segment to another. For example, if an employee obtains shares they will reposition from Segment 3 to 5; if a family member becomes an employee they will shift from 1 to 6, or if a family owner sells their shares they will shift from 4 to 1. Frustrations with the static nature of the Three-Circle Model motivated attempts to provide a model that captured the dynamism at the heart of businesses and families.

Three-Dimensional Development Model

Kelin Gersick, John Davis, Marion McCollom Hampton, and Ivan Lansberg built on the concept of three circles in their attempt to provide a more dynamic model that showed how family businesses might develop over time. Gersick et al. (1997: 15) argue 'our models must take time and change into account if they are to reflect the real world accurately'. The process of change is what creates many of the dilemmas that businesses and families have to face. Gersick et al.'s Three-Dimensional Development Model (Figure 2.2) provides a representation of some of the changes that might occur within each of the family, business, and ownership systems. Each of the three systems is represented by one axis, along which they move or develop over time, thus providing three dimensions and a development model as in the title. The family axis highlights that families develop through a variety of relationships including young couples, families with pre-school children, and retirees with elderly parents and grandchildren. Our adapted model in Figure 2.2 includes the potential for divorces and relationship break-ups, which might introduce step-children into the mix. Even though the family dimension is simplified, it is still messier than the other two dimensions, and the model highlights that changes in family circumstances create the potential for significant impact on a family business. The business axis captures simple stages in the development of the business; issues at the start-up phase will be very different to a business that is expanding and/or one that has reached a state of maturity. In the original model, the business axis only captures the upward trajectory of growth and we have added decline or renewal to more accurately reflect reality. The ownership axis represents movement from a simple controlling owner structure through a sibling partnership to a cousin consortium. The beauty of the Three-Dimensional Development (3DD) Model is that it introduces us to some of the complexity that family businesses might face. Movement along any single axis is associated with increasing complexity. In many cases, family businesses could be facing changes on all three dimensions at the same time. Non-family businesses do not have to concern themselves with some of the changes that we see in the ownership and family dimensions. It is this intertwining of family, ownership, and business issues that makes family businesses more complex and, we would argue, more interesting than non-family businesses.

Nothing so practical as a good theory   19

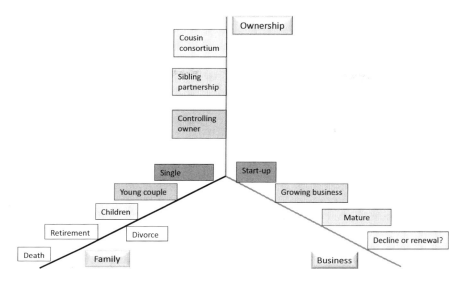

Figure 2.2 A Three-Dimensional Development Model (adapted from Gersick et al., 1997).

Practically, this model assists analysis of issues within family businesses by reminding us to consider what changes are happening on each of the family, business, and ownership dimensions that might be impacting on a particular issue. By identifying where an issue resides, the most appropriate forum for determining the way forward can be found. So, for example, in the classic family business issue of succession planning, who should succeed the current family CEO of the company is about management succession and might be most appropriately viewed as a business issue; whether next-generation member Cristina should study a particular university degree to better equip her to be a CEO in the future is a family issue; who should inherit shares is a family issue, but rules about how shares can be transferred is an ownership issue. However, it does not take much imagination to realise how such issues may overlap and become entangled. And the Three-Circle Model reminds us that individuals may have overlapping family, ownership, or business roles.

Whilst the 3DD Model provides a useful tool to gain insight into some elements of family business complexity, it is of necessity a simplification, as all models are. It is a 'stages' model and can be critiqued for the same shortcomings as other stages models. Families and businesses will not always start at the end of an axis: ownership could be a sibling partnership or cousin consortium at start-up; the business could be founded by parents and offspring working together. Movement might not necessarily occur neatly from one stage to the next: many larger family businesses have a complex array of family members with overlapping generations, as seen below when we look at genograms. Nor will movement always be in the same direction: family owners may be bought out to simplify the ownership structure; lack of heirs could lead to concentration of ownership rather than increased dispersion. In using the model, we need to be aware that only a few scenarios are included on each axis and there may be other situations that do not fit the model. The business axis appears to represent a positive maturing trajectory and, as mentioned above, does not include a decline phase, as most lifecycle models would. However, the model is helpful in reminding us that the three dimensions of family, business, and ownership are not static, and changes might be occurring in all three at the same time.

In the following sections we explain tools, concepts, and methods for analysing each of the three elements of a family business: family, ownership, and business.

Analysing the family: genograms

The two models explained so far in this chapter have both highlighted the importance of including the family influence in any analysis of a family business. In this section we explain how the construction of a genogram helps to identify who the relevant family members are, their roles, and their relationships. A genogram is similar to a family tree but provides more information. Genograms are used in family studies and family therapy to clarify relationships between family members, and are helpful in identifying how relationships might affect communication or impact on particular issues. In family business studies, a genogram can also identify overlapping generations and people's varying roles in and engagement with the family's businesses.

Figure 2.3 provides a genogram that represents five generations of the Moore family, who have one family business founded by John Moore, the first generation (1G), in 1952. A genogram is a tool of analysis, and, like all tools of analysis, its purpose is to help us better understand a situation or case, therefore it will be used and adapted as appropriate for the particular unit of analysis. In this case we are analysing the descendants of John Moore and have therefore not included his brothers and sisters and their branches of the family. We have also not included the names of spouses in order to provide a clearer picture of descendants. In alternative circumstances, who is included would be adapted to suit the analysis requirements.

Accepted components of a genogram include squares for males and circles for females; solid horizontal lines represent marriage and dotted lines represent living together. One line cutting through a marriage line indicates separation and two lines divorce. A crossed-out circle or square indicates that that person is no longer alive. Family therapists and psychologists often add additional components to indicate closeness and quality of relationships between individuals, usually from the perspective of the individual who is the focus of therapy. As family business analysts are more likely to be looking at the whole picture, and judgements about the quality of relationships are subjective, with variation between individuals, components about relationship quality would not usually be included. However, family business analysts would add information on ownership, management roles, and employment in the business.

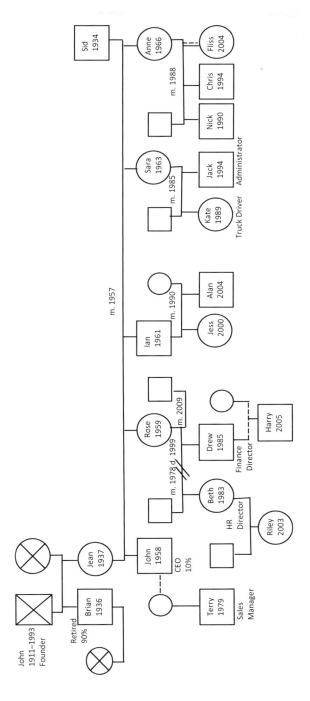

Figure 2.3 Genogram: five generations of the Moore Family in 2017.

The Moore family genogram provides us with a lot of information about the family and business relationships of five generations of the Moore family. John Moore and his wife (1G) are both deceased. We can see that John's son, Brian (2G), inherited the business and currently owns 90%. The CEO is John Jr who is in the third generation (3G) and owns 10%. John Jr is Brian's nephew, as Brian and his now deceased wife did not have any children. Brian's sister Jean and her husband Sid had five children, who are all still living. Only John from the third generation (3G) has a role in the family business. The dotted line between John Jr and his partner indicates that they are cohabiting. John's partner has one son, Terry, who is employed as Sales Manager. John Jr does not have any children of his own. The oldest direct descendant in the fourth generation is Beth, who is HR Director. Her brother Drew is Finance Director. Their cousins Kate and Jack are employed as a truck driver and administrator respectively. The genogram also shows us some other information about the family. We can see that Beth and Drew's parents were divorced and their mother Rose has remarried. The two lines, one solid and one dotted, between Fliss and her parents indicate that Fliss is adopted. Note also that there is overlap between the third and fourth generations: Riley, Harry, Alan, and Fliss were all born between 2003 and 2005.

Like the Three-Circle Model, the genogram is a snapshot of the family at one point in time. Changes in the family, e.g., births, deaths, marriages, will require changes in the genogram, as will changes in ownership and roles within the business. However, the genogram is an extremely useful tool to gain insight into the past history of a family business and highlight potential issues that might arise in the future. These insights will often lead to further questions. From the Moore genogram, we can see that Brian is in his 80s and John Jr is 60, and so ownership and management succession are likely to be a big issue for the business, made trickier by Brian and John having no direct descendants. We can see members of the fourth generation working in the business and we might ask whether there is a policy regarding employment of family members and whether any ownership and management succession plans are in place. We might highlight that the rights of stepchildren and adopted children need to be considered. We might also be concerned that the family is clear about the future role of Terry, who is the CEO's co-habiting partner's son and not a blood relative, but the oldest member of the fourth generation and employed in a management position. Interestingly, Beth and Drew, the CEO's nephew and niece, are employed in director roles, whereas Terry is employed as a manager, which could indicate that succession is expected to follow blood lines, but without further information we cannot assume this to be the case.

The Moore genogram highlights how complexity increases as family businesses move through the generations. It also highlights a weakness in the two models (Three-Circle and 3DD) presented earlier in this chapter. Ownership of the Moore family business is currently split between uncle and nephew. Further questioning reveals that John Jr received his 10% ownership on his 50th birthday after he had been appointed CEO. John Jr has thus moved through three segments of the three circles (family ⇨ family manager ⇨ family manager owner). The

Three-Circle Model for a particular family business can thus become out of date. The Moore family business also highlights limitations of the 3DD model. The business went from controlling owner (John Sr) to controlling owner (Brian) to two generations of ownership without being a sibling partnership nor a cousin consortium. The 3DD model assumes that ownership will become increasingly complex with each generation, but in this case it stayed simple for two generations and then became cross-generational, which is an ownership stage that is not represented at all in the 3DD Model. However, examination of the genogram indicates that a sibling partnership or cousin consortium could arise during the next succession for the Moore family business.

We can see therefore that a combination of models or tools of analysis are likely to provide a better understanding than relying on only one. Each model is of necessity a simplification of reality and no model can cover all eventualities. It is important therefore that family business analysts and scholars have a toolbox of models at their disposal rather than just one tool.

Further analysis of the family could include interviewing as many family members as possible, obtaining CVs, reviewing media coverage, reading family histories, which many older family businesses have produced, and comparing and contrasting the information provided. Depending on the issue that is being addressed, it is also frequently helpful to interview non-family employees and any family friends or advisors who are referred to by family members.

Analysing ownership

For some family businesses, like the Moore family, ownership is a fairly simple distribution among a small number of family members. For others, ownership can be a complex interwoven structure of individually held shares, shares held in trust, external investors, holding companies and subsidiaries, with variations in voting rights, pre-emptive rights, and shareholder agreements. Some longstanding family businesses have hundreds of family shareholders; some family businesses have a percentage of shares that are publicly traded and information is freely available; others are privately held and it is difficult to get information without access to a family member.

Analysis of the ownership needs to be at a level of detail that is appropriate to its purpose. For most purposes, it is sufficient to understand the distribution of shares, voting rights, who are the dominant shareholders, and what the policy is for the transfer of shares, whether through inheritance or sale.

An ownership structure chart is useful to provide a clear representation of the layers of ownership that might be found in a family business. Figure 2.4 provides an example of the ownership structure for a fictitious company, Agarwal Merchants, a private limited company registered in India. We have added additional information on the generation and gender of the owners. Combining the ownership structure chart with a genogram for the Agarwal family would give further insights into the relationship between family owners.

24 *Nothing so practical as a good theory*

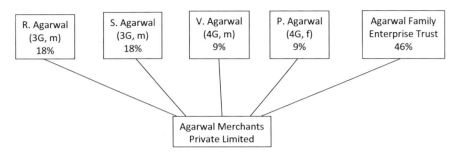

Figure 2.4 Ownership structure chart for Agarwal Merchants.

Figure 2.5 Portfolio ownership structure, Agarwal Group.

The ownership structure chart indicates that Agarwal Merchants is owned by two members of the third generation (18% each) and two members of the fourth generation of the Agarwal family (9% each), plus the Agarwal Family Enterprise Trust, which owns 46% of the company. Further investigation reveals that the two 3G members are brothers and the 4G owners are the offspring of a third brother who is deceased. Interestingly, the Trust holds a greater percentage of ownership than any individual or any combination of two individuals, which means that no individual shareholder has dominance. It could be useful to undertake further investigation into voting and other rights attached to shares in order to understand ownership decision making in this company.

However, digging a little deeper reveals that the ownership structure of Agarwal is more complex than examination of one company reveals. Figure 2.5 shows that Agarwal Merchants is at the head of a small group of companies. Many families in business will have a complex portfolio of companies with interwoven holdings, not all of which are obvious at first glance. Analysis of ownership structures often requires digging around in a variety of data sources to get the full picture. Interestingly, the two third generation brothers have shares in subsidiary companies in addition to their shares in the parent company, but their situation is very different. R. Agarwal has 10% of Baltimore Cuisine, leaving Agarwal Merchants as the major shareholder. S. Agarwal, however, is the major shareholder in Kaptil Developments through the 45% that he owns directly, plus a further 10% of shares held indirectly (i.e., 18% of the 55% that Agarwal Merchants own).

The Agarwal family business structure is a very simple illustration of how ownership structures can become complex when families own portfolios of businesses. Many families in business are much more complex than this simple illustration and it can be difficult to untangle the web of ownership. An ownership structure chart is a very useful tool for identifying and clarifying intertwining ownership relationships.

Analysing the business

There are a myriad of models and theories that help in analysing a business. From a family business perspective, we are probably concerned with whether the family's businesses are fulfilling their owners' objectives for them. From a policy perspective, we might be interested in whether family businesses outperform or underperform relative to other types of enterprises on particular indicators: e.g., productivity, employment, sustainability. Family business researchers might analyse various aspects of the business to understand the impact and intersect of family and business. Models and tools in use for analysis of enterprises in mainstream management and entrepreneurship disciplines can all be useful in analysing the effectiveness and performance of the family business. Institutional theory, resource dependency, and entrepreneurial ecosystem theories all highlight the relevance of considering the external context within which businesses operate. Strategic management provides us with tools such as SWOT, PEST (and its variants), Porter's Five Forces, Business Model Canvas, Dynamic Capabilities, and others, which are useful in analysing specific aspects of the businesses' strategy and performance. These models are very well explained in many entrepreneurship and strategic management texts and so we will not discuss them further here.

We should be careful of blunt comparisons between family and non-family-owned businesses. Results can vary with the definition of family and non-family businesses, i.e., they can be 'definition dependent'. In Chapter 3 we provide further insight into the varying definitions of family businesses and conclude that there is no single agreed definition.

Comparisons need to recognise and control for additional factors that might influence the dependent variable being examined, whether that is performance, survival, or sustainability. For example, family-owned businesses may occur more in particular industries, they may be associated more with smaller firms, or they may be over-represented in particular geographic regions. Analysis of a family business will recognise the overlapping family, ownership, and business dimensions that impact on purpose, objectives, and strategy. Family owners and managers may have a range of objectives, and success for some may not be only about traditional measures of financial performance. Some family owners and managers might have less interest in short-term financial performance and implement strategies in line with investing in future generations. A firm's direction and values may be influenced by specific family values. Governance structures, which we will examine in Chapter 4, will incorporate family as well as business needs. Family businesses are not all the same, and any analysis of family businesses needs to recognise the heterogeneity that exists within the sector, as explained further in Chapter 3.

Family and ownership analysis and solutions will be dependent on the business' size, industry, age, structure, and financial performance. The following chapters will examine specific aspects of family business, but in placing more focus on the family in the business, we must not lose sight of the importance of the specific business context.

Key learning point

All models are a simplification of reality and have their uses and limitations. Models and theories provide us with a range of very useful tools for analysis of family businesses. Employing a combination of these tools is likely to provide useful insights into family business issues and identify potential issues for further investigation.

Summary

Theory assists us to understand the likely issues that family businesses might face and the reasons for them. A good theory should be practical. Models provide us with useful tools for analysis of family businesses.

The Three-Circle Model was developed to analyse bivalent attributes, the particular characteristics that can bring both advantage and disadvantage to family firms. The model captures the overlap between family, ownership, and management domains and helps to consider issues and perspectives of people in different positions within the family business. The Three-Circle Model provides an extremely useful starting point for analysis of an individual family business but is limited to a static representation of a particular point in time.

The Three-Dimensional Development Model (3DD) highlights change and movement along family, business, and ownership axes. Practically, this model assists analysis by providing a picture of what changes are happening on each of the family, business, and ownership dimensions that might be impacting on a particular issue. Family businesses can become embroiled in discussing family issues in the business and business issues in the family. By identifying where an issue resides, the most appropriate forum can be sought. The 3DD Model has some limitations in common with other stages models.

Construction of a genogram identifies who family members are, their relationship to each other, and their roles. Genograms are a very useful tool for identifying issues that might occur in the future. Analysis of the Moore family genogram highlighted pertinent issues around succession and family governance that, if addressed early, could avoid disputes in the future.

This chapter also looked at how ownership and business dimensions could be analysed. It was highlighted that it is important to consider the wider context of family businesses and not assume that they are all the same. Chapter 3 picks up this theme.

Discussion questions

1   Employ the tools in this chapter to analyse a family business with which you are familiar. Compare and contrast the different tools' usefulness and shortcomings.
2   How might genograms be helpful in understanding conflict within a family business?

Case study 2.1: The prodigal daughter

Quality Tools is a Canadian wholesaler of tools with gross annual revenues of around $20 million, founded in 1960 by John Simon (all names anonymised) in Montreal. His wife, Esther, was not involved in the business much and focussed on raising their two daughters, Rebecca and Catherine. John started planning succession early and opened two new divisions to give each of his daughters some management experience. Rebecca and her husband led the Toronto office while Catherine and her husband managed the Edmonton one. Both daughters, along with their husbands, became part owners in Quality Tools Edmonton and Toronto as part of the ownership succession process.

Sadly, John died in 1980; his wife Esther unexpectedly took over managing the family business and quickly learned the ropes. Relations between Catherine's husband Harold and her mother Esther were fractious. Catherine was busy with three small kids so the management of Quality Tools Edmonton was mainly in Harold's hands, and he had little experience of running a small business. Esther did not trust Harold to manage the business and after the Edmonton office suffered in the economic downturn, Esther insisted that it should be separated from the core business to become the sole responsibility of Catherine and Harold. In return for gaining the Edmonton division, Catherine's shares in the Toronto division of Quality Tools were passed to her sister. Edmonton subsequently went out of business and Catherine and Harold later divorced.

Catherine went back to university, got a degree, and sought to re-engage with the family firm. She knew her cousin Dennis was running the Toronto operation but she was surprised to discover that her sister, Rebecca, held 60% of the shares and both Rebecca's children were employed in the business, whereas Catherine's three children had sought employment elsewhere. Catherine had been receiving an income on the shares she inherited from her father but had not really understood the financial updates she received from the company and she had not been to any of the annual meetings.

As a member of the original nuclear family that founded the business, Catherine believed that she was entitled to equal shares with her sister, but as the matriarch of a successful business, Esther had been concerned about Harold's competence and she stated that she had divided the company in the way she had to protect Catherine's shares from Harold. Esther, aged 78, now managed the company from Montreal with her new husband, while Dennis ran the Toronto division. Rebecca had little involvement in the day to day running of the business and was content to draw an income from her shares and live in luxury on the lake shore. On her return to the family fold, Catherine would like to have a formal role in the business but as yet nothing has been opened up for her.

It could be useful to map out the different parties onto a Three-Circle Model at key points in this case to consider how membership of family, ownership, and business circles changes. Also, consider where communications happen and why Catherine has become marginalised. What does the future hold for the business? Catherine's children are family members but have no ownership or business roles. Rebecca's children are family members and are active in the business. Rebecca's children are likely to take on increasing roles in the future, whereas it is uncertain what the future holds for Catherine's children.

The authors of this case highlight that the title relates to the Biblical parable of the prodigal son. In the parable, the father welcomes back with open arms a younger son who has spent his inheritance on profligate living, whilst the elder son, who has continued to work in the family business, is treated just the same as before. How would you view these actions from a family perspective? Is it the right thing to do? What about from a business perspective? Consider the point of view of each of the family members. This case highlights the complexity and intertwining of family and business.

Source: adapted from Trish Reay and Lloyd Steier (2004), *Family Business Casebook Annual 2004*, pages 77–90.

Note

1 You can find out more about the development of the Three-Circle Model from John Davis at http://johndavis.com/three-circle-model-family-business-system.

3 Family firms
Same or different?

By now you should be starting to realise that family firms are not all the same. But how do they vary? And do they differ that much from non-family firms? How do we distinguish between family and non-family firms?

Many studies have compared family and non-family firms, attempting to assess if one group performs better than the other financially, in terms of longevity, innovativeness, effectiveness of leadership, and various other measures. The most striking thing about these studies is the lack of consistency in their findings. For example, Anderson and Reeb (2003) found that family-owned firms perform better than non-family firms, Villalonga and Amit (2006) suggest that only family-owned, family-managed firms perform better than non-family firms, Bloom and Van Reenen (2007) found the reverse, whereas Westhead and Cowling (1997) found no overall difference in the performance of family and non-family firms.

To understand this apparent inconsistency in the findings, we should question whether the studies can be compared like for like. For a true comparison, studies should be testing identical measures of performance (i.e., dependent variables) and employing the same definition of family and non-family firms. In this chapter we will see that there is a whole range of definitions of family firms and that within any group of family firms there can actually be many variations or 'types' of family firms. For example, the afore-mentioned study by Villalonga and Amit (2006) examined three different types of family firms and found that family-owned firms with founder CEOs performed better than non-family firms and the other two types of family firms. By understanding the variations that can exist we will develop a more nuanced understanding of family business that will enable us to provide recommendations that are more appropriate to a particular firm or family. It will also allow us to consider what it is about family firms that sets them apart from other firms, and in so doing, provide the basis for the most appropriate, valid, and reliable definitions.

We begin by examining the lack of consensus regarding definitions of family firms. The reasons for varying definitions are analysed and the myth of homogeneity is busted. We then examine empirical and conceptual studies of the heterogeneity of family firms.

Learning objectives

Understand a variety of definitions of family firms and their implications for family business studies and practice

Develop skills in critical analysis of empirical and conceptual research, including consideration of definitions, reliability, and validity

Understand the criteria for identifying different types of family firms and relevant explanatory theories

Definitions of family business

If family businesses are to be distinguished from other types of business, it is important that we can reliably define them. Consensus on the definition of family businesses is, however, difficult to achieve because family firms are ubiquitous and range from very large complex organisations to very small owner-managed businesses. Definitions can be separated into those based on objective measures of ownership and involvement and those based on subjective assessments of family influence. Family business definitions that are in common use might require the family to own a majority of the shares, family members to be involved in the management of the firm, the family to have significant influence on the business, or other criteria. However, even within a group of similar firms there can be differences of opinion on whether a firm is classified as a family business or not.

Consider what you think should be the defining characteristics of a family business and then have a look at the following four examples of very large businesses to determine which of them might be defined as family businesses.

1. Mars is privately owned. The 3rd and 4th generations of the Mars family own 100% of the company's shares. Mars has 80,000 employees around the world and has a subsidiary, The Wrigley Company. In 2017 the chairperson was Victoria B. Mars, great granddaughter of Franklin and Ethel V. Mars, who founded the company in 1911. The CEO in 2017 was Grant Reid, who is not a member of the Mars family. The company is headquartered in Virginia, USA. Revenues were reported to be $33billion in 2014. In 2017 the Mars family were believed to be one of the richest families in the USA.

2. Tata is an international conglomerate of over 100 companies and is named after Jamsetji Tata, who founded the first company in 1868. Tata companies produce Land Rover Jaguar vehicles, Tetley tea, Tata Steel, and many less well-known products. In 2015/16, Tata's total revenues were reported to be $103billion, and they had 660,800 employees. Twenty-nine of Tata's companies are plcs. The major shareholder in Tata companies is Tata Sons, who typically own 20–30% in each company. Tata Sons is a holding company, which is owned by members of the Tata family and 66% by Tata Trusts. Tata Trusts is chaired by Ratan Tata, who was Chair of Tata Sons for many years. Each Tata company is

independently run, with its own board of directors and ownership configuration.
3   Walmart is a plc (public limited company). It was founded in 1962 by Sam Walton, who died in 1992. In total, the Walton family own just over 50% of the shares of Walmart through their holding company, Walton Enterprises, and individually. Walmart has 2.3 million employees in their various subsidiary companies, which at the time of writing included a stake in Asda in the UK. Walmart is believed to be the world's largest company, with revenues of $480billion in 2016. The Walton family are believed to be one of the richest families in the world, with a net worth of $149billion. Chair of the company is Greg Penner, who is the grandson-in-law of Sam Walton through marriage to the third-generation daughter of S. Robert Walton. In 2017 the CEO was Doug McMillion, who is not a family member.
4   FIAT was founded by Giovanni Agnelli and a group of investors in 1899. FIAT are owners of Ferrari, Lancia, Alfa Romeo, and, since 2009, Chrysler, when the company became FCA (Fiat Chrysler Automotives). Great-great-grandson of Giovanni Agnelli, John Elkann, is the Chair of FCA and also the Chair and CEO of Exor, who own 29% of FCA but have 44.3% of the voting power, through shares with additional voting rights. The Agnelli family own just over 51% of the share capital of Exor. The Agnelli family have also been controlling owners of Juventus FC since 1923.

The above examples demonstrate that defining a family business is not straightforward. Depending on the definition that is employed, each of the four examples could be included or excluded from being defined as a family business. If a definition requires that a family member should be the CEO of the company, then only Exor would qualify. If a definition requires majority family ownership, then Walmart and Mars would qualify, but FCA and the Tata companies would not. However, if a definition of a family business is that one family should have substantial influence on the firm/s, then all the above would qualify, including Juventus FC.

Importance of family business definitions

It is important to establish the definition that has been employed in a particular study or piece of work in order to identify how the findings might apply, or not apply, outside of that specific study. Where a narrow definition has been employed, the findings might be 'sample specific', in other words they only apply to firms in that sample. Definitions are also important if we wish to establish a valid and reliable body of knowledge. Studies can only be compared or combined if we know the definitions and assumptions that underpin each study. For example, if our aim is to establish whether family firms outperform non-family firms and we employ a family firm definition that requires the CEO to be a family member, we will likely get different results than if we apply a family firm definition that requires 25% family ownership, because the same firms will be classified as family firms under one definition and non-family firms under the other definition. Comparisons of such studies are thus 'definition dependent'.

Definitions are also important for policy makers who might aim to facilitate economic development by targeting firms that are most likely to contribute to long-term economic growth or to increases in employment. Without a clear understanding of which type of firms perform better on specific indicators – and in particular contexts – it is difficult for policy makers to provide fine-grained effective policies that achieve their aims.

Variety of definitions

Westhead and Cowling (1998) tested a variety of definitions of family firms and identified that the proportion of family firms within the same dataset varied from 15% to 80%, depending on the definition employed. Eighty per cent of businesses in the dataset had more than 50% of voting shares owned by a single family group. In 78% of businesses, the business was perceived by the leadership to be a family business. Businesses that satisfied both criteria accounted for 63.7%, indicating that some firms with majority family ownership were not perceived internally as family businesses. Variations in definitions of family businesses might be based on: majority family ownership; family management; family succession – or intention of family succession; family objectives; or family influence. Any of these criteria might be employed individually or as multiple criteria to define a family business. Some definitions require a sufficient level of family ownership for the family to influence strategic decision making, e.g., greater than 25%. Many definitions use two or more criteria: for example, Westhead and Cowling propose that to be defined as a family firm, the majority of the shares should be owned by family members related to each other by blood or marriage, and the firm should be perceived by the senior management to be a family firm.

A good operational definition should precisely identify the target group and exclude those not in the target group. Unambiguous definitions are important in ensuring that research results are reliable, in the precise academic understanding of 'reliable', which means that if a study was repeated employing the same definitions on the same population, the results would be the same, i.e., the study is 'replicable'. Studies of family businesses are notoriously 'definition dependent', which means that the results and models vary, depending on which definition of family business is employed. Unfortunately, some studies, particularly older ones, do not state the definition that they employed. Definitions based on objective criteria are more straightforward to operationalise. However, they may exclude businesses that are perceived by the owners or managers to be a family business (Westhead and Cowling, 1998).

The family business definitional problem is compounded by variations in understanding what constitutes a family. Most people would agree that parents and their offspring are all members of one family. It is less clear whether to include spouses of offspring, stepchildren, co-habitees, divorced spouses, parents-in-law, or cousins related by marriage when defining which family members are relevant to the family business. It is important that when defining a family business or comparing studies, there is clarity about who is included in the family aspect of the definition.

The EU Expert Group definition of family businesses (Mandl, 2008) states a firm, of any size, is a family business, if:

- The majority of decision-making rights are in the possession of the natural person(s) who established the firm, or in the possession of the natural person(s) who has/have acquired the share capital of the firm, or in the possession of their spouses, parents, child or children's direct heirs.
- The majority of decision-making rights are indirect or direct.
- At least one representative of the family or kin is formally involved in the governance of the firm.
- Listed companies meet the definition of a family enterprise if the person who established or acquired the firm (share capital), or their families or descendants, possess 25% of the decision-making rights mandated by their share capital.

Employing the EU definition, Mars, Tata Sons and FCA would be classified as family firms. Walmart would also be classified as a family firm because an in-law (i.e., spouse) is involved in governance. The individual Tata companies would not be classified as family firms where Tata Sons own less than 25% of the decision-making rights, even when they are the largest blockholders (i.e., they are the most influential shareholders because they own the largest block of shares). Interestingly, Juventus FC might also be classified as a family company, as the Agnelli family are the controlling owners and the chair is Andrea Agnelli, who succeeded his cousin John Elkann. Other football clubs that could be defined as family businesses (at the time of writing) include Watford, owned by the Pozzo family, and Blackburn Rovers, 99% owned by the Venky family. Typically, football-club-owning families have generated wealth through their other family businesses.

Scales of familiness

Definitions based on scales of 'familiness' have been proposed to capture the level of family influence on a firm rather than a binary definition of family versus non-family businesses. Such scales have attempted to capture the elusive family culture, which it was believed constituted the fundamental difference that family made to the business, arguing family culture was not necessarily directly related to objective measures of the amount of family ownership. Shanker and Astrachan (1996) developed a three-tier scale that went from little family involvement through some involvement to extensive family involvement.

Astrachan, Klein and Smyrnios (2002) developed these ideas and proposed the F-PEC Scale, which they believed would resolve the definitional issues that plagued family business research. Astrachan et al. (2002: 45) argue:

> The operationalization of family vs. nonfamily enterprises has been a matter of concern from the very beginning of family business research. In most studies, the categorization of firms has culminated in the use of the classification as an independent variable. This approach, while important, has contributed to several problems, such as the lack of comparability of empirical data, confusion over what is meant by the term family business, and unconstructive discussion among researchers.

Astrachan et al. argue that we should not be concerned with whether a business is a family business or not, i.e., a dichotomous classification, but we should examine the extent of family influence on a business to provide comparisons across businesses and understand the impact of variations in family influence on performance, behaviour, and other implications.

F-PEC is an abbreviation for Family – Power, Experience, Culture, which Astrachan et al. argue are the three defining elements of family influence on a business. The F-PEC Scale provides an index of family influence. Family Power measures the level of family involvement relative to non-family, in ownership, governance, and management. Family Experience indicates that as the family moves to second, third, and later generations, their influence is strengthened, and therefore the measure is weighted by increasing generations involved in ownership, management, and governance. The Family Culture sub-scale measures the overlap of family and business values, with higher scores indicating that family influence is stronger where there is greater overlap. The F-PEC scale is operationalised by combining scores for the three elements to produce a continuous scale that is purported to provide a reliable measure of the level of family influence on an individual business.

The F-PEC scale is a very useful reminder of the heterogeneity of family firms in its attempts to measure varying levels of family influence. However, some researchers have questioned the wider validity and utility of continuous scales that attempt to measure degrees of familiness, and instead have shown that distinct types of family firms can be identified and prove more useful in understanding the behaviour and performance of the family business sector. The following section further examines the heterogeneity of family firms.

Different types of family firms

The variation in definitions demonstrates that comparisons of family and non-family firms need to be undertaken and interpreted with care. As we saw in the introduction, studies that compare family and non-family firms have provided contrasting findings on the same phenomenon, which is often because they are employing dissimilar definitions to each other or because they are examining diverse populations of firms. Westhead and Howorth (2007) highlight that it is difficult to build a body of knowledge that provides us with reliable insights into variations in the performance of family and non-family firms because studies cannot be compared, and they suggest that this research stream has reached an impasse. Instead, we should look within the population of family firms to identify variations in performance and draw out the factors that might be impacting on performance, specifically for family firms. As family firms represent such a significant proportion of all firms, then regardless of which definition is employed, it makes sense to expect that they will not be a homogeneous entity and that there will be variation within the family business sector. We noted earlier that myths and inaccurate generalisations about family business abound, and that in practice some family firms are stuck in the past and some are very innovative; some family firms are very small and some are huge, and they grow at different times and varying rates. The performance of family firms cannot be captured in a simple linear regression because it is a complex phenomenon that incorporates intertwining family, ownership, and business objectives, varying balances between long- and short-term perspectives, generational capabilities, as well as all the business imperatives that impact on the performance of any firm.

Warm hearts, deep pockets

In an attempt to capture the family and business influences on performance, Pramodita Sharma (2004) examined variations in family firms' performance with regard to financial capital and emotional capital. She conceptualised four types of family firms, which, in her experience, provided insight into variations in family firm performance. Her model is a simple but insightful take on the realities at the heart of family business. Sharma's four types of family business were titled: *warm hearts–deep pockets*; *pained hearts–deep pockets*; *warm hearts–empty pockets*; *pained hearts–empty pockets*. *Deep pockets* indicate strong business performance that provides financial resources and vice versa for *empty pockets*. *Warm hearts* indicate good family relationships, whereas *pained hearts* indicate poor family relationships that might impact negatively on the business. Like any model, Sharma's two-by-two matrix model simplifies complex realities, but it is insightful in identifying the importance of considering the family business' ability to resource their strategies alongside the emotional complexities that might impact on achieving business goals. We could critique the model for not being theoretically grounded or empirically tested, but nevertheless it appears to have face validity, which means that when we look at the model, it makes sense to us as a basic model that might capture different types of family firms. ('Face validity' is the most basic measure of validity and is a subjective view on whether a model or test appears to capture what it purports to examine.)

A theoretically grounded and empirically tested model of family business types was provided by Westhead and Howorth (2007), who took insights from a complementary employment of agency and stewardship theories to identify six conceptual types of family firms based on company objectives, ownership structure, and the level of family involvement in the firm's management structure.

Agency theory and stewardship theory

In Chapter 2 we provided a very brief introduction to agency theory. It is important that we have a thorough understanding of this theory, which underpins a great deal of corporate governance codes and recommendations, as well as micro-economic studies of firms.

Agency theory provides insights and understanding of contexts where one person may be acting as an agent for another, who is known as the principal. The theory helps to understand issues arising in firms where ownership is separated from management. Managers are appointed to manage a firm in the owners' best interests and so act as 'agents' for the owners. Agency theory recognises that, in reality, managers may act in their own best interests, which could be at odds with the owners' interests – this is the classic 'agency problem' that gives rise to 'agency costs'. Agency problems are compounded by 'information asymmetries', which means that information is not equally available to both parties. Managers are likely to have a fuller picture of the firm than owners. Agency control mechanisms can be used to control agency problems, aiming to align managers' interests with those of the owners by, for example, introducing share options or performance-related pay, or providing governance structures that monitor the managers' and firms' performance for the owners. (For further reading, we would point you towards the seminal texts by Berle and Means, 1932; Jensen and Meckling, 1976.)

Where firms are owner-managed, it is assumed that agency theory is silent; in other words, agency theory does not have any predictive power because there is no agent. In closely held and managed firms there will be little outside influence or representation, and the firm's objectives are likely to be entangled with family objectives. There is, therefore, debate about the helpfulness of agency theory for examining family firms, and it has been suggested that it only provides a partial explanation of the dynamics of private family firms.

Stewardship theory has been presented to complement agency theory. Of particular relevance is the seminal article by Davis, Schoorman and Donaldson (1997), who note the limits of agency theory and particularly recognise challenges to agency theory's underlying assumption of people being self-serving and utility maximising. An earlier paper by Donaldson

(1990) provides an excellent, readable critique of agency theory, highlighting that agency theory emphasises the individual, and the theory suggests that managers will behave in ways that are 'opportunistic, self-serving, guileful and lazy' (p. 379). Donaldson contrasts this with management theories that assume a complex inter-weaving of management motivations, or systems theories that are based on an unproblematic assumption of people willingly co-operating in a shared effort.

Stewardship theory assumes that people can be organisation-serving and have higher-order motives than purely their personal financial gain or utility. Stewardship theory assumes a relationship-based system, with focus on non-financial objectives, and is therefore particularly relevant to family business, because the family itself is (usually) based on relationships, not on profit maximisation or individual gain. Family managers in particular may seek to protect the assets of the family and act as stewards by doing what they believe is best for the firm, rather than chasing after their own personal agendas. Stewardship theory is most relevant where the agendas of owners, managers, and employees are in line with those of the organisation. Strong psychological ownership and high levels of altruism might also be expected.

Six conceptual types of family firms

Westhead and Howorth (2007) employed this logic to distinguish between different types of family firms. They argued that if individuals were self-serving and focussed on financial objectives, profit maximisation would be emphasised and the rational economic objectives assumption of agency theory would hold. Westhead and Howorth suggest that this is more likely where there is separation of ownership and control, and owners may adopt agency control mechanisms to align managers' motivations with their own. However, as we saw in Chapter 2, the introduction of a family system on top of ownership and management systems increases complexity, and some family firms may emphasise non-financial family objectives more than the short-term financial performance of the firm. The key elements that Westhead and Howorth employed to distinguish between different types of family firms were therefore ownership structure, management structure, and the relative emphasis on a range of family objectives or business objectives. We can see that these elements are similar to the underlying elements of the F-PEC scale outlined above (which was purported to capture family influence through ownership, management, governance, and values), but Westhead and Howorth arrived at their model via a different theoretical logic. In their conclusions, Westhead and Howorth argue their empirical tests indicate that a continuous scale of family influence is probably less useful than a typology that is able to identify varying permutations of family firms' ownership, management, and therefore influences.

38 *Family firms*

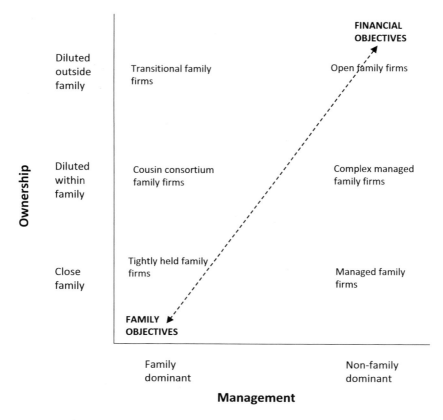

Figure 3.1 Different types of family firms (adapted from Westhead and Howorth, 2007).

Figure 3.1 provides a pictorial representation of the six types of family firms that Westhead and Howorth (2007) derived conceptually. The vertical axis distinguishes between three different ownership structures: firms that have close family ownership (i.e., shares are owned by a small number of family members), firms that have diluted family ownership (shares are owned by a large number of family members), and those where ownership is diluted outside the family (shares are owned by family and non-family members). The horizontal axis distinguishes two variations of management structure: family firms where management is dominated by family members and family firms where management is mainly non-family members. The variations in ownership and management thus provide six potential types of family firms.

Objectives are a cross-cutting theme, and it was expected that financial objectives would predominate when ownership and management were separate and when there was more non-family involvement, in line with the above discussion of agency theory. Family and non-financial objectives were expected to be more important in closely held and family-managed firms, in line with stewardship theory. The line that runs diagonally from bottom left to top right thus represents movement from non-financial towards more financial objectives, as ownership and management are diluted away from the family.

In our adapted Figure 3.1, six theoretical family firm types are labelled as follows: 'Tightly held family firms' are closest to the stereotypical family firm, have closely held family ownership and management, and emphasise family objectives. 'Managed family firms' have closely held family ownership with mainly non-family management and will report a mix of family and non-family objectives but probably emphasising family. 'Cousin consortium family firms' have diluted ownership within the family but retain family-dominated management. 'Complex managed family firms' have more non-family management and likely a mix of close and distant family owners so are expected to place increasing emphasis on financial objectives. 'Transitional family firms' are transitional because they have diluted ownership outside the family, but family members still dominate management. They are expected to be transitional because outside owners are likely to require more non-family managers alongside an increased emphasis on financial objectives. This type of firm might typically be seen during a transition from family to non-family ownership, e.g., a sale or management buyout. 'Open family firms' have diluted ownership outside the family, and non-family management dominates. Some of the large companies discussed earlier in this chapter (e.g., Tata, Walmart) might be typical of this type of family firm. 'Open family firms' are most likely to emphasise financial objectives, and might have some of the agency problems associated with separation of ownership and control.

Westhead and Howorth tested their theoretical framework of family firm types on a sample of 237 small, privately held UK family firms. They derived an 'empirical taxonomy', or classification of family firms, that closely matched the conceptual model outlined above, employing statistical methods that are able to distinguish clusters of firms that are statistically and significantly distinct from each other (if you are interested in the methods used we would recommend reading the original article, which provides a thorough explanation). Using 17 variables representing relevant aspects of ownership and management structures and objectives, they identified seven distinct types of family firms, four of which matched the conceptual types. Two conceptual types (transitional and complex managed family firms) were not validated by the study. As the empirical data were from small private firms, this is not surprising, as these types are more likely to be found in larger family firms.

Variation within types

The key difference between the conceptual types and the empirically identified types of family firms was that within the 'tightly held family firm' type Westhead and Howorth identified three distinct types of family firms with closely held family ownership and management that performed very differently. 'Average family firms' were closely held, family managed, and held a mix of family and financial objectives, with family objectives dominant. 'Entrenched family firms' were also closely held and family managed but had entrenched family objectives, few financial objectives and very weak performance. Such family firms are likely to be high risk in the long term, as they spiral down into entrenched family agendas with insufficient financial resources for long-term sustainability. 'Multi-generational average family firms' were similar to average family firms in many ways but distinct in being older, with greater emphasis on inter-generational objectives and sufficient financial emphasis to ensure continuity.

The most important result of the study by Westhead and Howorth is that distinct types of family firms can be identified conceptually and empirically, i.e., using both theory and data. This finding dispels any assumption that family firms are all the same. There are clearly a number of types of family firms in varying stages of development and with very different needs. Not all family firms emphasise family needs at the expense of the business. And even among those family firms who do put family first, the empirical study showed that there are very distinct groups.

Key learning points

The key learning point is that we cannot generalise about family firms and we should be careful about making broad assumptions that they will behave or perform in a particular way. We need to acknowledge the heterogeneity of family firms and recognise that different types exist in order to gain genuine insights into the fascinating world of family business.

Melin and Nordqvist (2007) go further and argue that the assumed homogeneity that underpins the institutionalisation of family business could lead to mimetic and normative pressures on family businesses themselves to conform to a stereotype that might not be appropriate to their specific context or circumstances. We need to avoid over-simplification and pay attention to the differences within the family business category as well as the similarities.

Advisers, policy-makers, and family firms themselves need to recognise how family firms vary. Awareness of family firm heterogeneity is important in ensuring that enterprise policy interventions and initiatives are designed effectively. Consideration of the specific context and circumstances of a family firm enables advice to be relevant and appropriate.

Summary

This chapter set out to explore definitions and types of family firms. While students and researchers may desire that the notion of a family firm be distilled into a single, essential, all-encompassing definition, this chapter has demonstrated that the sheer variety and constitution of family businesses make a single explanation inappropriate. The chapter established that attempts to compare family and non-family firms have provided conflicting results, probably due to differences in definitions and sample frames. No unequivocal definition of what makes a family firm has yet been agreed upon. It is important to know which family business definition is being employed to provide valid understandings, advice, and policy for family businesses.

Family firms exist across the spectrum of sizes and types of businesses, including small owner-managed businesses and large, complex, multinational organisations. Majority ownership is often employed in definitions of family business, but some large family firms might be dominated and controlled by very powerful families owning only a minority shareholding. Family business definitions are also dependent on what constitutes a family. Opinions vary on how many generations and whether spouses, stepchildren, co-habitees, or ex-spouses should be included.

A widely used definition was developed by the EU Expert Group, employing multiple criteria relating to family ownership and governance. The 'EU definition' requires families to own the majority of shares in privately held firms or 25% in publicly listed firms, and have involvement in governance, in order to be classified as a family business. Others argue that it is the family influence that is key to defining and understanding family businesses. Scales of familiness, such as the F-PEC scale, have been suggested to capture the extent of family influence on a business.

Typologies of family firms provide a helpful way of understanding the variation that exists within the family business sector. The validity and generalisability of research evidence could be compromised if contrasts within the group of family firms are not recognised. Assumptions about stereotypical family firms should be avoided if assistance and advice is to be appropriate for a particular family firm.

Discussion questions

1 What is the best definition of a family business and why?
2 Why do definitions of family business matter?
3 How might you classify different types of family firms?
4 Could you ever define Manchester United as a family business?

Case study 3.1: When blood boils over

All happy families are alike; each unhappy family is unhappy in its own way, wrote Tolstoy in *Anna Karenina*. It is too easy to generalise about family businesses. Some believe they are all harmonious havens of industry, run by relatives whose blood is much thicker than water, but there are numerous examples where family blood boils over and might even be spilt.

Historically, the E. and J. Gallo family provides an example of a family firm that was the opposite of a harmonious, happy family. Family relations erupted in a fairly explosive way. Fiery Californian Joe Gallo started his winery in the early 20th century and married Susie, the daughter of a fellow California winery owner. Susie twice threatened to divorce Joe, but the union produced three boys – Ernest, Julio, and, nine years later, Joe Jr. Life was tough for the older brothers who had to work in the vineyards and got the rough edge of their father's temper. By the time Joe Jr arrived the family business was established and the family were becoming wealthier. Ernest became increasingly dissatisfied with his position and started pushing his father to give him an ownership stake in the family business. Eventually he gave his father an ultimatum, either give him a partnership with equity or he would quit. This led to an angry exchange and Joe pulled out a shotgun and threatened to shoot his two older sons, who promptly fled. It was some months before a rapprochement ensued and the boys returned to the family business. Two years later tragedy struck when Joe and Susie were found murdered, a crime that was never solved and which the coroner recorded as murder–suicide.

At the time of their parents' deaths, Joe Jr was in his early teens, whereas his brothers were in their twenties. Their father died intestate and the older sons took charge. Joe Jr signed everything his brothers put in front of him, including a document giving them full power of attorney. Ernest and Julio put all the assets of both their parents into a partnership – Gallo Bros Ranches. The unhappy family continued to be unhappy in its own way. Julio struggled following his parents' deaths and suffered a series of mental breakdowns that hospitalised him. When he returned to the company he led the vineyard operation whilst Ernest led winemaking. Over the following decades, the commercial aspects of the business flourished but were blighted by low morale and high staff turnover. Ernest had a relentless business drive and treated his own sons with the same rough manner that his father had employed, stressing they should be rigorous, relentless, and ruthless. Julio's youngest son died of suicide, prompting Julio to think about leaving the company, but his younger brother Joe, who was now working with him, persuaded him to stay. Ernest and Julio once more joined forces in the consolidation of a subsidiary, freezing their younger brother Joe out of converting his shares. A row erupted and triggered a series of court cases between the brothers. Joe Jr set up an independent business but was blocked from using the family name. Then Joe Jr found a document from the 1980s that he believed showed his brothers had defrauded him in dealing with their parents' estate. He took them to court but lost, and his involvement with E. and J. Gallo ended in rancour.

Julio died in a car crash in 1993, while Ernest and Joe Jr died in 2007. Despite the bad blood between the three brothers, E. and J. Gallo became the second largest wine producer in the world. The brothers' children and grandchildren continued family ownership, eschewing their forebears' battles and emphasising the importance of attracting and motivating high quality, non-family management.

What do you think are the reasons for the issues described in this case? Which of the 'types' of family business helps to give insight into the case? How did the parental role models influence the family business?

Source: adapted from Grant Gordon and Nigel Nicholson (2008), *Family Wars*, pp. 60–67.

4 Professionalisation and governance

One of the dynamics introduced in Chapter 2 was the need for firms to formalise governance structures and processes as they grow, in order to professionalise their business. Family firms are sometimes portrayed as lacking professionalisation. However, empirical studies highlight that this is an unfounded generalisation and another of the myths about family firms. In fact, there is wide variation in the level of professionalisation among families in business, just as there is wide variation in the types of family firms, as we saw in Chapter 3. For families in business there are two areas of governance: their businesses and their family in business. As a group of interconnected shareholders, the family need to govern the family side of their business as well as the businesses themselves. The way in which a family business is governed can potentially be effective and create value or it can be detrimental and – over time – destroy value.

This chapter explains the options available to families to professionalise the governance of their businesses and of their families. Family councils, family offices, and family charters are explained. Professionalisation is not the binary option that is portrayed in threshold models or common assumptions about family firms. Instead, families in business professionalise in waves that intensify with changes in ownership and management. This chapter explains the influences on professionalisation.

Sir Adrian Cadbury (2000) argued that there are three essential requirements for family firms to achieve success once they have moved beyond the stage of being owned and managed by one or more founders. The first is clarity of roles, which relates particularly to the relationship between business and family. In Chapter 2 we explored the intertwining of family and business objectives and needs. Cadbury argued that good governance for family businesses needs to separate family affairs from those of the firm. Cadbury suggested that all family members, be they executives, owners, or an incoming generation, should be clear regarding the role they can take in enabling the success of the family firm. In this chapter we will examine the structures and processes that enable this clarity of roles. Second, family firms need to have an effective board. It is often argued that families need to bring in external directors to provide objectivity and broaden the perspective. However, families who recruit in their own image or among a close group of family friends could negate the benefits of external directors. This chapter will examine what makes a board effective. The third requirement is to have a logical organisational structure. Cadbury (2000) argues that the structure of the family firm should be aligned to its purpose. Chains of command and decision-making processes need to be clear in order to avoid arguments within the family about fairness and responsibilities.

Learning objectives

Understand the issues that family businesses face in ensuring good governance of their firms.
Be able to explain the roles and relevance of specific family firm governance structures, including Family Council, Board of Directors, Family Charter, Family Office.
Apply relevant concepts to the practical issues of governance.

What are the relevant issues for governance?

In Chapter 2, we highlighted the intertwining of family and business issues. Family can be a force for good and provide a positive influence on the business, encouraging commitment, loyalty, long-term perspective, and good relations within and outside the business. Networks of family members can be drawn upon to enhance the business, as we will see later in the book when we examine internationalisation of family businesses. The business can provide an unrivalled learning experience for the next generation. The Dennis family business (Case 4.2) highlights that there are four areas of learning in developing a family business: learning about business; learning about your family business; learning to lead; and learning to let go. Good governance will enable this learning to take place.

The best families in business can be creative, innovative, and provide the entrepreneurial drive to enable their businesses to excel. The best family businesses are often altruistic, trustworthy, and held up in society as providing a positive influence in their communities. They use their wealth and influence to benefit others, to the extent that some have called them 'natural philanthropists' (Breeze, 2009). However, as we saw in the E. and J. Gallo case (Case Study 3.1), families can also be a melting pot of conflict, embroiled in past hurts and entrenched rivalries, made worse by nepotism, free riding, and destructive self-interest. If such behaviours are brought into the family business, the consequences can be disastrous.

Good governance is required for all businesses, but family businesses have the added complexity brought about by family relationships. Families in business are advised to consider what they would do in the event of a divorce, what are the rights of stepchildren, the rights and involvement of spouses, and whether this is the same for cohabiting couples. Some family owners may wish to only have a family CEO or chairperson, in which case the process for appointing and selection becomes a family issue as well as a business one, and it would be wise to have a considered policy and process. Families are advised to have clarity over inheritance rights, including tax implications, which have been the death knell of some families in business (File and Prince, 1996).

Governance can be formal or informal, i.e., contractual or relational. Where there is strong family cohesion, a collectivist attitude, and alignment of interests, governance may be relational, with fewer formal structures (Pieper, Klein and Jaskiewicz, 2008). Whilst this chapter will emphasise and explain the formal governance structures that can be put in place by family firms, it should be noted that, in some contexts, formal governance structures and contracts may be counter-cultural. Studies tend to be dominated by American or European perspectives, which arise from countries with strong institutional frameworks where contractual and formal structures are the expected norm. In developing economies, legal mechanisms to enforce contracts may be less prevalent, and therefore more informal governance may be the norm. Many of the recommendations of 'good governance' are based on agency theoretic assumptions that ignore social forces and relationships. Some would argue that strong emotional and relational ties are more effective than formal governance mechanisms.

The key point with formal governance structures is to have policies and structures in place before there is a crisis, rather than attempting to make decisions in the heat of the moment. It is not unusual for families in business to be faced with considering who will be the next successor in the middle of grieving over an unexpected death of the incumbent. Gert Boyle of Columbia Sportswear was faced with exactly this dilemma.

In 1970 Gert Boyle's husband Neal died of a heart attack at the age of 47. Neal was the CEO of the firm that had been founded by Gert's parents, making hats and outdoor clothing in Oregon, USA. Gert had little involvement in the business and was shocked to discover that it was struggling financially. The bank recommended that the business be sold. Gert and Neal's son, Tim, was in his first year at university and they had not considered succession. In the middle of grieving for a husband and father and the shock of a sudden death, Gert and Tim had to start learning about the business, weighing up different advice and determining the future for the company. Their story had a happy ending, as mother and son turned the business around and the Columbia Sportswear Company became an international leader in outdoor sports clothing, but many other family businesses have failed under similar circumstances. The title of Gert's book – *One Tough Mother* – indicates how challenging it was for the family. The issues for Columbia Sportswear stemmed from a lack of governance processes, which meant that family members and employees had little involvement or knowledge of the management of the business and made false assumptions about its financial status. The problem was compounded by dependence on one dominant family CEO, who was trusted and who did not share information about the business.

Many cultures would not deem it acceptable to question or challenge family members who are more senior. Some senior family members hold a powerful position over other family members, dominating decision making and constraining the latter's contribution to their business. A well-known issue is senior family executives clinging on to their positions long after the usual age of retirement, refusing to give way to the next generation, who might be in their 40s or 50s but are still deemed not ready to take over. Dominance by one or more senior family members has the potential to hamper business performance and create family conflict or resentment. Intra-generational factions might develop. Younger family members might vote with their feet and leave the family business. Innovation could be stifled by not enabling a diversity of ideas, views, and perspectives to be shared. Good governance could temper the power of dominant family members, providing a control mechanism but also, on the positive side, ensuring that the business benefits from the skills and experience that can be provided by drawing on a broad range of contributions.

The intertwining of family and business can allow family issues to spill over into the business arena. Unconditional love associated with families could reduce the incentive for some family members to put effort into their work, leading to problems of shirking and 'free-riding'. Family members may shy away from tackling bad behaviours by other family members. Particular family members might be favoured in ongoing nepotism, which could lead to resentment elsewhere in the family or firm. Sibling rivalries can bubble up and destroy a company. Nepotism can be reduced by having an agreed policy for the education and employment of family members. The impact of sibling rivalries (illustrated so potently in the example of E. and J. Gallo in Chapter 3) can be reduced by having a forum such as a family council, where issues can be aired before they become destructive.

Family issues tend to become more impactful as the family business moves through the generations. With each additional generation the number of family shareholders is likely to expand: some family businesses have hundreds of family owners in a complex array of cousins, aunts, uncles, parents, grandparents, and siblings. Family owners who are more distant from the business may be more likely to focus on their own self-interest and the dividends they earn rather than the long-term strategic objectives of the company. Focus on dividends is compounded by the illiquid nature of shares in many family businesses, which do not have a ready market for exchange. An expanding group of shareholders can lead to factions developing, for example, between different branches of the family or between executive and non-employed family owners.

In 1992–1993, Clarks Shoes, which was founded in 1825 and had grown to over 14,000 staff, had hundreds of family shareholders who fell out spectacularly over the future of the company. Despite the private nature of this Quaker-founded family business, the dispute was widely reported in the press as 'open warfare' (e.g., *The Independent*, 28 March 1993). As the company made losses and dividends dwindled, two factions had developed, with one group supporting the non-family chairman and the others demanding his resignation. As the factions deepened, the fires of the dispute were fanned by a proposal to accept a bid to buy the firm, which one faction supported and the other faction vehemently opposed, determined to keep the company in family ownership. Clarks came through that dispute by electing a 15-person council to represent the shareholders and take shareholder issues out of the boardroom. It was agreed to keep the business in family ownership on condition that the company was listed before 1998 (this deadline was later extended). The Chair resigned and Roger Pedder, brother-in-law to some of the warring directors, with substantial retail experience, took over as Chair. In 2003 this former 'family at war' was given the JP Morgan Award for Family Governance, partly in recognition of the gracious and professional way they had managed the dispute, which could have been the end of the family business.

Family businesses tend to generate a higher level of emotions than non-family businesses. Psychological ownership, family relationships, attachments to the past, promises made, and expectations of the future all have a bearing on family businesses. As mentioned in the introduction, it is usually recommended that family business owners separate family issues from business issues. Decisions need to be made about employment of family members, successor selection and process, retirement and length of tenure, family share ownership, who can inherit and how shares can be traded, next generation education, and how to develop shareholders' understanding of the business. All these are issues where the family overlaps with the business, highlighting that for family businesses, family governance is also important.

Family governance

Families are a relationship-based system underpinned by emotions such as love. For loving families with high levels of trust, the idea of implementing a formal family governance structure might be anathema. However, many families have found that formalising family governance enables them to address issues before they become problems.

Family business associations and consultants are very active in promoting the development of formal family governance structures. The sceptics might argue that promoting family councils and family charters keeps family business consultants in business, but it could equally be argued that consultants might have increased business if there were higher levels of conflict to require their services.

Parada, Nordqvist and Gimeno (2010) demonstrated the influence of voluntary family business associations on the introduction of recommended

> **Box 4.1 Reasons for family governance.**
>
> 1. Provide a forum outside the business for family dynamics to be addressed.
> 2. Encourage a collective view with input from all generations, and avoid older generations claiming superiority in terms of experience and younger generations thinking their parents or grandparents are 'past it'.
> 3. Clarify roles, rights, and responsibilities of family members.
> 4. Manage family shareholder relations, increasing transparency and understanding of the business.
> 5. Invest in education of the next generation – for their future role as shareholders and possibly employees.
> 6. Avoid or address conflict before it becomes an expensive or destructive battle.

forms of family governance and on conforming to accepted values. Family business associations provide seminars, education, and networking events for their members, and many family businesses see them as an important source of learning. Although there is no coercion, family members who are involved in voluntary family business associations may experience mimetic and normative pressures to conform to specific models of family governance (Parada, Nordqvist and Gimeno, 2010). This relates to institutional theory, which indicates that organisations may morph into similar structures and ways of working through coercive, mimetic, or normative pressures (DiMaggio and Powell, 1983).

Box 4.1 summarises the reasons why families in business might seek to put family governance mechanisms in place. The following sections review the most frequently used methods of family governance.

Family charter

A family charter, also known as a family constitution or family protocol, is an agreement by members of the business-owning family that sets out the principles by which they will manage their relationship with the business and specifies the family's commitment and responsibilities to each other. The agreement is usually developed collectively and written up as a document that can be revisited at specified regular intervals. Each family charter is specific to a particular family and so can include anything that the family deems relevant. The family charter will often provide the basis on which the

> **Box 4.2 A family charter might include processes and policies relating to the following.**
>
> 1. Definition of the business family (who is included and who is not).
> 2. Strategic objectives, family values, and aspirations: why we are in business.
> 3. Family involvement in business: principles, employment, roles, responsibilities.
> 4. Next generation involvement, education, rights.
> 5. Purpose of the family council.
> 6. Responsibility, representation, and relationship between family council, board of directors, and family members.
> 7. Membership of family council, roles, and responsibilities.
> 8. Finance – compensation, expenses, budget.
> 9. Process for amending charter.
> 10. Anything else the family deems relevant and appropriate.

family council will operate, specifying its mission, boundaries, and rules. Families can have a family charter without necessarily establishing a family council, particularly where families have smaller and less complex businesses. Some possible elements of a family charter are listed in Box 4.2.

Why would you need a family charter?

A family charter sets out the principles and processes by which a family in business agrees to govern itself. The family charter can be as simple or detailed as an individual family requires. Clarity regarding rights and responsibilities is provided. For example, the family charter might provide a policy regarding working in the business, such as: all family members have the right to gain work experience within the family's businesses, or family members do not have any preferential right over non-family members to work in the business, or family members must gain five years' work experience outside the business before applying to the family business. The process of agreeing a family charter provides a helpful forum for family members to air and discuss issues that they consider pertinent to their relationship with the business, hopefully before they become contentious. The process allows family members to interrogate time-honoured customs and practices. By having agreed principles and processes, the family charter will not necessarily prevent conflict or disagreements, but it will provide a reference point for family members to air issues and try to resolve them.

A family charter becomes more important as complexity increases. Additional generations may bring new attitudes and increasing numbers of family members with ownership rights are likely to generate greater divergence of interests and motivations. A thoughtfully developed set of principles and processes by which the family's relationship with their businesses is governed provides stability and clarity for the long-term sustainability of the business and ensures that the family are not caught in the ebb and flow of different opinions.

Family meetings

Family meetings enable the family to discuss their interaction with the business outside of the formal business structure. Small family businesses with simple structures may find that family meetings are sufficient for their needs. Some families may rely on ad hoc family meetings for specific purposes, e.g., to discuss succession planning or to respond to a crisis; other families may install a regular pattern of meetings. Smaller family businesses likely find that meeting every six months is sufficient. Membership may be open to all (over a particular age) or specific to a sub-set of family members. For family meetings to work well, the family needs to establish clarity of purpose, roles, and decision making. Families may find that family meetings are a good means of integrating new spouses into the family business, increasing interaction and engagement between family owners and the business, building entrepreneurial learning, improving communication, and developing decision-making skills among family members (Eckrich and McClure, 2012).

Family assembly

A family assembly is an inclusive forum for all family members, often with a minimum age limit. Each business family can determine who is to be included in their family assembly. Larger families may hold retreats or away days with a structured programme of activities and meetings appropriate to different groups, e.g., small children, next generation, shareholders.

The purpose of a family assembly can include education, communication, relationship building between distant family members, as well as governance and contributing to business development. Family assemblies tend to incorporate social activities, and families suggest that they are an important element of ensuring they have fun together. Through social activities and the interactions within a family assembly, dispersed family members can build stronger relationships that might help reduce conflict and increase understanding of varying points of view.

Family council

A family council is a formal governance forum specifically for family members to meet outside of the business and discuss issues relevant to the family's relationship with their businesses. The majority of family businesses do not have a family council, but those that do tend to find it an extremely useful means to manage the interaction of the family and the business. As highlighted in Chapter 2, the owning family influences the business in a variety of ways, and therefore family is a legitimate concern of the business. Many business families have discovered that the implementation of a formal family council is a positive step in managing the interaction of family and business.

The purpose of a family council might vary from one family to another. Overall, family councils are expected to improve stewardship of the family's enterprises by engaging and educating family members, clarifying roles, and addressing family issues outside of the business. Eckrich and McClure (2012: 79–81) provide a useful summary of some of the purposes of family councils. Eckrich and McClure suggest that a family council can promote family mission and meaning by articulating shared values, capturing the family's history and sharing philanthropic activities. Family councils might review the strategy and performance of the family's enterprises, examining opportunities and challenges, and discussing new visions. Family councils provide a means to communicate information between dispersed family members. Many of the issues specific to family businesses arise out of the overlap between family and business. A family council provides the mechanism to extract family issues out of the business and make decisions, resolve problems, and address grievances. A major purpose for many family councils is the education of family members, particularly their younger generations. Family councils might provide an education programme for different age groups that helps them to learn about business generally and their family business specifically, as well as understanding the rights and responsibilities of ownership and wealth. Most family councils will have a concern for ownership continuity and succession and they will take responsibility for reviewing the family constitution to ensure that it remains relevant and effective. Family councils can also be the locus for exchanging information, sharing good times together, building relationships and understanding between family members.

Family office

Larger families in business may adopt a family office, either purely for their own benefit or in collaboration with other families. The key role of the family office is to manage family wealth centrally, but many family offices provide additional services, such as insurance and financial services brokerage, legal advice, tax management, real estate and asset management. In addition, the family office might organise activities such as education and mentoring of younger family members or a family newsletter, which might otherwise sit within the family council; or professional services such as physical security and concierge services for family members. Some family offices manage philanthropic services for family members.

The family office provides a process and means to diversify the family's wealth. Families in business need to consider the risk of retaining nearly all their assets within one business. Some wealthy families choose to diversify the risk by investing in other businesses and in assets not related to business.

There are three variations on the family office model: a) a not-for-profit family office controlled by one or more family owners, providing services exclusively for the family; b) a for-profit family office controlled by family owners, providing services for other clients in addition to their own family; c) a for-profit family office owned by professionals or consultants who provide services to various families. When a family decides they wish to set up a family office, the decision on which type will depend on the amount of their wealth, the willingness and ability of family members to take on roles within the family office, and the level of trust between groups of family owners and professionals. Family offices might be organised as a separate company with a board of directors and paid managers, depending on the resource available.

Some advantages of setting up a family office include the sense of unity and belonging it provides for family members, generating a centripetal force to counteract the natural centrifugal force that occurs as the family expands through generations (Corbetta and Salvato, 2012). A family office can increase the professionalisation and education of family owners and future family owners.

To summarise, individual families can determine the remit of any aspect of their family governance, therefore the exact role and structure might vary. For example, philanthropic activities might be considered within a family council and/or a family office. Corporate governance is more regulated and certain aspects are required by law; although such law might vary in detail from one country to another, it most certainly will include the requirement for companies to have a board of directors. However, the following section notes that the extent to which boards of directors are: a) active and b) effective might also vary.

Corporate governance

Following some very high-profile scandals and the financial crisis of 2008, many countries have adopted codes for corporate governance, most often aimed at publicly listed companies (plcs). The majority of family businesses are privately owned and therefore such codes are not directly applicable, but we can see from the Guinness case study (Case study 4.1) that corporate governance has serious implications in family businesses – for business success, all stakeholders, and for society. From 2018, in the UK, all companies meeting a minimum size criterion (>2,000 employees) must report which corporate governance code they have applied and how they have applied it. In line with this regulation, the Wates Corporate Governance Principles for Large Private Companies were developed to provide a code of governance more applicable to privately owned

> **Box 4.3 The Wates Principles (2018).**
>
> 1 Purpose. An effective board promotes the purpose of the company and ensures that its values, strategy, and culture align with that purpose.
> 2 Composition. Effective board composition requires an effective chair and a balance of skills, backgrounds, experience, and knowledge, with individual directors having sufficient capacity to make a valuable contribution. The size of a board should be guided by the scale and complexity of the company.
> 3 Responsibilities. A board should have a clear understanding of its accountability and terms of reference. Its policies and procedures should support effective decision making and independent challenge.
> 4 Opportunity and risk. A board should promote the long-term success of the company by identifying opportunities to create and preserve value, and establishing oversight for the identification and mitigation of risks.
> 5 Remuneration. A board should promote executive remuneration structures aligned to the sustainable long-term success of a company, taking into account pay and conditions elsewhere in the company.
> 6 Stakeholders. A board has a responsibility to oversee meaningful engagement with material stakeholders, including the workforce, and have regard to that discussion when taking decisions. The board has a responsibility to foster good stakeholder relationships based on the company's purpose.
>
> Further details from www.frc.org.uk.

companies. Box 4.3 lists the six Wates Principles, which all relate to the role of the board of directors. Many countries have developed a governance code specifically focussing on family businesses, some in conjunction with the international Family Business Network (FBN) and some of these provide checklists for family businesses to follow e.g., Gulf Countries, Switzerland. Governance codes tend to aim to achieve a balancing of power, clear structures and processes, and representation of different interests.

Boards of directors

Whilst increasing concerns about corporate governance have led to inquiries and legislation for boards of directors, we should not miss the point that effective boards add value to the firm by providing strategic oversight (Cadbury, 2000) and are not just a means to monitor stakeholder interests. Pendergast, Ward and Brun de Pontet (2011: foreword) suggest that

> A well-functioning board of directors can play an essential role in providing insight and oversight to help businesses succeed – yet many family businesses do not make use of this valuable resource.

Pendergast, Ward and De Pontet (2011) suggest that an effective board of directors is one that meets at least three times per year, is well organised and managed, and includes at least three independent, external directors. However, smaller family firms, if they have any external directors, are more likely to have only one or two (Westhead and Howorth, 2006). Many family business boards include family owners who are not employed in the firm but can be personally very influential through their (usually senior) position in the family. The combination of external directors' objectivity and experience with family owners' commitment and insights can add substantial value to family firms' boards of directors when they work well.

It is important to understand the issues that family firms might face in establishing an effective board of directors. By law, companies are required to establish a board of directors, but there is considerable variability in how effective or active boards of directors are. A board's legal duties are to appoint (and remove) executive directors, set executive remuneration, determine dividends, and ensure that the company is fulfilling its statutory obligations. In addition, many boards review and approve budgets, strategic plans, major policies and significant capital expenditure, and oversee the audit processes. Boards of directors are only applicable to companies, not partnerships or sole proprietors.

Westhead and Howorth (2006) examined family companies' governance and management structures to determine if there were any associations with particular board structures and the performance of the firm. Their findings indicate that family firms do not gain advantage purely from the appointment of particular permutations of directors, for example the ratio of non-family to family directors, but that variations exist in the effectiveness of boards of directors. It has often been suggested that family firms should appoint non-family non-executive directors to provide an external perspective and control the family influence. Westhead and Howorth (2006) did not find any association between the appointment of an external non-executive director and family firms' performance. Some families in business appoint close friends and longstanding business associates as non-executive directors; some non-executive directors are inactive or compliant. The value of non-executive directors' external influence can be limited in those circumstances. It is important therefore to explore how family firms can ensure that their board of directors is effective and not just a statutory body that the family owners do their best to circumvent or ignore.

> The job of the board is all about creating momentum, movement, improvement and direction. If the board is not taking the company purposefully into the future, who is? It is because of the failure of boards to create tomorrow's company out of today's that so many famous names in industry continue to disappear.
>
> (John Harvey Jones in Cadbury, 2000)

Whilst acknowledging that the effectiveness of a board cannot be improved just by imposing a particular structure, it is important to consider the evidence and recommendations regarding board composition.

Family directors can provide a strong connection to family values, strengthening stewardship perspectives and ensuring that the family business preserves the strategic objectives of the family owners, as well as shielding the business from any dysfunctional family effects like sibling rivalries that might be detrimental to the firm. However, a predominance of family directors could potentially lead to over-emphasis on family priorities – to the detriment of the business – and family issues could spill over into the boardroom.

External directors traditionally provide a monitoring and mentoring role, bringing an external perspective to the boardroom and extending the social capital of the business. A high-trust relationship with family directors can enable external directors to provide a challenging, objective perspective – for example, restraining any tendency to over-emphasise family agendas or challenging entrenched positions and escalating commitments. External directors might also be more able to take the heat out of emotionallycharged situations than a family director. Most researchers would argue that family business leaders need to recognise the value of external, non-family directors. However, as highlighted above, family business leaders may select trusted friends and business associates who are not fully independent. High trust might enable freer exchanges but could reduce the capacity for external directors to fulfil the challenging, objective role that is expected of them.

The role of external directors will vary with the size and context of the family business. Founder-led family businesses will be less embroiled in family agendas and likely to value the external director's mentoring role, whereas later generation, complex, family-owned businesses are more likely to require external directors to provide independent, monitoring expertise. Thus, the selection of external directors is important in matching them to the expected role. The Dennis family (Case study 4.2) demonstrates the use of a skills gap analysis to determine exactly what they needed from external directors. For smaller family firms who are not yet ready to include external directors on their board, an advisory board can provide a helpful alternative. Setting up an advisory board retains control but provides the helpful mentoring and advice of an external perspective. For some family firms this might prove a useful transitional stage.

Very few studies have examined board processes or tasks in family firms and therefore we do not know under which circumstances an informal or formal structure is most effective. In the following section we examine the process of introducing more formal structures and professionalising the family firm.

Professionalisation process

Family managers are sometimes contrasted with non-family 'professional' managers, terminology which implies that family managers are not considered to be professional (Hall and Nordqvist, 2008). However, this is another example of a myth about family firms and, as we have already noted, generalisations such as this are neither accurate nor helpful. Indeed, many family managers are highly educated and skilled (Stewart and Hitt, 2012), particularly those from later generations, where the firm's success has provided the family with resources to invest in the next generation's development.

Until recently, professionalisation has been conceptualised as a binary variable, or a threshold that a firm must achieve to move from being an entrepreneurial firm to becoming a professional firm (Daily and Dalton, 1992). This is out of line with what happens in practice, where firms introduce changes in process, systems, and governance procedures over time (Dekker et al., 2015). The Dennis family took five years to implement all the changes mentioned in our case study (Case study 4.2). Howorth et al. (2016b) provide a helpful conceptualisation of the professionalisation process in family firms, which they suggest occurs in waves triggered by changes in management or ownership, and contingent on the specific context of a particular family firm.

If we consider the characteristics we might associate with 'professionals' (e.g., solicitors, doctors, lawyers, professors), we would probably list specialised expertise, high morals, capability, and integrity (Stewart and Hitt, 2012) and notably not increased bureaucracy (Howorth et al., 2016b). Howorth et al. (2016b) suggest that the highest level of professionalisation is 'Mastery', characterised by reflexive management in line with the common perception of other 'professionals'.

Figure 4.1 is a simplification of Howorth et al.'s (2016b) model of the Waves of Professionalisation. Professionalisation develops from an ad hoc contingent approach through formalisation and standardisation, followed by adaptation contingent on firm-specific needs towards mastery. Howorth et al. observed that external drivers, including the introduction of external advisers, investors, and non-family managers, alongside increased risk management, appear to be the most powerful drivers of professionalisation, which include implementation of many of the governance mechanisms and structures discussed in this chapter.

The Waves of Professionalisation model indicates that initially family firms will adopt diverse systems and controls contingent on their specific contexts.

58 Professionalisation and governance

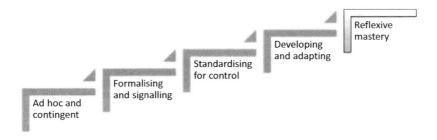

Figure 4.1 Waves of Professionalisation (adapted from: Howorth et al., 2016b).

The introduction of non-family managers is likely to have a funnelling effect, whereby diverse control systems converge into a standardised set of controls and governance mechanisms. Howorth et al. (2016b) developed their model from a longitudinal study of family firm management buyouts (MBOs) and management buy-ins (MBIs). Prior to the MBO or MBI, variations were observed in the extent and specifics of control and governance mechanisms. Entering into the MBO or MBI process was associated with formalisation of policies and processes and structuring the firm for sale. If formal governance mechanisms, regular and frequent reporting systems, and planning and control systems were not already in place, the new ownership would implement them, resulting in standardisation and convergence. Post-MBO/I, professionalisation continued, but the actual mechanisms and controls diverged, contingent on firm-specific circumstances. This study showed that professionalisation focusses on operations when stewardship relationships predominate, but on agency control mechanisms when there is increased potential for agency costs, providing insights into why governance structures might vary with different family firms.

Key learning points

This chapter has considered governance of family firms, highlighting that family firms, unlike non-family firms, have to consider governance of the family's relationship with the business as well as corporate governance relating to business issues. The various elements of family governance should not be taken as prescriptive, but instead are options that business-owning families can consider and determine whether relevant for their specific context and circumstances. Many family firms have found that implementing formal family governance structures has provided them with the mechanisms to tackle issues before they become damaging. Families have also found that formal family governance mechanisms provide a means for the family to strengthen relationships and improve understanding of the business.

Good governance needs to comply with statutory responsibilities and be effective for the firm and the family. Any suggestions that family businesses can be contrasted with 'professional' businesses is an incorrect generalisation. Many family businesses are extremely professional and responsibly managed.

Openness to external advice and scrutiny are key elements of good governance. However, privately owned family businesses are at risk of dominant family executives resisting external advice and controls, which on occasion has led to their downfall. Policy makers in various countries are therefore increasingly interested in implementing governance codes of practice for businesses.

Summary

While good governance is required for all businesses, family businesses have the added complexity brought about by the intertwining of business and family relationships and imperatives. The best family businesses are responsible, well-managed, and trustworthy. However, the negative aspects of family relationships can have disastrous consequences if brought into the family business.

Good governance for family business requires:

Clarity of roles – particularly clarifying the roles, rights, and responsibilities of family members.
An effective board – as outlined in the Wates Principles.
A logical organisational structure – including business and family governance mechanisms.

Many of the recommendations of 'good governance' are based on agency theoretic assumptions, which ignore social forces and relationships. Emphasis tends to be on formal rather than informal governance mechanisms. Some would argue that strong emotional and relational ties are more effective in particular contexts than formal governance mechanisms.

The key point with formal governance structures is to have policies and structures in place before there is a crisis, rather than attempting to make decisions when disaster strikes or in the heat of the moment, as highlighted in the case of Columbia Sportswear.

Family governance is important, particularly as family businesses move through generations and become more complex. Family governance mechanisms include Family Charters, Family Councils, Assemblies, Meetings, and Family Offices.

Professionalisation is not a once-for-all threshold where family businesses step from being weakly governed and 'unprofessional' to become 'professional' with strong governance. Instead, it is a process that appears to occur in waves, stimulated by changes in management or ownership, and contingent on the specific context of each firm. Businesses implement more formal controls and systems as they professionalise, up to a point where they develop mastery and confidence to loosen controls and increase flexibility.

Discussion questions

1   Family councils might be good for the family, but are they good for the business or are they just an expense that the family business can do without?
2   Institutional theory predicts that family businesses will conform to a prevailing governance structure. What influences might family businesses face in attempting to determine a governance structure that best suits their needs?

Case study 4.1: Succession and governance in the Guinness family

Guinness is not only a world-renowned brand, it is also the name of a family who were a bedrock of British and Irish aristocracy. The Guinness dynasty presided over a business that sold its beer all over the planet, founded a finance house, Guinness Mahon, and bought country estates that played host to royalty on numerous occasions. Famously, founder Arthur Guinness signed a lease on the St James Gate Brewery in Dublin for 9,000 years in 1759 at an annual rent of £45.

Share ownership and managerial responsibility stayed within the family for generations, and the preference – like royalty – was for male heirs, a time-honoured tradition that the Guinness family believed was the best way to stem any dissension among the expanding family. Competence came second to carrying on the family line, a lineage that was badly scarred by the Second World War, when prospective chairman Arthur Guinness died in battle. His father, Rupert, stayed on as chairman until he was 88, handing over to his grandson, Benjamin, when he was just 25 years old.

Benjamin had no professional training in management, was shy and lacking in leadership experience. Under his tenure, direction and vision were absent. Increasing numbers of non-family executives assumed senior positions and set about diversifying, much of which was unsuccessful and with very little accountability or board controls. The family's stock dwindled to 20%. In stepped a new CEO, Ernest Saunders. He turned the company round by concentrating on the company's *raison d'etre*, the unique stout that is sold everywhere. Saunders then led a successful takeover of Scottish drinks giant Distillers. On the face of it, it appeared that Ernest Saunders had restored strong governance and renewed the company's direction, but the means by which he achieved the turnaround attracted the attention of regulators and legislative enforcement bodies: Saunders' alleged involvement in share price manipulation saw him jailed and the company's name blackened with something other than roasted barley. Corporate governance had been weak, and in 1997 Guinness merged with Grand Metropolitan to develop a new company Diageo, whose name stemmed from diēs, meaning 'day', and geo, meaning 'world', which refers to the company slogan 'Celebrating Life, Every Day, Everywhere'. The Guinness family continue to own a significant percentage of shares in the combined company.

What do you think are the advantages and disadvantages of the Guinness approach to succession?
How might the approach to governance have changed following the merger with Grand Metropolitan?

Source: adapted from Grant Gordon and Nigel Nicholson (2008) *Family Wars*, pp. 125–131.

Case study 4.2: Professionalisation for long-term sustainability in the Dennis family

Bert and Dawn Dennis' engineering and construction business in Australia had grown steadily from its inception in 1965, weathering upturns and downturns in the country's economy to become a major property developer and builder, with operations across Australasia and joint venture projects in China. Their company reached a point at which it could be sold for a handsome sum, or it could be transformed into a family business powerhouse.

Bert and Dawn Dennis discussed the options with their four adult offspring: Adele, Grant, Natalie, and Marshall. Both Grant and Marshall had joined the family business, while Adele and Natalie had pursued other options. They quickly determined to eschew the idea of a sale and instead instigated a process of professionalisation around a new mission statement: 'To build a long-term, sustainable, and profitable family business for present and future generations'. In order to build long-term sustainability that could withstand demands from each family member, their spouses and future generations, it was decided that the ad hoc arrangements they used to manage their various business interests needed to be formalised.

To achieve this, they determined to amalgamate the various businesses under the umbrella of a single entity, the newly formed Dennis Family Corporation. This would be run by the Dennis Family Council, comprising the six blood relations, all of whom would have equal shares and interests. The family agreed on a shared set of values that should underpin their business, which included:

mutual trust, respect, and understanding;
honesty and openness;
encouraging and supporting each family member;
and always acting in the best interests of the family and the company.

With the help of consultants and benchmarking themselves against other successful family businesses, the Dennis family implemented a governance structure that was as comprehensive as any plc. A Family Constitution was written, establishing the Corporation as an entity that was greater than its individual parts. Provision was made for contingencies such as divorce, a family member wishing to pursue a particular career direction within one of the Corporation's companies, and even for a family member or spouse 'going off the rails'. A board was set up, which included external members, sourced nationally to meet a specific brief following a skill gap analysis. The principles for remuneration were clarified and salaries, directors' fees, and dividend policies agreed.

The initiative involved a big learning process for all concerned. Although all family members knew about business, they needed to learn more about their family business; they had to learn to lead, and Bert, the originator of the business, had to learn to let go of his creation.

What aspects of this case would you consider to be good practice? Which elements do you think are necessary in a family such as this, which is characterised by high levels of trust and good relationships?

Source: adapted from Justin Craig and Ken Moores (2004) *Family Business Casebook Annual 2004*, pp. 91–122.

5 Families in business
Expansion and entrepreneurship

In this chapter we will examine the strategies that some family businesses have adopted that enable them to be truly 'masters of entrepreneurship'. Expansion and internationalisation of businesses requires entrepreneurial actions and enterprising individuals. The focus of this chapter is on entrepreneurship in family businesses, including portfolio entrepreneurship and new venturing.

Earlier chapters have introduced us to some family businesses that have grown to become corporate giants, among the largest businesses in the world. Many have built family business groups, owning groups of interconnected companies that dominate their industries. Some families are very active entrepreneurially through developing portfolios of small businesses. We can learn from their stories what the elements of successful expansion and entrepreneurship are. We can also learn from others who have been unsuccessful or made costly mistakes.

Family members might share their resources, networks, and knowledge to enhance the family's businesses. Often, we also see collaborations between business families who seem to share a bond or cognitive understanding. We noted in Chapter 2 how the complex social interactions and relationship dynamics that characterise family businesses have been labelled 'bivalent' because they have both positive and negative implications. Relationships among a wide range of family members, who may or may not have a formal role in the business, introduce a complexity that non-family businesses do not face. Individuals' relationships with others outside the business and family can influence the family's businesses positively if they are shared and provide expansion opportunities, or negatively if jealousy, conflict, and broken relationships in the family harm family members' businesses.

Bonds and connections within and outside the family, which academics conceptualise as social capital, may underpin the familiness that distinguishes family businesses from other business forms (Pearson, Carr and Shaw, 2008). In this chapter we will examine social capital and explore how it is particularly relevant to family businesses and how it influences families' entrepreneurial efforts to expand their businesses.

Families might expand their businesses locally, nationally, or internationally. They might grow the core business or develop a portfolio of businesses. Throughout history, international trade has flourished through families drawing on their resources and expanding their interests. This chapter will examine how family businesses expand, looking particularly at social capital and the tendency for families to interact with other family businesses. We will examine portfolio entrepreneurship and look at how and why families expand and internationalise their entrepreneurial activities through family business groups and family entrepreneurial teams. In doing so, we will uncover the importance of trust and we will examine theories of trust to provide further insights into the bivalent attributes of familiness.

Learning objectives

Understand influences on family entrepreneurial activities to expand existing businesses and create new ventures.
Knowledge and understanding of portfolio entrepreneurship, including the formation and strategies of family business groups and family entrepreneurial teams.
Knowledge and understanding of the theories of social capital and trust and their applicability to family business entrepreneurship.

From family business to families in business

In previous chapters our emphasis has been on the family business. Chapter 2 examined theories of family business and demonstrated the intertwining of family, ownership, and business systems that makes family businesses unique and complex. In Chapter 3 we noted the lack of consensus with regard to family business definitions and the variation that exists across the family business sector. Chapter 4 examined the governance that a family business might need to consider. However, entrepreneurship in a family business context can take a variety of forms and many families have multiple businesses. The unique environment of families in business is said to provide 'an idiosyncratic bundle of resources and capabilities (termed "familiness") which provides a potential agency advantage in new venture creation' (Habberson, 2006: 879).

In this chapter we shift the emphasis from a single family business unit (i.e., individual firms) to examine the family in business that might have a portfolio of firms. We examine how these families act entrepreneurially and how they expand and grow their firms. A vast amount has been written on entrepreneurship, including many books, but it is noticeable how many of them ignore the family influence on entrepreneurship. Entrepreneurship is rarely enacted by individuals in isolation and yet the myth of heroic individual entrepreneurs continues to prevail. The lack of examination of families in entrepreneurship is surprising when we consider that the majority of firms are family-owned and many more depend on family support, particularly in the start-up phases. For example, it was Mary Gates, Bill Gates' mother, who introduced Microsoft to the chairman of IBM and thus triggered the relationship that proved crucial to her son's early success.

The connection between generations is at the heart of transgenerational entrepreneurship, a concept that is particular to families in business. Transgenerational entrepreneurship is about the long-term enterprising behaviour of families, emphasising the renewal and growth potential that each generation can bring to a family's businesses through expanding existing businesses and creating new ventures. It highlights the family in business as a relevant unit of analysis, rather than individual family firms. Transgenerational entrepreneurship also highlights the challenges and issues associated with transferring entrepreneurial spirit from one generation to the next. This will be picked up in Chapters 6 and 7, where we examine succession and learning.

By looking at the family in business, this chapter provides valuable insights into the practice of entrepreneurship. General theories of entrepreneurship, strategy, and international business are not examined here because they are well covered in other texts. Instead, we focus on concepts that are specifically relevant to the family in business. As we have seen previously, the family bring a relationship perspective into the business and therefore theories that are specifically relevant to family entrepreneurship focus more on relational aspects that impact business. The sections that follow examine social capital and trust theories because they are particularly relevant to families acting entrepreneurially together. We then explore different models and outcomes, bearing in mind the understanding we have gained from these theories.

Social capital

Any examination of the expansion and internationalisation of family businesses needs to understand the importance of social capital. All businesses will employ social capital to a greater or lesser extent to expand their activities, looking to who they know or who they should get to know in order to help them access particular resources or markets. Business contacts come and go, varying in the length of time they are sustained and accessible as social capital. Family relationships, however, are enduring, so families in business are more likely to retain the distinctive social capital that exists in relationships between family members. All a family's relationships are intertwined through a shared past and expectations of a shared future. It has been argued that it is social capital that underpins the very familiness that makes family businesses distinct from other types of businesses (Pearson, Carr and Shaw, 2008).

Social capital has been defined as the goodwill that is available to individuals and groups (Adler and Kwon, 2002). Social capital is an enabler and it does not exist outside the networks and relationships within which it is embedded. Social capital enables individuals, businesses, or other types of organisations to access resources that are available through people they know and that might not otherwise be available to them. Although assessments can be made of the number and form of networks that an individual or group might be part of, social capital itself does not belong to an individual or group, it resides in the links between individuals and groups. Social capital cannot therefore be objectively measured and is instead considered in relative terms, based on the size and form of networks and relationships available to an individual or group. Social capital arises from relationships, shared values, mutual obligations, and personal attachments; embedded within networks of relationships, it enables people and groups to collaborate and share information, ideas, and resources, and therefore, because it has the potential to add value to the family business, social capital is viewed as an asset. Unlike physical assets, however, social capital is tacit. Social capital is also an inimitable asset – in other words, it is unique to each family in business. Businesses or families looking to expand their activities and engage in entrepreneurship will employ social capital to access new markets, find suppliers, and gather information, but every family or business will vary in their configuration of relationships.

Families are a relationship-based phenomenon and social capital is at the heart of how families in business function. In order to understand family businesses we need to understand the social capital embedded in often complex family and business networks, particularly the social capital within and arising from the family, because this is what provides a fundamental difference between family and non-family firms. In Chapter 2 we highlighted how family members without a formal role as owners or employees can influence the business. A unique advantage of families in business is that they can extend their social capital through such family members.

So, for example, your aunt may be on holiday and become friends with someone with business interests in a different country. If the aunt is knowledgeable about your business, she might recognise the value of making introductions. You can imagine the conversation going along the lines of 'My niece's business is looking to expand in your country and I'm sure you'd have interests in common. I must introduce you'. In this way, the aunt, who might have no connection to the business other than being related to you, is able to actively expand the family business' social capital.

Social capital can be expanded through a whole range of family connections. Consider the value of next-generation family members studying or working within an international environment and making friends with people from a variety of countries. Some innovations and new markets have been opened up for family businesses through such connections. William Grant and Sons, famous whisky distillers founded in Scotland in 1886, began exporting to Canada in 1905 after discovering that the Canadian High Commissioner was a distant relative. Clarks shoe manufacturers' 'desert boot' was the result of young Nathan Clark serving in the British Army in India and being impressed by the comfort and the practicality of boots brought from Egypt by other British officers. On returning to the UK, he shared the design with the family firm and the desert boot was adopted as the 'cool' footwear of choice for a whole generation of young people from the 1950s to 1970s. Clarks' connections with family member Nathan Clark – and through him with the British Army – opened up an important new market to the company that became a mainstay of their product line.

Business families might proactively engage in formal networks to expand their social capital. This is not unique to family businesses; many businesses strategically engage in particular networks, but family businesses are able to engage in national and, importantly, international networks exclusive to family businesses, such as the Family Business Network (FBN), a global network of family businesses. As noted above, the shared understanding of being a family in business appears to enable trusted relationships to grow between some business families. This 'shared understanding' relates to the cognitive element of social capital.

Social capital and familiness

Earlier, we highlighted that familiness was perceived to be an idiosyncratic bundle of resources and capabilities (Habberson, 2006), of which social capital is an important element. Social capital can be divided into three dimensions, structural, cognitive, and relational aspects, which can help us break down and better understand the familiness construct (Pearson, Carr and Shaw, 2008). By examining familiness in this way, it helps us to understand how social capital is employed and how it might influence the strategies of family businesses. The structural dimension of familiness consists of the interactions, patterns, and ties within the family, some of which will arise from the governance structures discussed in Chapter 3, while some will be linked with the family's history, and others will arise from current or new relationships within the nuclear and extended family. Ties might be classified as strong or weak (Granovetter, 1973), with strong ties denoting relationships that are close, such as family or friendships, and weak ties representing more distant relationships, such as associates and transient relationships. Strong ties are more likely to be associated with shared understandings, interpretations, and systems of meaning (Nahapiet and Ghoshal, 1998), which is captured in the cognitive dimension of familiness.

It is this cognitive dimension that is at play when family members talk about them 'all being on the same page', or having an innate understanding of what is important in their business, or what it means to be a member of their family. Many successful business families will capture the cognitive dimension in a formal articulation of their values, which might then form the basis for company values.

The Bibby Line Group is a 200-year-old family business, starting out as a shipping line in 1807. As of 2019 the group included Bibby Line, Bibby

Distribution, Bibby Hydromap, Bibby Financial Services, Garic UK and Costcutter supermarkets. Bibby Line Group is one of the largest privately owned businesses in the UK, operating in 16 countries with revenues of £1billion and 4,000 employees. The Bibby family are actively involved in the management of the group and, until 2018, Sir Michael Bibby was the group's managing director. As you enter the Bibby Line Head Office in Liverpool you see their values written large on the wall.

> People are the most important part of our business ... all of us, at all times strive to: Work Together; Be Better; Trust Each Other; Be Innovative; Do the Right Thing.

By sharing and displaying these values so prominently, the Bibby owners and management aim to share with employees (and promote to suppliers and customers) some of the values that they believe to be important, in other words their shared cognitive understanding of the values that underpin doing business the Bibby way.

The cognitive dimension of social capital is also seen between members of different family businesses, who develop deep friendships through their shared understanding of what it means to do business in a family business context. In addition to Chambers of Commerce and generic business organisations, family business owners might be members of specialist family business associations such as FBN (Family Business Network) or IFB (Institute for Family Business) that build ties with other family businesses. Chapter 4 highlighted the role that family business associations play in introducing mimetic and normative pressures to conform to specific models of governance. Connections through family business associations can provide weak ties but with a shared understanding of family business, which could provide excursions into unknown territory, physically and metaphorically, and thus generate new ideas and entrepreneurial opportunities.

The shared understandings that arise from the cognitive dimension of social capital can also have a downside. Strong or close ties, such as those often found within family or friendship groups, can lead to embeddedness, and families can become entrenched in 'groupthink', which might limit entrepreneurial or creative thinking. Alternatively, families might assume they are all on the same page but in practice have very different understandings. By their nature, cognitive understandings are tacit, and if there are no mechanisms for articulating values and beliefs, incorrect assumptions might prevail.

The third dimension of familiness is the relational dimension and consists of all the elements that make relationships work (and threaten them when they are not present), including trust, norms, obligations, and identity (Pearson, Carr and Shaw, 2008). When trust, norms, obligations, and identity are strong and focussed on the collective, family members will be more committed to each other, and they may be more likely to get involved in or support entrepreneurial initiatives to expand their family's businesses. Thus, the relational dimension of familiness provides an extended resource for the family in business through their social capital.

Not all families have strong, trusting relationships, and many families have one or more family members who do not 'fit in'. Where the relational dimension is characterised by jealousy, conflict, low trust, or lack of identification with the family, the effects on the family and the family's businesses can be destructive. In some families, it only takes 'one bad family member' to undermine the family firm (Kidwell et al., 2013), a phenomenon that has been called the 'Fredo effect'. Fredo is the middle Corleone son in the American movie *The Godfather*. He is considered to be the 'black sheep' of the family and not suited to take a leadership role but instead given a side activity. Fredo sees this as rejection and engages in behaviour that is disastrous for the family and the business. Kidwell et al. suggest that the 'Fredo effect' occurs in many family businesses. It is compounded by guilt towards a difficult child, undeserved rewards, ignoring bad behaviour, and putting more faith in a family member than is justified. This exacerbates damaging behaviours, increases a sense of entitlement and leads to increased conflict, all of which can undermine a family that wants to engage in entrepreneurship together.

Stewardship influence on entrepreneurship

In Chapter 3 we explained the principles of stewardship theory and suggested that family firms provide a context where stewardship behaviours might be more likely. Stewardship theory complements social capital in that it relates to commitment and shared vision. A stewardship perspective would influence family members to focus on strategies that protect or build their shared assets, rather than pursuing their individual interests (Donaldson and Davis, 1991). Thus, family members will provide access to their social capital to further the interests of the collective.

It is interesting to consider what that collective might be: this is most often assumed to be the family business (singular), but families in business frequently build portfolios of businesses either through structured family business groups or through interconnected permutations of family members or family entrepreneurial teams. For some, stewardship may relate to one family business that is served by generation after generation of the same family; in other families, commitment may be to the shared interests of the family rather than one particular business. In the latter case, family members will seek opportunities for the family rather than for one specific business, and the portfolio of the family's interests would be emphasised more than any individual component. In some cases, focus on stewardship of the family's shared interests leads to very entrepreneurial families, while in others it could lead to risk-averse strategies that aim to protect the family's wealth.

Difficulty arises where there is variation in attitudes to risk within the family and this can lead to conflict. For some families, particularly 'cousin consortium' family businesses, more distant family owners might adopt risk-averse positions focussing on short-term financial rewards, i.e., dividends from their shares, rather than long-term investment. In such cases, some businesses 'prune the family tree' to a smaller group of family owners, thus restricting ownership to family members who are more likely to have the same focus. This may involve a share buy-back, where the firm purchases shares from some family owners to consolidate ownership, or in extreme cases a management buy-out (see Chapter 8).

It should be noted that the etymological roots of stewardship emphasise that good stewards aim to grow the assets they have, not just protect them in a caretaker role. A stewardship perspective that is true to these roots would be entrepreneurial, and family members who wish to expand the wealth, assets, and opportunities of the family would be active entrepreneurially.

However, as we saw in Chapter 2, families in business are not internally consistent nor externally homogeneous (Westhead and Howorth, 2007). Not all families will adopt a stewardship perspective and those that do may find that there are pockets characterised by self-interested attitudes and behaviours that destroy rather than build value. If some family members indulge in self-serving behaviours, others may feel betrayed and less motivated to contribute towards the general good. Discua Cruz, Howorth and Hamilton (2013) indicated that where individual family members are self-serving rather than collective-serving, there is likely to be more fragmentation of entrepreneurship within the family. In such cases, the expansion of the original family business may be constrained, as individual family members develop their own businesses independently or small factions of family members join in founding new businesses together.

Trust

Social capital is efficacious when it is threaded through with trust. It has been suggested that 'entrepreneurial behaviour cannot be understood without taking into account the phenomenon of trust' (Höhmann and Welter, 2005: 4). Trust, norms, obligations, and identity are interdependent, and trust probably underpins many of the theories used to explain behaviour in family businesses.

A widely used definition of trust is 'the willingness of a party to be vulnerable to the actions of another party [who] … will perform a particular action important to the trustor, irrespective of the ability to monitor and control that other party' (Mayer, Davis and Schoorman, 1995: 712). When you trust someone you are willing to open yourself up to their actions; if their actions have to be monitored or controlled, this suggests a low level of trust. The formal governance mechanisms that were explained in Chapter 4 have a strong element of monitoring and control, but trust is still required so that individuals will 'perform a particular action' (as in Mayer et al.'s definition). Within expanding family businesses, different individuals or 'parties' (e.g., family members, owners, managers) need to depend on one another, thus making themselves 'vulnerable to the actions' of the other party. Trust between the relevant parties is likely to be crucial as families in business work entrepreneurially together to create, expand, and internationalise their businesses.

Trust exists in different forms or strengths (Lewicki and Bunker, 1996); the weakest form of trust is based on calculated risk and is called calculus trust. If somebody is basing their expectations on calculus trust, they will consider the trustworthiness of another and the decision whether to trust them or not within a specific calculated context or contract. Knowledge-based trust is stronger than calculus trust and is based on relationships and the knowledge arising from the other's previous actions within that relationship. In making an assessment of trustworthiness under knowledge-based trust a person will consider, consciously or subconsciously, what they already know about the other and how they have acted previously. The highest and strongest form of trust is unconditional, identification-based trust. Identification-based trust does not have to be thought about, it extends across a variety of contexts and it is less likely to be broken. Within families, trust is more likely to be the strongest form, based on identification, as family members identify with each other and frequently share values and behaviours they would understand as normal (Discua Cruz, Howorth and Hamilton, 2013). Thus, because family members are more likely to have a strong identification-based trust of each other, they may be more willing to be vulnerable to other family members' actions in comparison with their willingness to be vulnerable to non-family members' actions. This is a major reason why family members frequently go into business together or support each other's business ventures.

Perceptions of trustworthiness vary with context. Mayer, Davis and Schoorman (1995) break trust down into trust in another's ability, their benevolence and their integrity. In practical terms, we might trust that our parents will be kind to us (benevolence) and that they will be honest in their dealings with us (integrity), but we may not trust that they will be good at a particular task (ability). In an alternative context, or with a different task, our perception of their trustworthiness may change. Conversely, we may trust that someone is very skilled and capable of doing a task but we might not trust their integrity. Within a family business, family members are likely to have perceptions about the trustworthiness of others, and, as family members usually have longstanding relationships with each other, some of these perceptions could be quite entrenched, whether for good or ill.

Trust explains some of the classic family business behaviours. Where families in business demonstrate a preference for employing internal family candidates over external candidates with more demonstrable skills and experience, this might not be a non-rational decision if the families place greater emphasis on trust in integrity and benevolence than trust in ability.

Family businesses which do not expand or change but continue doing the same old things in the same old way might be perceived to be risk averse, but at the heart of their risk aversion might be low levels of trust in each other, in employees or in the markets. Conversely, families with high levels of trust in each other will be more likely to take risks together. Families in business who avoid taking on debt talk in terms of differences in their values and those of investors and the financial markets; underpinning such talk is a lack of trust, which arises because there is a different cognitive understanding of what is important.

Having examined some of the theories that help to explain entrepreneurship, expansion, and internationalisation in a family business context, where relationships might have a powerful influence on business behaviour, we shall now examine different forms of entrepreneurship that families in business might engage in to expand their interests.

Portfolio entrepreneurship

Some individuals are 'habitual entrepreneurs' (MacMillan, 1986; Ucbasaran, Wright and Westhead, 2003) who engage in entrepreneurship on a repeated basis, either as 'serial entrepreneurs', who have one business at a time, or 'portfolio entrepreneurs' who have more than one business at the same time. Serial entrepreneurs found one firm, close or sell it, and then found another firm. Serial entrepreneurs will frequently use tangible and intangible resources from a closed firm to found a new start-up. Portfolio entrepreneurs found more than one firm, owning two or more firms at any one time.

Many habitual (and non-habitual) entrepreneurs found their businesses with others, some in enduring 'entrepreneurial teams', which will be examined below, and others in permutations of family, friends, and colleagues. In the same way that individuals might be habitual entrepreneurs, some families are also habitual entrepreneurs, founding more than one firm, most often in portfolios rather than the serial model. Some families undertake portfolio entrepreneurship in order to provide opportunities for the younger generation to develop their entrepreneurial skills. Others build a portfolio because one business is not sufficient for the family's needs, particularly where market opportunities are limited in developing economies (Rosa, Howorth and Discua Cruz, 2014). The portfolio model enables risk management because, through founding distinct new businesses rather than expanding the existing business, the support of more experienced family and non-family members is available to young entrepreneurs but the main family business is not put at risk. New businesses can provide an effective training ground for nascent entrepreneurs in the younger generation. Younger family members may have an interest in business and may demonstrate entrepreneurial tendencies, but they may have little interest or skills in the specific industry that the family is currently operating in. Family portfolio entrepreneurship enables such members of the younger generation to develop in an industry where they are more likely to flourish.

Many families develop portfolios of businesses inadvertently in an evolving process, without a particular strategy or purpose in mind, particularly in the early stages, as they engage in a succession of linked entrepreneurial adventures. Portfolio entrepreneurship in a family context is not necessarily planned or strategic, and could be viewed as non-rational from an economic standpoint. However, from a family viewpoint it may be very rational to invest in each other and develop opportunities for family members to flourish. It might also be rational for a family to try something out with a low level of investment.

A family's portfolio of businesses might develop in line with an effectuation logic (Sarasvathy, 2001). Effectuation logic is presented in contrast to causal logic where there is a pre-determined goal and a planned approach to achieving the goal. In entrepreneurship, causal logics are captured in the stages approach of seeking, evaluating, and exploiting opportunities (Shane and Venkataraman, 2000). Effectuation logic is a way of thinking about entrepreneurship that starts with the means (what have we got) rather than the end (what we want to do). When the Lobo family developed their soya enterprise (La Empalizada, Case study 5.2), they had an expanding family, a challenging market for their existing products, and an empty flour mill. Conversations with people they knew highlighted the potential for retooling their flour mill for soy. Low initial investment allowed products to be trialled, methods adjusted, and commitments obtained, resulting in expansion of the Lobo business portfolio. This is a classic effectuation approach (more details on effectuation logic are at effectuation.org and Sarasvathy, 2001).

Different approaches to portfolio entrepreneurship in the family business context include coordinated approaches, such as family business groups and family entrepreneurial teams, and uncoordinated approaches. An uncoordinated portfolio is a loose grouping of businesses by one family that could result through ad hoc ventures into entrepreneurship by various family members. For example, in a fictional case, Catarina Cruz has a group of four shops that she has developed with the help of investment from her parents, who are retired and live on the family farm. Catarina's daughter develops an equestrian facility in which her grandmother and grandfather have a 20% share each. Catarina's son develops a business in a nearby city, selling autoparts. Catarina closes two of her shops and rents out the properties. Her son manages the properties for her and together they set up a new property management business. This portfolio of businesses is all connected to the same family but there is no overall control by a family group and no central coordination.

A coordinated approach will have a formal structure, such as a holding company. Family business groups emphasise the organisational structure, whereas family entrepreneurial teams emphasise the entrepreneurs themselves.

Family business groups

A family business group is a coordinated group of firms, owned or controlled by a group of people with family ties. Family business groups (FBGs) may consist of a few or a large number of companies but the key point is that they have interconnected shareholdings and are coordinated, usually through a central holding company. Pyramidal structures that disconnect ownership and control are frequently used. Shareholdings can be quite complex as different companies own equity in each other and so the equity of each family (or other) owner is not immediately obvious and may need a little detective work to disentangle. Understanding who has the major influence or control can be complicated by variations in classes of shares, wherein the voting rights of shares differ.

Large family business groups often develop through acquisition. Businesses in the group may be undiversified, or related in some way, e.g., in the same industry or part of a supply chain, or they may be diversified to spread risk in a classic portfolio strategy. Synergies may arise through access to resources, markets, knowledge, capital, and collective power. Costs may be reduced through vertical or horizontal integration. In this, families in business are no different from any other type of business group that is looking to expand their portfolio of businesses. However, families may expand the business as the family expands to provide opportunities for family members, and/or to follow interests of family members. In the best cases, the family can bring together identifiable, trusted individuals who likely share values and entrepreneurial understanding.

The institutional environment of families is an important influence on the type and structure of businesses. Family business groups exist throughout the world, but it is noticeable that they are prevalent in developing countries (Rosa, Howorth and Discua Cruz, 2014). In Southeast Asia, Carney and Gedajlovic (2002) showed that FBGs contributed significantly to the rapid rise of the region's economies post World War Two. Despite their cultural variations, across a range of ASEAN countries (Thailand, Philippines, Indonesia, Malaysia, Singapore) a similar diversified FBG organisational form developed, run by migrants or their descendants from mainland China. Chinese migrants owned a majority of private businesses in these countries despite being a very small minority of the population in all nations except Singapore. Before World War Two, Chinese entrepreneurs typically acted as middlemen for colonial British, Dutch, or Japanese trading houses. Unfavourable environments for entrepreneurship post World War Two led to migration from China and the setting up of businesses overseas. Employing a group structure rather than one large business, FBG structures enabled Chinese family business owners to protect and diversify their wealth, limit their visibility in an environment of discrimination, and control non-family managers whom they did not fully trust by restricting their influence and tying their performance to smaller business units.

Similar reasons are provided for FBG structures in other hostile environments. For example, family business owners in Honduras, Central America, employ FBG structures to disguise the extent of their wealth in a hostile environment where the wealthy are targeted and kidnapping is prevalent. The FBG structures enable them to control the risks by employing non-family managers. Central American business families spend considerable periods of time out of their home country, with Florida and California being especially popular.

Some business families find it impossible to hide their wealth and are very much in the spotlight. In Chapter 3 we introduced Tata, an international conglomerate of over 100 companies, headquartered in India. Tata is an example of a large, complex FBG. Tata companies include Land Rover Jaguar, Tetley tea, Tata Steel and many other brands with the Tata name. In total, Tata companies employ nearly 700,000 people, equivalent to twice the entire population of Iceland, and they have revenues of over US$100 billion (2017), which is higher than the GDP of two thirds of the world's countries. The major shareholder in Tata companies is Tata Sons, who typically own 20–30% in each company. Tata Sons is a holding company, which is owned by members of the Tata family and 66% by Tata Trusts. Tata Trusts is chaired by Ratan Tata, former Chair of Tata Sons. Each Tata company operates independently, with its own board of directors and ownership configuration. Twenty-nine of Tata's companies are publicly listed companies (plcs).

Family entrepreneurial teams

Entrepreneurial teams usually have the purpose to identify and pursue entrepreneurial opportunities together. They might be formed as a result of someone identifying an opportunity and putting a team together to pursue it, or they could be formed by a group of entrepreneurs wanting to work together who then seek opportunities after they have formed the team. Sometimes the former can lead to the latter when a team values working together. An entrepreneurial team is defined as two or more individuals who engage in the identification and pursuit of business opportunities to establish or purchase a firm, have an equity stake in the firm, and a direct influence on the strategic choice of the firm at the time of founding (Wright and Vanaelst, 2009).

Family entrepreneurial teams will include two or more family members and sometimes they might in addition include one or more non-family members. Within families, members may feel and behave as if they have an ownership stake before they actually have any financial ownership, as discussed in Chapter 2 with regard to psychological ownership. Younger family members might expect to become owners through inheritance or succession. They may be fully involved in creating a new business with family members but, at the time of founding, younger family members might not have an actual financial stake. The definition of a family entrepreneurial team takes this into account and is therefore

> two or more family members, related by kinship or marriage, who engage in the pursuit of business opportunities to establish, purchase, or expand a firm, have an actual or planned equity stake in the firm and a direct or legitimate influence on the strategic choice of the firm.
> (Discua Cruz, Hadjielias and Howorth, 2016)

Unlike family business groups, family entrepreneurial teams are more likely to own 100% of the equity in their businesses. Although family entrepreneurial teams might be a vehicle for increasing the wealth of the family or protecting the family's assets, the chief driver appears to be a desire to be in business together for the long term and members emphasise the importance of family unity and considering future generations (Hamilton, 2013). Family entrepreneurial teams can develop as a planned entrepreneurial strategy, but this is likely less usual than in non-family entrepreneurial teams. Many family entrepreneurial teams are associated with new generations growing up and expanding the business family. Some family entrepreneurial teams evolve out of a dissatisfaction with the established family business or a lack of opportunity for junior generations within existing businesses. Others provide a vehicle to exploit identified opportunities that do not sit within the existing business structure. Within family entrepreneurial teams, sub-teams might be developed to exploit particular opportunities and to provide leadership opportunities for different family members. Having a portfolio of separate businesses diversifies risk for families in business.

The connections and bonds through social capital enable entrepreneurial teams to be drawn from (mainly nuclear) families. The cognitive dimension of social capital indicates the importance for family entrepreneurial teams to have a shared understanding, particularly around stewardship of the family's assets. Successful family entrepreneurial teams will articulate why they are in business together and what they are aiming to do. This might be in the form of a formal set of values, a stated purpose or mission statement, or it might be through shared narratives about what is, and is not, done in their particular family or team.

Family members are not automatically included in a family entrepreneurial team and decisions on who is included in the entrepreneurial team, and who is not, are related to relational aspects of trust and shared values (Hamilton, 2013). Discua Cruz et al. provide an example where a particular son was excluded from the family entrepreneurial team, as explained by his sister:

> My father was really sad … but realized he could not work with him anymore in the businesses. He was very eager to engage in very risky businesses that would harm the legacy my father wanted to leave all of us.
> (Discua Cruz, Howorth and Hamilton, 2013: 37)

In the La Empalizada case (Case study 5.2), only two of a potential 12 members of the next generation joined the senior generation as members of the family entrepreneurial team. The reasons for exclusion include pull factors like choosing alternative careers or push factors such as not demonstrating an inclination for hard work. Further examples of why specific family members were excluded from family entrepreneurial teams highlight the importance of trust and shared understandings:

> They do not have that facility to see things the way we see them ... they are very nice but I am not certain of their business spirit ... with uncles or aunts [it] is difficult ... I don't trust their business acumen.
> (Discua Cruz, Howorth and Hamilton, 2013: 37)

Putting entrepreneurship into context

This chapter has examined family aspects of entrepreneurship, but it is important that we insert a caveat. We cannot examine family entrepreneurship (or indeed any aspect of family business) in isolation from its institutional, geographic, cultural, and economic context. We provide a few examples to illustrate this point.

The institutional context can influence strategy and structures of families in business. Where institutional environments are less developed, for example, legal structures are weaker and contracts less enforceable, there may be greater emphasis on trust, networks, family ties and relationships, and we may see more prevalence of family businesses. Where minority shareholders have fewer protections, we may see increased use of family business groups with elements of public ownership.

Families in rural or isolated communities may have stronger family ties than those in urban environments, leading to more interconnected businesses, but they may have fewer weak ties, constraining the identification of opportunities for innovation or entrepreneurship. Particular regions or cities will vary in their employment opportunities, which could influence the propensity for entrepreneurship.

In developing countries, where economic activity is constrained, plural modes of income generation (or pluriactivity) are common and various members of a household might engage in a whole range of activities, some related to entrepreneurship and some as employees (Rosa, Howorth and Discua Cruz, 2014). In some developed countries, farms, which are often family businesses, are encouraged into diversification through financial incentives (e.g., EU subsidies) or market constraints.

Cultures vary in their approach to family and who is included in the definition of family, with more and less emphasis on extended family, or tribes. Business families in cultures that emphasise independence and individuality may prefer to support family members to set up individual businesses, whereas in cultures that place importance on the collective there may be more prevalence of collective ownership and shared leadership of businesses.

These are only a few examples that show it is important to consider the context of a particular family or business and avoid making sweeping generalisations.

Key learning point

By examining the family in business rather than individual family businesses, we get a much better understanding of the entrepreneurial activities of a family.

The connections, understandings, and relationships that family members share, as captured in the concept of social capital, are at the heart of them coming together in business, whether as family entrepreneurial teams, family business groups, or with uncoordinated portfolios. The dark side of social capital, including disconnects, inconsistent understandings, embeddedness, groupthink, and destructive relationships help to explain how family entrepreneurship can falter.

Summary

Entrepreneurship is rarely undertaken by individuals in isolation and family members often provide resources, connections, and knowledge to enhance each other's businesses. Many families also have interconnected portfolios of businesses, which can be uncoordinated and develop in an ad hoc process, or formally coordinated through family business groups or family entrepreneurial teams. If our unit of analysis is always focussed on individual family businesses, we will miss the unique advantage that families in business can gain from their interconnections. This chapter therefore advocates considering the family in business as the most appropriate unit of analysis for examining entrepreneurship in a family context.

At the heart of families in business is social capital, which provides the structures, cognitive understanding, and relationships that facilitate collective entrepreneurial activities. The dark side of social capital can undermine or in extreme cases destroy entrepreneurship for families in business.

Trust is an important aspect of doing business together and high levels of trust facilitate family entrepreneurship. Trustworthiness can be broken down into ability, benevolence, and integrity, and family members who act entrepreneurially together likely need to trust each other on all three dimensions.

Many families develop portfolios of businesses in an evolving process, without a particular strategy. Family business groups adopt a more structured approach and include interconnected, sometimes very complex, groups of businesses that are owned or part-owned by members of the same family.

Family entrepreneurial teams provide a vehicle for family members with the desire to be in business together for the long term. Family entrepreneurial teams may thus have longer horizons than non-family entrepreneurial teams. A long-term approach is associated with stewardship. For families in business, stewardship is more likely associated with the family's assets as a whole, rather than a specific family business.

Finally, we warn that we should not examine entrepreneurship in isolation of its context. Institutional, geographic, cultural, and economic contexts all influence the opportunities, approaches, and success of entrepreneurial activities.

Discussion questions

1   How does portfolio entrepreneurship impact the definition of a family business? When is the family business the most appropriate unit of analysis and when would it be better to examine the family in business?
2   Why do families engage in portfolio entrepreneurship?

Case study 5.1: Families across borders, across boundaries

When Danfoss, Denmark's largest industrial company, was looking for a partner company with which to set up a joint venture (JV) in Poland, it opted to join forces with a Japanese company, Saginomiya. On the face of it, these two organisations made unlikely bedfellows, but one of the big attractions for each company was the fact that they were both family businesses.

Danfoss CEO Jorgen Mads Clausen, son of the founder, Mads Clausen, stated that the JV was successful because theirs was a fusion of two family-owned companies who trusted each other and kept their promises. As market leaders in their field of engineering control technology, both firms had a large reservoir of research expertise and development capability, but it was the jointly held values of trust and reliability that enabled the partnership to thrive. Danfoss became Saginomiya's agent in Europe and the USA. When Danfoss closed their sales operation in Japan, Saginomiya became their distributor and took on a portion of the redundant workforce.

The firms share sales and operations outlets to distribute their products in multiple worldwide locations. They also share learning. The JV in Poland has adapted to the Japanese mindset and introduced a quality control system based on the Japanese principle of kaizen, or continuous improvement. Products such as cartridge controls, used for high- and low-pressure safety controls in refrigeration units and the automobile industry, began to experience record sales, with companies like Honda and Toyota becoming big customers. The big growth for Danfoss is in green transport solutions and green energy. The city of Taipei has introduced a fleet of all-electric buses, powered by Danfoss drivetrains, while, nearer home, the company has also pioneered the world's strongest all-electric ferry, operating between Ærø and Als, the Danish island that is Danfoss' home. The company strives to attract motivated graduates for whom the search for cleaner, greener energy is a priority, and their partnership with Saginomiya is helping knowledge move seamlessly across continents in the quest for a more sustainable future.

Source: adapted from Boyd, B., Goto, T., & Hollensen, S., (2010) *Family Business Casebook*, 2009, pp. 1–24.

Case study 5.2: La Empalizada – power of networks versus power of land

Porfirio Lobo Sosa, former President of Honduras, has access to extensive social capital arising from his political activities and the networks of himself and his family. His father Don Pepe (Porfirio Lobo Lopez) was the second generation to own and manage La Empalizada, the extensive family estates near Juticalpa in Honduras. Since its founding in the early 20th century, the family agricultural business has expanded locally, nationally, and internationally as each new generation brings ideas, expertise, and social capital to their entrepreneurial endeavours. Diversification of products and crops provided stability and revenue protection. As their managers' knowledge and experience grew, more sophisticated techniques and machinery were employed. Profits enabled reinvestment and further success. By the 21st century, the Lobo family entrepreneurial team owned four separate agricultural businesses, employing approximately 450 people in food exports, agricultural machinery, soy mills, and real estate.

The story of La Empalizada emphasises that successful entrepreneurship arises from a combination of factors, some of which are beyond the control of even the most powerful and experienced entrepreneurs. However, when things go wrong, social capital increases the options.

Lobo Sosa had 12 offspring; the two eldest sons, Porfirio Lobo Alonzo and Jorge Lobo Alonzo, graduated in agricultural engineering and business management respectively, providing valuable expertise to the family's businesses. As Lobo Sosa's political career took off, the two eldest Lobo Alonzo sons took over management of the businesses and the father and two sons formed an entrepreneurial team to develop their business ideas.

By the early 2000s climate change and several plagues were attacking traditional crops and changing the chemistry of the soil so much that the team had to consider new crops. A diversification into motor dealerships had previously been closed. Cantaloupes and watermelons were trialled but were unsuccessful. The family had to find new crops that worked with the land and the conditions that they faced.

Political connections provided the business family with insight and understanding of regulations, policies, and, importantly, new regulations that might be on the horizon. Connections with the agricultural research community and representatives from large multinational food suppliers enabled the brothers to be at the forefront of tackling agricultural pests and diseases. Crop trials and conversations with industry contacts identified soy bean production as a high yielding crop ideal for their vast amounts of land. However, despite the vast amount of resources ploughed into it, the first crop of soy failed to find a ready market and Porfirio Snr had to persuade his business contacts to take it up.

Agricultural products cannot be changed in the short term and the family were committed to soy production. It was at this point that Porfirio Jnr learned from a former university tutor that soy flour was much more sought after, which traditional mills could easily be retooled to produce. The family already owned a traditional mill and silos to store the flour and so a very successful diversification into soy milling was born.

Source: based on Philip Roscoe, Allan Discua Cruz and Carole Howorth (2013) 'How does an old firm learn new tricks?' pages 53–72.

6 Succession issues and alternatives

In the north of England there is a saying 'clogs to clogs in three generations'; in Japan it is 'rice paddy to rice paddy in three generations', and in many countries it is 'shirtsleeves to shirtsleeves …': every country seems to have its own version of the proverb that suggests families in business will revert to poverty in three generations. Such sayings prevail because we can always find examples of family businesses that have failed within three generations, or where succeeding generations have taken the wealth created by hard-working parents and whittled it away on 'profligate living' – such a dramatic, old-fashioned phrase! However, there are also frequent examples of successful family businesses that have survived for many generations. We can learn from both failed and surviving family businesses, avoiding their mistakes, mirroring best practice, and learning from the challenges they have navigated as they attempt to transfer ownership or management through succession.

Succession is often perceived as a problem that needs to be faced. However, it can also represent an opportunity for regeneration, innovation, and expansion. Family businesses that aim to thrive into the next generation need to understand succession and the dangers and opportunities it brings. Earlier chapters have hinted at some of the issues associated with succession, such as older generations not willing to let go, intertwining of family and business values, competing objectives, and complexity of governance. Chapter 5 indicated that succession can also bring about renewal, innovation, and a boost to entrepreneurial endeavours.

As family business research gained momentum in the late 20th century, it was awash with studies of succession, models of succession planning, and recommendations. In a concern not to let succession overly dominate, we have deliberately included it later in this book because succession is not the only issue that family businesses face, occurring only infrequently. Succession is more likely to run smoothly if family businesses understand and address the points discussed in earlier chapters.

Succession is much more than handing over a baton at a particular point in time. Instead, succession is a process of learning and development, where one generation learns to lead and another generation learns to let go. Succession is also much more than choosing the next CEO: we need to be clear about the difference between management succession and ownership succession. Management succession is about developing the next generation of managers and directors of the family's businesses, both family and non-family members. Ownership succession most often relates to how and when family members gain shares in their family businesses, but for some it might also include decisions to sell some or all of the equity in the family business. We elaborate on the issues and alternative strategies for management and ownership succession in this chapter. In the following chapter we examine the succession process, including the identification and development of successors.

In Chapter 4 we highlighted the relevance of family governance mechanisms, alongside corporate governance policies and processes. Succession will be smoother if agreements and policies are in place before succession becomes critical, such as the criteria for choosing a CEO, family employment, next generation education, transfer of shares, and dispute resolution. This chapter will refer to some of the governance mechanisms introduced in Chapter 4. We therefore recommend that you read and understand Chapter 4 before reading this one. In Chapter 5 we demonstrated that many families have portfolios of businesses. It is important, therefore, that when considering succession we do not fall into the trap of assuming all families have only one business and one succession route.

Learning objectives

Knowledge and understanding of issues related to family business succession and ability to distinguish between management succession and ownership succession issues.

Critical analysis of prescriptions and models for family business succession.

Understanding of alternative strategies for family business ownership and management succession.

What are the issues for succession?

In order to highlight some of the issues for succession, we shall look briefly at the British Royal Family and refer to the LVMH case study (Case study 6.1). But first a warning. It is too easy to generalise and assume all family businesses or family business leaders follow a particular model or way of thinking. Whilst the issues we raise here are common, they do not apply to all family businesses nor all family business leaders.

Incumbents not letting go

In reference to their royal duties, the British Royal Family apparently call themselves 'The Firm'. In 2019 Queen Elizabeth II was 93 years old, her son

Charles was 70, his sister Anne was 68 and there were two younger brothers, Andrew, 59, and Edward, 55. Should the monarch step aside to allow the next generation to take control? A similar circumstance can be seen in the LVMH case study. Bernard Arnault is nearly 70, his eldest is in her mid-40s and has significant leadership experience, yet Arnault does not want to step away from the business. Should the next generation have to wait for the incumbent to die or become infirm before they get their opportunity to lead?

Incumbents not letting go is a major issue for family businesses and has been associated with the decline or even demise of some companies. As we discussed previously, emotional attachment to a family business can be very strong and it can lead to reluctance to let go for a variety of reasons. An incumbent might gain huge enjoyment from their work and feel they still have plenty to contribute. A leader's identity is strongly associated with the role they hold and they may have worries that their identity will be lost if they step down. Some see stepping down as admitting their mortality, and they might fear retirement as being only one step away from death. Handing over the leadership might feel like a demotion and entail a reduction in power, status, and identity, which is especially problematic for family business leaders who have had very active, powerful roles. Many family business leaders, particularly founders, do not want to lessen their hold on the business because they do not believe that anyone could run it as well as them. They look at the next generation and think they are not sufficiently capable or ready yet.

Incumbents may look back at the successes they have had and expect the business to continue in the same mould going forward. Where the next generation express opposing views to the incumbent generation, there may be resistance to giving them control. The incumbent may try and mould successors in their own image, and indeed potential successors may try and mould themselves in the image of previous leaders, particularly where those leaders are lionised, as can be the case for some longstanding family business leaders (or a queen who has reigned for 60+ years). However, as we highlighted in previous chapters, the influx of new blood can bring renewal, innovation, and a surge in enterprising initiatives for family businesses. Younger generations may be more connected with newer trends, technology, and ideas.

It is a fact of life that senior generations will at some point depart the family business. Variously attributed to Mark Twain, Benjamin Franklin, and Edward Ward, a famous quote suggests there are only two certainties in life – death and taxes. Clearly, both are important in succession planning! However, as Terry Pratchett wrote in *Reaper Man*:

> He said that there was death and taxes, and taxes was worse, because at least death didn't happen to you every year.

Successor selection

Selection of a successor raises various issues. The British Royal Family have traditionally followed the rule of male preference primogeniture, whereby the first-born son will succeed the current monarch, making Prince Charles the heir apparent. Note that, strictly speaking, primogeniture means the first-born, but is popularly used to refer to the tradition of first-born sons inheriting, which should be more accurately termed male preference primogeniture. In Queen Elizabeth II's own case there was no male heir, so as a young woman of 24 the Princess Elizabeth became queen of seven independent Commonwealth countries, including the United Kingdom, and Head of the Commonwealth. However, had she had a younger brother, he would have taken precedence. In the LVMH case study, male preference primogeniture would make Bernard Arnault's successor Antoine, in preference to his older sister Delphine. Interestingly, the UK Succession to the Crown Act 2013 replaced the law of male-preference primogeniture with absolute primogeniture, which means that male and female successors have equal rights in line to the throne. However, we continue to see male preference primogeniture in some family businesses, particularly in countries where males dominate economic activity.

Although rules like primogeniture do not necessarily provide the best qualified or most capable successor, they provide clarity, remove ambiguity, and reduce the grounds for dispute. Studies of procedural justice indicate that a sense of fairness is associated as much with process as outcome. So if a family (or business) has agreed particular rules and/or criteria, for example to select a successor, and those rules are applied, then the outcome is more likely to be seen as fair than if exactly the same outcome/selection is made but it is unclear what criteria or rules have been applied.

Applying primogeniture, family businesses can identify the chosen one, or ones, from an early age and train them up in the role they are expected to fulfil. However, potential successors are not given choices under this model, or, if they are given a choice, it is often only to agree or veto their allotted path, which has potential to create discord in the family.

Limitations of the gene pool

There is evidence to suggest that family firms that allocate the CEO position based on primogeniture (i.e., to the eldest son) are, on average, more likely to be managed poorly and perform worse than other firms (Bloom and Van Reenen, 2007). Clearly, a particular gene pool is much more limited than the world at large when seeking family business leaders, making the numerical odds of getting an outstanding candidate lower. A key decision in succession is whether family business leadership positions are restricted to only family members or whether they are open to family and non-family.

Early identification of successors will enable families in business to educate and develop their next generations to increase their chances of success. Indeed, the resources available to wealthy families in business enable their next generations to benefit from some of the best education and development opportunities in the world. Clearly, business families in a less privileged position may be less able to support their next generations but they can still provide the best opportunities at their disposal to mitigate the constraints of the gene pool.

Commitment

Family members may be more committed to the family business long term, through psychological ownership that provides a strong affective commitment. Meyer and Allen (1997) suggest there are three levels or types of commitment: affective commitment; continuance commitment; and normative commitment. Employees with affective commitment really want to be there, they feel a strong sense of identity with the organisation, its values and its purpose; they love their job and have high job satisfaction, an effect that is probably self-perpetuating as affective commitment increases job satisfaction, which increases affective commitment, etc. Continuance commitment is associated with a fear of loss and a loss/benefit analysis of exiting. Commitment is maintained because the benefits of exiting are outweighed by the losses, e.g., loss of friends, status, salary. Normative commitment is all about a sense of obligation to stay with an organisation because it is the right thing to do.

Family members may have a higher commitment than non-family members through affective and normative drivers, and so family businesses may consider it is worth the risk of a restricted gene pool to gain the commitment that comes from appointing family members over non-family members. The Bloom and Van Reenen (2007) study referred to previously indicates that the negative performance effect of family successors only applies to primogeniture. Family-owned and professionally managed firms perform just as well as non-family firms in management practices and financial performance measures.

Divorce, cohabitation, and stepchildren

Had her uncle King Edward VIII not abdicated, Queen Elizabeth II's life would have been very different. Edward stepped down because he wanted to marry a divorcée, which was not acceptable at the time. Princess Elizabeth was not planning to be a successor and her father, who became King George VI, had not been trained as a future king (the film *The King's Speech* beautifully highlights some of the difficulties he faced in this unforeseen succession). Succession plans need to allow for changes in the planned course; divorce is one issue that can disrupt plans and add further complexity, particularly to ownership succession. In North America and Western Europe, 40% or more marriages end in divorce. Ownership shares in the family business could form part of a divorce settlement. If an ex-spouse remarries then pre-deceases their partner, offspring of the divorced couple could lose the potential to inherit family business shares through sideways disinheritance. Ownership thus can move outside of the business family through divorce.

Some business families use trusts to protect from this scenario. Ownership trusts are found throughout the world but particularly in countries that have their roots in the English legal tradition. A trust involves the transfer of assets into a separate formal structure, managed by trustees. In this case, it would be ownership shares that were transferred into the trust, but it could include property or cash. The trustees (not the trust itself) become legal owners of the shares but must always act in the interests of the beneficiaries, whose rights (e.g., to receive dividends) will be set out in a trust deed. Family business shares can be transferred into a trust, trustees nominated and beneficiaries specified to protect against ownership dispersion.

Traditionally, hereditary succession excluded the children of couples who were not married. Henry VIII famously had six wives because he desperately wanted a son who could succeed him, leading to horrendous consequences for some of his wives. His 'illegitimate' son Henry Fitzroy was the son of one of Henry VIII's mistresses, Bessie Blount, and Henry openly acknowledged him as his son, making him Duke of Richmond and Somerset, the highest-ranking peerage in England, but he was still not perceived as a rightful heir. In some countries, such attitudes persist in family business hereditary rights, but social changes are increasingly bringing them under scrutiny.

In many countries, there is an increasing trend for cohabiting in preference to marriage. Antoine Arnault, in our LVMH case study, has two sons with his girlfriend Natalia Vodianova. Natalia also has three older children who live with them. It will be interesting to see how these five children feature in future succession plans for LVMH. How family businesses assimilate stepchildren, children born to non-married parents, and indeed adopted children, is likely to vary between cultures and between families. The key point is that decisions about such children are relevant to succession planning.

Motivation of successors

Earlier we explored three types of commitment and we suggested that family members may have increased levels of commitment relative to non-family employees in a family business. But 'clogs to clogs', 'shirtsleeves to shirtsleeves', or 'rice paddies to rice paddies' in three generations indicate that this is not always the case and successors may not have the same drive and motivation as earlier, and particularly founding, generations. In Scotland, they have a saying (ignoring women, i.e., 51% of the population): 'the father buys, the son builds, the grandchild sells, and his son begs'. The scenario of wealthy succeeding generations being less motivated to work as hard as their parents has been termed the 'Carnegie effect' after the influential philanthropist Andrew Carnegie who is quoted as stating, 'The parent who leaves his son enormous wealth generally deadens the talents and energies of the son, and tempts him to lead a less useful and less worthy life than he otherwise would'.

In Chapter 5 we explained how some family members might be excluded from entrepreneurial endeavours because they have different attitudes to risk, work ethics, or understandings of what it means to be in business. Family owners will vary in the importance they place on providing employment to family members within their businesses. Some families believe it is important to provide opportunities for all, particularly those less able to find employment elsewhere. It is understandable that families want to look after their kin, but such a value may compete with business values around efficiency and effectiveness. If successors are motivated by the belief that it is easier to get a top job in the family business, they are more likely to suffer from the 'Carnegie effect'.

Typology of post-succession retirement styles

Management succession planning often focusses exclusively on the successor: how they will be selected, trained, and inducted (we examine succession processes in the next chapter). Ownership succession planning often emphasises tax reduction. However, for an incumbent family CEO (Chief Executive Officer), the key issue is what they will do next. What will their role be? Will they lose status? Who will they be if they are no longer the big cheese? Will they have the funds to support their choices?

An early, but still relevant study by Sonnenfeld (1988) examined retiring CEOs and identified different patterns of behaviour, which he named monarchs, ambassadors, generals, and governors. Sonnenfeld's book, titled *The Heroes' Farewell: What Happens When CEOs Retire* examined family and non-family businesses, but the findings are particularly relevant for family business leaders who are considering 'what next'. As we examine Sonnenfeld's categories of retiring CEOs, we will highlight some of the dangers of each type.

'Monarchs' rule their business and do not let go until they die. They resist any succession planning and structure their businesses to be very dependent on them. Long-serving monarchs provide continuity and stability that enables long-term planning for the business. As they age, monarchs may become so fragile that no-one wishes to raise the thorny issue of succession in case it upsets them or makes them ill. The consequences for the business can be catastrophic if knowledge transfer does not occur, as monarchs often retain a high level of power, tacit knowledge, and social capital.

'Generals' similarly retain high levels of control and struggle to let go of the business. They fear that surrendering their status and the associated prerogatives will make their life meaningless. Generals provide strong determined leadership and organise their 'troops' to achieve targets. Generals may plan succession but not implement it, or they may even undermine it to provide them with continuing status. Some generals can become tyrants and it may take a coup to oust them.

'Ambassadors' retire gracefully from their business but continue to undertake a role promoting the interests of the business and brokering opportunities for their successor. Ambassadors tend to take pride in the achievements of their successors. They may represent the business at external events. If the continuing role of an ambassador is not clearly specified it may create confusion for stakeholders and could unintentionally undermine the authority of a successor, particularly where employees, customers, or suppliers hold the ambassador in high regard, or where the retiring CEO has a very high profile. Decision making and lines of responsibility need to be clear to all and ambassadors need to be careful not to overstep their new (reduced) authority.

'Governors', like ambassadors, find it easier to let go of the business. Just like governors in other contexts, they view their period leading the family business as a job with a finite timeframe. Governors often go on to other career opportunities and may renew their entrepreneurial spirit, or undertake philanthropic activities, or advisory roles. If their departure is not well planned and governors walk away, they can create a leadership vacuum in the family business. Succession is more likely to be successful if there is an adjustment period where the governor can continue to contribute leadership advice, wisdom, coaching, and support. Note that there is an implicit assumption here that the 'governor' has been a successful and effective leader of the business.

A fifth category of leadership departure is the 'hedonist', who takes off to do their own thing with little planning or knowledge transfer and subsequent negative consequences for the family business. However, where there is a strong management team and a weak leader, the impact of a hedonistic departure could be minimal. It is more likely that a hedonist will have been disengaged from the family business for some time prior to their departure, thinking about what they will do next.

This typology of variations in retirement styles highlights that we need to understand the particular context of a family business and of the people involved. Whilst issues may be common, the individual circumstances will vary hugely, depending on characteristics such as leadership style, team composition, personal circumstances, and the structures and stage of the family business. The five categories or types of retirees are simplified caricatures that help us to identify different behaviours and mitigate their negative implications. Not all CEOs will match a specific type.

Up until this point, it may have been assumed that succession is one in, one out. However, family businesses often experience a swathe of successions, with siblings or cousins retiring in close succession to each other. Obviously, this can accentuate all the issues associated with specific retirement styles, and, in particular, increase the potential for a leadership vacuum in terms of soft skills, wisdom, and experience.

The incumbents' plans for what they do next may require ownership succession as well as management succession. For some family owners, retirement plans may require them to liquidate some or all of their shares in the family business. Ownership succession might therefore not be a straightforward inheritance of shares by the next generation of family members and alternatives may need to be considered.

Succession alternatives

The alternative succession strategies available to family businesses involve varying degrees of family ownership and management. Determination of an alternative will depend on the hopes and aspirations of family and non-family owners, managers, and employees; strategic objectives; business and family values; business performance; lifecycle stage of family, business, and ownership; alternative or competing opportunities; and pre-existing agreements, legal requirements, and provisos. These relate to themes discussed elsewhere in other chapters of the book.

Management succession

Management succession is mostly concerned with criteria used to select and prepare a successor and the best way to ensure a successful succession. In smaller firms, management succession might only relate to a managing director. For larger companies with layers of managers and directors, succession will be relevant at various points in the hierarchy. Regardless of the size of company, many of the principles and issues for management succession in family businesses are similar, but increasing size brings greater complexity. Our focus is on leadership succession, which is management succession specifically concerned with determining the next holders of the most senior roles in the family business, usually the CEO and Chair of the Board.

When we discuss management succession for family businesses, the key question boils down to the degree and type of family involvement. Family owners may have an ongoing agreement, either formal or informal, that specifies one or more of: how many family members will be on the board (minimum and/or maximum); roles reserved for family directors; whether the CEO and/or Chair should be a family member; how many family members can be employed, and criteria for selection. Such an agreement might form part of the family's governance structure (see Chapter 4). The family agreement (constitution or charter) is integral to succession planning. For instance, family members employed in the business may be required to gain a particular amount and/or type of external experience and education to prepare them as potential successors.

Frequently, management succession in a family business context is framed in terms of a 'crown prince or princess', where a family member is anointed at an early age and groomed to take over when the time is right. The stereotypical succession from a senior family CEO to the 'chosen one' is an individualistic, monarchist model based on primogeniture, where an heir is identified, often from early childhood, and brought up to expect that they will be the next CEO. The 'chosen one' will be educated with this future in mind, they will be introduced into relevant networks and may take part in a structured training programme to gain the skills and experience they are expected to need.

In centuries past, the Crown Prince was nearly always the first-born son, but this is becoming less frequent and in many countries it is no longer the unquestioned norm. However, despite variation between countries and cultures, there are still far more men than women leading family businesses in every country of the world. KPMG Australia indicates that 78% of family businesses are led by men (KPMG, 2018). EY's survey of the largest family businesses in the world indicates that only 30% are 'strongly considering' having a woman as their next leader (EY, 2012). In Saudi Arabia, before 2018, women could not run a business without permission from a male 'guardian', usually a husband, father, or brother, and therefore women's explicit involvement in Saudi businesses is extremely limited.

Succession is often assumed to consist of passing the baton from one family member to another, but in practice there are many alternatives that family businesses adopt.

The most extreme case of management succession is a 'forced succession', where the incumbent becomes seriously ill or dies. If no planning has been undertaken, the business is likely to suffer, sometimes catastrophically, because all the tacit knowledge of the former incumbent will be lost. They may have had particular skills, knowledge, and/or networks that were crucial to the business. Often, businesses do not realise just how much tacit knowledge they depend on until it is no longer there. Tacit knowledge is not just an issue for the CEO; businesses can identify how exposed they are to this risk by considering the implications of specific role holders no longer being available. Those businesses most at risk are likely to have one or two central figures who hold large amounts of knowledge 'in their head'. Forced succession in the case of a death is more complex because leadership and ownership succession are likely to be required at the same time. Emotional responses to the death or illness are likely to make it more difficult to disentangle family from business decisions.

The case of Eliza Brown (Case study 6.2) highlights a commonly expressed responsibility among family successors that they cannot let the business fail on their watch. Eliza had not only to demonstrate to employees and other family owners that she was capable of leading the company, but she had to implement a strategy to turn around the company that was losing money and in danger of failing. At the same time, her family were all grieving for her father and she was pregnant and then a young mother. The case highlights how family and business issues intertwine.

Non-family management

Alternatives to family management succession involve employing non-family managers, who are sometimes deemed 'professional' managers and contrasted with family managers (although in Chapter 4 we argued that suggesting family managers were somehow not professional is an incorrect generalisation (Hall and Nordqvist, 2008)). Some family businesses will determine that their business needs are best suited by the employment of a non-family manager, often an experienced CEO from outside the business. Not all families in business will have a next generation family member who is ready, willing, and able to take on the senior management role at the time that succession is required. Frequently, a pairing of family and non-family in the most senior roles of CEO and Chair of the Board is sought to provide a balance. Most often, family members will occupy the chair position alongside a non-family CEO but sometimes the board of directors will appoint a non-family chair alongside a family CEO. Obviously, any combination of family and non-family directors is possible. We explained the governance procedures around this in Chapter 4.

The employment of non-family managers in the CEO position can be contentious for some families. Family owners may be concerned that a non-family CEO might have different values, less attachment to the business, and increased focus on securing their own interests at the expense of the business. Clarks is an international shoe retailer founded in 1825 by brothers Cyrus and James Clark. In 1992–1993, Clarks hit the UK national headlines as family members fought over the future structure of the company as it came to light that it was suffering financially. Arguments included whether the company should be taken public and whether it should remain under direct family management. Two factions developed, both of which believed they knew what was best for the future of the company. Following an Extraordinary General Meeting open to over 400 family shareholders and a large number of employee shareholders, the late Roger Pedder took over leadership of the company. Pedder was an experienced business leader who had married into the Clarks family. Over a number of years, he was able to placate the warring factions and lead a business turnaround. Clarks illustrates that family owners can have very strongly held views about whether a business should be managed by family or non-family.

Some might argue that a non-family 'professional' CEO should improve the performance of the firm as they would be a more skilled and effective manager. Westhead and Howorth (2006) tested the impact on performance of employing a family or non-family CEO in a sample of UK smaller family-owned firms. They hypothesised that a family CEO would be associated with inferior performance but their hypothesis was not supported; family CEOs were not associated with inferior nor superior performance across a range of variables. These findings indicate that it is not whether a manager is family or non-family that is important, as both can include good and bad managers.

Stop-gap manager

In the following chapter we examine how the succession process identifies and prepares next-generation family members to be ready, willing, and able. If a next-generation family successor has been identified but is not ready yet, then family businesses may appoint a 'stop-gap manager' as CEO. A 'stop-gap manager' is someone who is appointed on either an explicit or implicit understanding that eventually a particular family member is expected to take on the CEO role. As the average tenure of CEOs in many large companies is less than five years, a stop-gap arrangement may suit both family owners and the non-family CEO. Where a family business prefers to retain family management in the long term, a non-family CEO can be appointed for a period of time to provide space for the next generation to mature and gain experience.

The downside is that a non-family CEO may steer the business in a different direction to that expected by the family owners, particularly where the owners have a long-term perspective on the business and the CEO is more interested in the short term. A non-family CEO may have lower levels of affective, continuance, and normative commitment, which is heightened if they expect to be in the role for only a few years. Similar to any employee on a fixed-term contract, a 'stop-gap manager' is likely to always have an eye out for career advancement and job opportunities. Agency theory suggests that managers are likely to act in their own self-interest. They may focus on short-term wins to boost their career prospects elsewhere, to the potential detriment of the long-term success of the business. They may aim to gain as much out of the business in perks and rewards as they can. This is a classic agency problem in line with agency theory, introduced in Chapter 2 and explained further in Chapter 3.

Agency theory teaches us that such risks can be reduced by aligning the interests of the principal (owners) and the agent (CEO). Family businesses employing a 'stop-gap' CEO can mitigate the above agency risks by ensuring that the contract and reward structure of the CEO is tied to the objectives of the owners.

Joint CEOs

Some family businesses appoint two family members as joint CEOs. This can reduce dependence on one person and their tacit knowledge and mitigate the risks of potential forced succession through illness or death. It avoids the issue of having to choose between two siblings and the potential jealousies and rivalries that might arise, as so graphically demonstrated by Gordon and

Nicholson in *Family Wars* (2008). Joint CEOs also multiply the experience, social capital, insight, and skills in the CEO position. However, it is important that specific roles are identified and responsibilities are clear. The joint CEOs need to have the personality to be able to work collaboratively, and the success of this structure hangs on them having a trusting, positive relationship.

Many small family businesses are set up under a co-leadership model, particularly when two married or cohabiting partners found a business, known as 'copreneurs' (Fitzgerald and Muske, 2002). Some evidence suggests that co-leadership models in family businesses are increasing (LeCouvie, 2016). In accordance with Chapter 2, we need to be clear that what works for one family may not work for another. Effective co-leadership requires sharing. If siblings do not have a history of sharing well, then appointing them as joint CEOs is probably not a good idea. This does not mean that joint CEOs need to have the same opinion on everything; indeed that would negate the advantages of a shared leadership model. Joint CEOs will be more effective if they have: a shared vision for the business; shared values; high levels of trust in each other; and the ability to subordinate their egos (LeCouvie, 2016). A strong board will help control the power of joint CEOs and ensure that decisions are scrutinised. A co-leadership model will require compromise and decisions may take longer. On the one hand, decisions may be more considered and better as a result, but, on the other hand, having to consult on every decision can make the business less nimble.

Kick4Life is a charity, social enterprise, and family business, founded by brothers Steve and Pete Fleming in 2005. Kick4Life runs a unique football club based in Lesotho, aiming to change the lives and long-term prospects of vulnerable young people through a wide range of health, educational, and social activities. Steve and Pete continue to be joint CEOs, Steve in the UK and Pete in South Africa. In 2015 both Steve and Pete Fleming were named in the Beyond Sport Inspirational 50 List of leading figures who have inspired and facilitated change through sport. Steve and Pete are both passionate about the work they do. Steve suggests that challenges come when they have different ideas about the direction of the organisation and that they need to work through these to ensure that their ideas align. Clearly defined roles and responsibilities are key, as well as respecting their complementary strengths. As they are based in different countries, regular communication is especially important so that concerns can be brought up early before they develop into contentious issues (Power, 2018).

Bettys and Taylors is a fourth-generation family business based in Yorkshire, England, and is the company behind Yorkshire Tea, Bettys Tearooms, and Taylors of Harrogate coffee. Family member Lesley Wild chairs the Group Board. Former CEO Jonathan Wild retired in 2011. The Executive Board has since been structured as a five-member 'Collaborative CEO' and includes managing directors of Bettys and of Taylors but no single

CEO. Chair of the Collaborative CEO and the Finance Director sit on the Group Board (Bettys, 2018). Bettys and Taylors state,

> The Collaborative CEO take shared responsibility for organisation strategy and development, and the operation of the Bettys and Taylors businesses. This role would traditionally be fulfilled by a single CEO, but this structure signals our commitment to a peer-based leadership approach and promotes the ways of working that we are developing through the business (Bettys, 2018).

Ownership succession

As highlighted previously, management succession does not necessarily occur at the same time as ownership succession. In Chapter 3, when we examined typologies of family firms, we explained different degrees of family and non-family ownership and management that led to six conceptually derived types of family businesses. Family businesses may be 100% family owned and family managed, in which case ownership and management succession are likely intertwined. However, if businesses are family owned but 100% non-family managed then there is clear separation between ownership succession and management succession. In reality, family businesses may have varying degrees of family and non-family ownership and management. Therefore, whilst in smaller family businesses ownership and management succession may coincide, it is important to recognise a distinction between the two.

In Chapter 2 we explained that ownership can become dispersed and more complex as family businesses move through the generations. A simple ownership succession might progress from a controlling owner to a sibling partnership to a cousin consortium as succeeding generations involve increased numbers of offspring. For example, Mum and Dad found a business together, each owning 50%; they have three children who inherit one third each; their children have two children each who inherit one sixth of the family business. In this way, shareholdings are diluted from half to one sixth per person in three generations. What is more likely is that each of the three second generation members would have varying numbers of offspring; if they have one, two, and three children, each of those children would inherit one third, one sixth, or one ninth of the business respectively. Cousins will likely have varying percentages of ownership, for no reason other than the number of siblings they and their parents had, which could potentially lead to jealousies, resentment, and varying levels of attachment and commitment by family business owners.

If shares are inherited on the passing of a previous generation, the family owners might believe the only consideration in this case is ensuring that inheritance taxes are not burdensome. However, just as with management succession, the business is likely to be more successful if the next generation has been prepared for their new role and responsibilities. In the next chapter we will examine some recommendations for developing the next generation of family business owners.

As family businesses move through the generations, the ownership structure can become quite complex, with overlapping generations, large numbers of cousins, and distantly related family members owning smaller percentages of shares. Where each branch of the family can determine how they transfer their shares, ownership may become very dispersed over the generations, leading to hundreds of shareholders, as in the Clarks example above. Some families gift a small number of shares to the next generation, for example on their 18th or 21st birthday, enabling the next generation to learn about ownership without them having enough control to put the business in jeopardy. As explained above, some business families control ownership succession by putting shares in trusts, or by stipulating how shares can be transferred. Often this is to reduce risks associated with widely dispersed share ownership.

Alternatives to family ownership succession

Alternatives to family ownership succession are very rarely discussed in the research literature but it is not a foregone conclusion that family business owners will pass the business to the next generation, or that the next generation will wish to take on the family business. Every year many family businesses are sold through trade sales, acquisitions, or management buyouts. Like other types of businesses, some will be liquidated or fail.

Succession studies and guidance have concentrated mainly on longevity of the firm. We should also consider longevity of the family in business. Succession can provide a trigger for entrepreneurial action, and alternatives to gifting the business to a succeeding generation can provide resources for expanding a family's portfolio of businesses. New owners and managers can also bring renewal and revival to businesses. Alternatives to family succession can thus be a positive strategy for the family and the business.

Selling the family business

Family business owners vary in how wealthy they are and some need to monetarise the value from their business assets to fund their plans post-succession. Some owners may have no potential successors available and others have no wish to pass the business on to their kin. The decision to harvest their investment can be a positive choice for family owners and for the firm, allowing owners to invest elsewhere, whether it be in pursuit of their own or their family's leisure, supporting other business interests, or supporting their retirement plans. Business families with a portfolio of interests may sell one or more of their businesses to provide resources to invest elsewhere or to adjust their portfolio to suit the next generation.

However, as we learned in earlier chapters, family businesses can generate powerful emotions in other family members and even those who have no financial stake may have strong opinions about the sale of what they consider to be 'their' family business, particularly where the business was founded by a close family member (e.g., a parent). In Chapter 8 (Finance) we examine the issue of how to put a value on a family business, which we will see can be laden with emotion. In the same chapter we also examine 'pruning the family tree', which involves buying shares from more distant family members to reduce ownership dispersion.

Options available to owners wishing to harvest their investment include selling shares to other family members (which might include their own offspring), a management buyout or buyin, a trade sale, or liquidating the business.

Management buyout

A management buyout (MBO) is the purchase of a firm by its existing management, typically four to six senior managers who are employed in the business, using their own funds often coupled with private equity and bank loans (Howorth, Westhead and Wright, 2004). Management buyouts provide an ownership succession that releases the value of the business to the family owners whilst retaining some or all of the same company management. For family owners, management buyouts might be preferable to a trade sale because the ethos of the business, employee job security, and the name of the firm are more likely to continue the same (Howorth, Westhead and Wright, 2004).

A management buyin (MBI) is similar to an MBO except that the purchasing management team is external to the company, sometimes with one or two internal managers. The MBO/I team may also include family members, often from the next generation. In both MBOs and MBIs, the management team become owner-managers in their acquired business. MBOs have been used in some family businesses to prune the family tree, restructuring and reducing ownership to a small number of family members who are actively involved in management. Where MBO/I negotiations are positive and good relationships between the old and new owner-managers pertain, previous owner-managers may be retained to secure knowledge transfer and a smooth takeover. Sonnenfeld's (1988) typology of retirement styles (above) provides helpful insights into the implications of different exit behaviours for the business going forward.

Trade sale

A trade sale involves the sale of the whole or part of a business. Businesses may be bought by a company in the same supply chain (i.e., vertical integration) or by a competitor (horizontal integration). Following a trade sale, the former family business may have a change of name, be incorporated into the acquiring business, and potentially jobs may be rationalised. Some owners sell the business but retain ownership of premises, which they lease to the business' purchasers.

Liquidation

Family business owners may decide to liquidate the business as an alternative to a trade sale or MBO/I. Liquidation is likely to yield a lower return than selling the business as a going concern. It involves realising the value of all the assets of the business, such as premises, plant, and stock. Liquidation is most often employed when there is no desire or opportunity to sell the family business as a going concern.

Key learning points

Although they can overlap, family businesses need to distinguish between management succession and ownership succession.

Succession foregrounds decisions about the extent to which family members are ready, willing, and able to be involved in management and ownership of their business/es.

Summary

Clogs to clogs in three generations is not inevitable for family businesses but succession does represent a critical juncture where the future of the business is at risk.

Succession can be an opportunity for regeneration, innovation, and expansion.

Succession issues include: incumbents not letting go; primogeniture; limitations of a family gene pool; varying levels and types of commitment; motivation of non-family managers.

Retirement styles of the incumbent may influence the future success of the business. A typology of retirement styles outlined the positive and negative implications of monarch, general, ambassador, governor, and hedonist retirement styles.

Management succession entails choosing and preparing the next senior leaders, most often the CEO and chair of the family business.

Management succession requires consideration of the advantages and disadvantages of family or non-family managers. There is little evidence to suggest that family or non-family managers are generally better or worse for the performance of the business. Both groups include good and bad managers.

Ownership succession includes consideration of how and when family gain shares in the family business, but it also encompasses alternatives to family succession that could involve selling some or all of the family's equity. Alternatives include a management buyout, trade sale, or liquidation.

Discussion questions

1 What are the potential succession issues that LVMH might face in the future and how might they be mitigated? Further information on LVMH and the Arnault family is widely available online.
2 What are the implications of increasingly dispersed share ownership in family businesses?

Case study 6.1: LVMH Moët Hennessy Louis Vuitton

Bernard Arnault, Chair and CEO of LVMH Moët Hennessy Louis Vuitton, is one of the richest men in the world, owning Christian Dior and a host of luxury brands.

LVMH was formed in 1987 as a merger of Louis Vuitton and Moët Hennessy. All the companies involved in the LVMH merger were rooted in family businesses. Moët et Chandon was founded in 1743 by Claude Moët, becoming Moët et Chandon when in-law Pierre-Gabriel Chandon de Briailles joined Claude Moët's grandson in 1833. Moët Hennessy had arisen from a merger in 1971 between Moët et Chandon and Hennessy, the world's largest cognac producer. Fifth generation family member, Kilian Hennessy, led Hennessy at the time and remained on the advisory board of the merged company until his death in 2010 at age 103. Louis Vuitton (LV), founded in 1854, specialised in luxury goods and was previously controlled by three generations of the Louis Vuitton family. Ironically, in 2004, after it was revealed that LV had profited from the Nazi occupation of France, LV managers declared that to be ancient history from when they were family run, even though LV today is majorly owned and managed by the Arnault family.

Soon after the LVMH merger, disagreements led to talk of a de-merger. Into the fray stepped Bernard Arnault, head of Christian Dior. After graduating in engineering in 1971, Bernard joined his father's civil engineering company Ferret-Savinel, reformed in 1976 into Férinel. Bernard became CEO in 1977 and succeeded his father as president of Férinel in 1979 at age 30. In 1984, through the acquisition of holding company Financière Agache, they acquired Christian Dior along with some other companies. Between 1988 and 1989, with the support of Guinness, Arnault bought sufficient shares to block the de-merger and in January 1989 was elected as chair of the LVMH management board.

The Arnault Family Group own over 40% of LVMH shares and a majority of the voting rights (2017 data). Bernard Arnault is the majority shareholder, Chair of Christian Dior and Chair and CEO of LVMH. He has five children aged 20–43 from two marriages; four have senior roles within LVMH companies, the youngest is studying at Imperial College. The eldest and only daughter, Delphine, is director and executive vice-president of Louis Vuitton, and she is on the boards of various companies. Her brother, Antoine, is on the board of LVMH, CEO of LVMH brand Berluti and chair of Loro Piana. Delphine and Antoine's half-brother Alexandre, age 26, is one of the youngest CEOs in fashion, heading luggage brand Rimowa, and Frédéric, age 23, is head of connected technologies at LVMH company Tag Heuer.

In 2019 Bernard is 70, and succession is becoming increasingly relevant. Two of Bernard Arnault's children are considerably older than their father was when he became president of his father's company. There are a number of very well qualified non-family CEOs and senior directors within the various companies. Yet, Bernard Arnault is believed to be planning to lead LVMH for at least another decade.

Source: the Authors.

Case study 6.2: Forced succession at Brown Brothers wine estate

In 2001 Eliza Brown left a senior role in advertising to join her father, Peter Brown, in the family business, All Saints Estate, which had been making wines since 1864 and was part of the Brown Brothers empire. Four years later, when she was 32, her father was tragically killed in a motorbike accident. As the oldest of three siblings in the fourth generation, Eliza succeeded her father in the role of CEO. The tragedy of her father's death coupled with the responsibility of taking over from him weighed heavily and made for a very difficult transition. Six months after her father's death, Eliza returned from six weeks maternity leave and the general manager resigned. She was shocked to discover that the business was losing money.

> The first few years were tough. There was no option to fail. I had to convince family members (many well entrenched in the business) that I was the right candidate, and was prepared to work hard … I had to show that I was taking charge and was up to the task.
>
> (KPMG, 2018)

The business was turned around as Eliza insisted on focussing on specific products and improving processes. The business is owned by Eliza, her sister Angela, director of Sales and Marketing, and her brother Nicholas, General Manager. About the relationship with her siblings and family members, she says:

> We have an extraordinarily close working relationship. We each have different skillsets and integrate fairly seamlessly. We work together and socialise together. I firmly believe that a family that plays together, stays together.
>
> (KPMG, 2018)

As well as continuing to be CEO of All Saints Estate, Eliza is now a director of Brown Brothers. All Saints Estate is highly respected externally and described in glowing terms:

> Set amongst one of the most spectacular vineyard settings in Australia, the historical and iconic estate is a must-see destination for wine and food lovers. The wines are amongst Australia's and the world's greatest, internationally extolled for their richness and lusciousness.
>
> (Kazzit.com)

Source: the Authors, with quotes from KPMG (2018); All Saints Estate; Kazzit.com.

7 Succession processes and the next generation

As we highlighted in the previous chapter, succession is a process, not an event. Succession presents family businesses with a variety of alternatives, including, but not limited to, intergenerational succession. Time is required to make decisions, develop successors, ensure knowledge transfer, and put processes in place to ensure a successful transition. In an earlier chapter we saw how the absence of succession planning at Columbia Sportswear put the family business at risk of failure when Neal Boyd died suddenly. Sadly, this is not an uncommon scenario.

Succession can be contentious. Issues, resentments, and rivalries that have previously been contained might come to the fore in a succession crisis. It helps to mitigate a succession crisis if some decisions have already been agreed and preparations made for the process of succession. Well-thought-out policies and processes provide clarity, reducing the potential for conflict and the dangers of emotional decision making. Succession can then become an opportunity for renewal and innovation.

Succession is much more than handing over a baton at a particular point in time. Instead, succession is a process of learning and development. If a family business decides to follow the process of intergenerational succession, one generation will learn to lead as another generation learns to let go. Successors, whether they be owners or managers, need to learn about business, learn about family business, and learn about their own business. In this chapter we will explain how the succession process is as much about learning as it is about decision making.

We recommend that you read Chapters 6 and 7 in order because Chapter 6 provides some background to this chapter. Further relevant ownership topics are covered in Chapter 8 (Finance), where we consider how to value a family business and how family business owners might approach decisions about internal and external equity.

Learning objectives

Critically analyse different prescriptions and models for the succession process.
Knowledge of the principles of relevant concepts, including power, fairness, and procedural justice.

Understand next-generation perspectives on family businesses.
Knowledge of how theories of learning might be applied in family business.

Why many family businesses avoid succession planning

In earlier chapters we have seen how lack of succession planning and disagreements over the choice of successors can put family businesses at risk of failure and cause emotional upset or sometimes huge rifts for business-owning families. And yet, many family business leaders ignore succession and do not undertake any succession planning. We examine here some of the reasons why family businesses may avoid succession planning.

Resistance to change

Resistance to change is a common response for people in many situations, but is especially prevalent where the change is perceived to be a threat to social relationships. Change is more likely to be resisted when it is imposed from outside rather than generated from within the group experiencing the change. Stepping down from the family business or changing the leader can be a huge change for family businesses and there may be resistance even to considering the prospect. Succession could require changing something that is familiar and comfortable and might be working very well. Within a family business, some members may perceive succession as threatening their own position in the business and/or in the family. A family business leader may be concerned about who they will be if they step down. Will they lose status or power? We noted in the previous chapter that it is difficult to accept that we are all mortal and incumbents may avoid succession planning because it involves recognising that one day they will die. Resistance to change is therefore understandable, but if it leads to lack of succession planning it can have negative implications.

Whilst resistance to change is very well recognised as a relevant concept, it is not always recognised by the persons experiencing it. Those who avoid succession planning because they do not want change are likely to articulate reasons why succession cannot be addressed just now: we don't need to worry about succession yet; let's concentrate on what matters to us now; this project is much more important. Family members can also use emotional blackmail and play on relationships to ensure the topic stays off the agenda, e.g., 'Are you suggesting you want me to die?' Resistance to change is also associated with some perverse behaviours that attempt to undermine the impending change. In a succession scenario, potential successors may be undermined or sidelined, teams or boards may be constructed to strengthen the power of incumbents, new projects or relationships may be pursued that increase dependence on those in power. Such behaviours may lead to suboptimal performance of the business and/or threaten family relationships.

Sibling rivalry

For some, succession planning might bring increased risk that negative emotions will surface, undercurrents of conflict might become full-blown battles. Both parents and offspring can hold on to issues, attitudes, or resentments going back many years, sometimes to childhood. Brothers and sisters may hark back to a particular event that occurred many years ago but still upsets them. Phrases beginning 'I remember when you …' or 'You've always …' may be an indication of deeply held resentments. In some cases, negative attitudes or issues will be well known within the family, but, in other cases, they may be hidden until an issue such as succession brings them to the fore. Sibling rivalries can be especially severe. The Gallo case study (Case study 3.1) highlighted that sibling rivalries can be devastating for both business and family. Family business leaders may therefore deliberately avoid raising the issue of succession planning in an attempt to avoid stirring up negative emotions and rivalries.

Sibling rivalries can stem from concerns about fairness and equity, but they can also be about gaining power. Extremely competitive behaviours and attitudes can occur between siblings, cousins, or different branches of a family. An early example is the story of Cain and Abel, which goes back to the beginning of the Hebraic religions (i.e., Christianity, Islam, and Judaism). Cain and Abel were the sons of Adam and Eve. Cain was jealous of his younger brother Abel, whom he perceived to be more favoured. Cain murdered Abel and was banished from the family, wandering the land of Nod until he settled down with his wife to build his own separate enterprises. Interestingly, in the story, God forbids anyone from taking vengeance on Cain, thus avoiding the spiralling of a family feud and highlighting the influence that a powerful father figure can have in reducing family conflict. Regardless of religious beliefs, the fact that we find this story in the creation narrative suggests that competitive behaviours and the seeking of power and favour are as old as time and inherent in humans.

Power

Resistance to change, competitive behaviours, and rivalries can all give rise to 'power games'. Psychologists suggest that high-power individuals likely exploit opportunities to seek rewards for themselves, whereas low-power individuals seek to avoid risk and harm. 'Power games' is a popular term for the behaviour adopted by individuals seeking more power: for example, they might align themselves strategically with people or initiatives believed to have the potential to give them what they want; they might seek allies; create divisions; manipulate emotions; include and exclude particular individuals from specific activities. Behaviours might range from innocuous power plays to full-blown Machiavellian plots. Avoiding succession planning might be part of someone's power game or it may be an attempt to avoid bringing rivalries out into the open and possibly escalating them.

Power is central to all aspects of social life and everyone operates within a web of power relations. Power is popularly conceptualised as an individual possessing power over others, for example having the ability to administer rewards and punishments. However, power is a prerequisite for agency, it is needed to do things. If you have agency, you are able to take action. Therefore, rather than thinking about power as something that is possessed, it may be more helpful to consider it as the ability to do, as in 'power to …'. Power flowing through the electricity cables enables you to switch the light on. You do not possess that power but it enables you to do something, i.e., it gives you agency. Power 'to' also includes power 'not to', or the power to stop things happening. Power 'not to' is exercised when issues (such as successor selection) are not prioritised, are sidelined, or are kept off the agenda. We may see this playing out in the succession process. For example, a senior family business leader may have the power to keep successor selection off the agenda, perhaps benignly to avoid warring factions of the family escalating their differences or more aggressively to retain power until a preferred younger family member is in a position to be considered.

Power is therefore an important concept to consider when examining succession, and particularly the enabling of a succession process. Power can influence the selection of successors for good or bad. More subtly, power can be used to enable the development of successors and put them in positions that help their advancement; alternatively, power can be used to restrict the development of unfavoured ones, or take the business in a direction that suits particular individuals' agendas. Power may be used to keep succession off the agenda but it can equally ensure that succession is considered and planned.

We saw in the previous chapter how incumbents who continue to exercise power after succession can be disruptive and undermine their successors. Successors need to have the necessary power to undertake their new role. As we will see below, this is not always straightforward and there may be obstacles to overcome.

Sensitivity

Avoidance of succession planning may also occur because of sensitivity to someone else's feelings. Management succession may be avoided if younger generations are reluctant to broach the subject of parents no longer being capable of doing their job. Discussions about ownership transition may be avoided because it could require considering what happens after older generations die. Brothers and sisters may not want to be seen to be promoting their own interests above another's. There may be a family member with greater needs or less competence, but sensitivities to feelings mean that no one wants to address how this might be fair or not fair to that person and to others. Any of these or similar sensitivities might lead to avoidance of succession planning.

There are likely cultural differences in how open families are regarding sensitive issues. Although we cannot generalise to whole nations, cultural variations are perceived to endure within particular groups. Some groups in the UK, for example, are believed to have a 'stiff upper lip' and avoid discussing sensitive issues. More collective and less individualistically oriented groups, such as in some Central and South American countries, may be characterised by increased openness between family members. We need to recognise that families will vary in their relationships, as well as in their openness, and we must beware of assuming that families will behave in particular ways based on our own experiences or cultural assumptions.

Too busy

Stressed, resource-constrained business leaders may be so busy managing the day-to-day operations of their business that they do not allocate time to planning for the long term. Some may wonder what is the point of planning so many years ahead when the context will almost certainly be very different. It is commonly believed that particularly small businesses tend to be resource constrained and have a tendency towards fire-fighting, and there is evidence to suggest that for some small businesses this is the case. However, business leaders that are more successful do manage to get away from working 'in the business' to working 'on the business', and this is an important contributor to long-term success. Family business leaders need to take time out to consider the future.

Summary of reasons

Reasons for avoiding succession planning might thus include a resistance to change, reluctance to allow negative emotions to surface, inability to address conflict, power games, lack of knowledge of what is required, and generally a tendency to hide their head in the sand, ostrich fashion. So while there are very good business reasons why succession planning is recommended, there are many family and individual (people) reasons why it might not happen. However, if the long-term viability of the business is important to them, then family business leaders will want to ensure that their successors have the skills, motivation, and knowledge to enable the business to thrive.

Families in business that wish to secure the future viability and longevity of their businesses will want to educate the next generation to be responsible and committed owners. At the heart of families are births, growth, maturing, and renewal. Families are thus by their nature dynamic and changing. Good parenting focusses on developing the next generation for adulthood and the various roles they might take in the home, workplace, and society. Formal family business roles may be as owners, managers, or employees. Additionally, family members without formal roles will also be connected to the business purely because they are members of the owning family, although not necessarily owners themselves.

The succession process

The succession process is likely to consider criteria for the selection of successor/s, timing of the process, as well as how to ensure a smooth transition. Most succession plans will be concerned about transfer of knowledge, resources, and social capital. Better succession plans will also consider contingencies or mitigation in case a decision turns out to be a poor one, as well as the aspirations of retiring leaders. In the sections that follow we will examine how family businesses can pay attention to the process of succession.

Succession planning, particularly in family business books, is in danger of dwelling on the family aspects at the expense of the business. From the business' point of view, a succession policy is likely to be concerned with: prospects for non-family managers; ex-post performance; continuity and discontinuity; and long-term plans. If a succession plan specifies that the CEO should always be a member of the owning family, this could demotivate non-family managers. This succession plan may then consider how non-family managers, who have no prospect of promotion to the top job, will be rewarded and motivated to ensure the success of the business. Some family businesses provide an employee share ownership scheme, often with the condition – to control ownership dilution – that shares must be sold back to the business should an employee leave. Some family businesses structure their firms to provide separate divisions or subsidiary companies that can be led by non-family managers, whilst overall control is retained by a family CEO. Business concerns about performance, continuity, discontinuity, and long-term plans will require successors to be well-prepared, experienced, and skilled in areas that are important for the business. The succession plan may specify that management successors should be trained and have experience in specific areas. Ownership successors need to understand their rights and responsibilities and their role in governing the family business, so the succession plan may include a learning plan for potential owners.

The succession process involves determination of a strategy, policy for selection of successors and transfers of ownership, successor selection, training and learning, knowledge and resource transfer, and shift in roles. Box 7.1 provides recommendations for a successful succession. A smooth transition could take many years or a few months, depending on the ages and experience of different parties. Various models for the succession process have been devised. We present three models here which illustrate the key principles and which we find helpful.

> **Box 7.1 Recommendations for successful succession.**
>
> Start early.
> Learn about succession: read, ask other family businesses about successes and regrets.
> Plan knowledge transfer and reduce reliance on current leaders.
> Identify and prepare successors.
> Plan for business objectives.
> Seek advice and undertake tax planning.
> Share values and dreams with family members.
> Address conflict, jealousy, and resentments.
> Prepare a formal but flexible succession plan.
> Consider alternatives to the obvious.
> Ensure trust and communication.
> Do not believe that checklists like this will provide all the answers!

Succession as a relay race

Succession is often talked about in terms of 'passing the baton'. Dyck et al. (2002) expanded on this colloquialism and used the analogy of a relay race to examine key aspects of succession. They suggest that, just like a relay race, succession is a team event that requires consideration of sequence, technique, timing, and communication. Decisions need to be made about who is the best person for each stage (sequence). The team needs to engage in training to ensure they have the requisite skills for their particular role (technique). Timing of the handover needs to be planned so that the receiver is ready and the one holding the baton knows when to let go. Finally, communication is vital to ensure a smooth handover of the baton; each member of the team gives and receives instructions. Behind the scenes, a successful relay team will have a host of professionals supporting them, planning, advising, providing coaching, skills training, psychological and physical support. Prior to any training, there will have been selection decisions about who is to be included in the squad and then who from the squad will be in the team.

The relay race analogy transfers well into succession planning, incorporating selection of possible successors (the squad) and allocating people to specific roles (the team). Just like the relay team, a family business may have a host of advisers and professional support, some of whom will be employees in the business while some may be appointed externally for a specific task. Passing the baton is just a small part of the succession process and the culmination of a long sequence of events. However, when Dyck et al. (and many others) discuss succession they are referring to management succession. Their model is less applicable to ownership succession.

Succession as a dance

Wendy Handler (1990) proposed a model of mutual adjustment, which she likened to a slow and subtle dance. Just as when we are dancing, in a succession process we need to avoid stepping on each other's feet. As the successor steps forward, the incumbent needs to step back to provide room for the successor to take on the new role. Handler's model suggests that successors take on increasing responsibility in a staged approach that enables them to develop skills, joining first as a 'helper' before becoming a manager and finally the chief decision maker. At the same time, their predecessor takes a decreasing role, moving from being a 'monarch' to being an 'overseer/ delegator' and finally a consultant. The principles underpinning the 'mutual adjustment' model are more easily applied to management succession than ownership succession. The need for an incumbent to let go, provide space for a successor, and not interfere as they take on a new role are well recognised as important to successful management succession. A staged approach allows successors to gradually take on more and more responsibility, developing skills and experience, until they have the most senior role; transferring first experience, then knowledge, followed by authority, decision-making power, and finally equity. Retaining the predecessor as a consultant facilitates knowledge transfer for the successor. However, successors may suffer from the shadow of a founder hanging over them, negative interference by their predecessor or stifling of innovation, particularly where there is a strong loyalty to the predecessor.

It is less common for ownership succession to follow a staged approach but some larger family businesses provide shares to junior family members at particular ages, for example on their 21st birthday, which enables them to become involved in shareholder meetings and learn the rights and responsibilities of shareholders before they inherit large volumes of shares. Many younger family members may engage with the family business through summer jobs, 'helping', internships, and formal training programmes. Family businesses might allow junior family members, who do not yet have any shares, to be included in away days, owners' retreats, or particular elements of shareholders meetings. Next-generation members may join a training programme, either within or external to their own family business. In all these ways, the next generation can begin to develop their understanding and knowledge of what ownership entails, gradually becoming more involved in ownership issues. Ideally, future owners will develop knowledge of how business works, issues of particular relevance to family businesses, and how their own business works.

Correlates of success

Morris et al. (1997) examined what they term 'correlates of success', in other words the factors that are most important in ensuring a successful succession, defined as a smooth transition between incumbent and successor. Their quantitative analysis indicated that preparation, relationships, and planning were all associated with successful successions, and, of the three, relationships were the most important factor. Relationships are believed to be the most important factor because good relationships between family members enable more effective communication, sharing of values, and a more collective view. Generally, where there are fewer self-interested behaviours in a family business, there is likely to be less conflict and succession is expected to proceed more smoothly.

Morris et al. suggest that family businesses should pay more attention to relationships than tax and estate planning. However, Morris et al. had no evidence of a generalisable pattern between 'successful' succession and post-succession performance.

In looking at many models of succession, there is a tendency to assume that conflict is bad and smooth processes are the ideal. However, a smooth process is not ideal if everyone goes along with a decision that is not good for the business or damages family relationships in another area. Some conflict has been shown to be good for innovation (Eisenhardt, Kahwajy and Bourgeois, 1997) and some issues give rise to conflict that may be necessary and even beneficial. Open and honest communication might sometimes entail challenging or painful discussions that in the end have better outcomes for the business and individuals.

Fairness and procedural justice

Succession is likely to proceed more smoothly when those involved perceive it to be fair. Fairness is always a perception not a fact, because what one person believes to be fair, another may perceive to be unfair. Perceptions of fairness are closely associated with levels of trust between the parties. Where there are high-trust relationships, participants are more likely to perceive a fair process and vice versa. Of the three elements of trustworthiness (ability, benevolence, and integrity: see Mayer, Davis and Schoorman, 1995), integrity is an especially important element of perceptions of trustworthiness during the succession process. (For more on trust and perceptions of trustworthiness, see Chapter 5.)

Perceptions of fairness are usually higher where a decision or process follows agreed criteria, whereas unfairness is more likely to be perceived if the process deviates from what was previously agreed. This is the concept of 'procedural justice'. Procedural justice relates to the fairness and transparency of decision-making processes. It is different to distributive justice, which relates to fairness in the actual distribution of rights or resources. Participants who have been involved in determining the criteria and/or involved in the process are more likely to perceive it as fair. In family business ownership succession, equity may be distributed unevenly but if it is on the basis of agreed criteria, participants are more likely to perceive the distribution to be fair. Similarly, participants are more likely to perceive successor selection to be fair if the decision was made according to agreed criteria.

Perceived fairness is important because individuals will likely act more favourably where a process is perceived to be fair. Similarly, perverse behaviours are more likely where individuals perceive unfairness. In the case of succession, if criteria for the selection of an heir have been agreed, then, even if I disagree with the choice of heir, I am likely to perceive the decision as fair if the selection was made according to the agreed criteria, particularly if I have been involved in determining said criteria. This is why there are remarkably low levels of disagreement with successor selection decisions based on primogeniture: the selection criteria are unambiguous, even though some might believe the principle to be unfair.

Succession planning enables criteria and processes to be agreed prior to them being needed. We would expect that family businesses that engage in succession planning are more likely to have a smooth transition and less likely to have conflicts and negative behaviours post succession.

Tax considerations

As well as considerations aimed at ensuring that the business continues and has every chance of success, succession planning may include practical considerations aiming to ensure that ownership succession is 'tax efficient', which is usually taken to mean reducing the 'burden' of tax. Although attitudes towards the responsibility of paying taxes vary between families and individuals, it is important to understand the impact that inheritance taxes can have when an inheritance is tied up in business assets not cash, including the real possibility in some countries that ownership succession and continuity of the family business can be jeopardised. Inheritance tax and capital gains tax are key considerations. Some people call inheritance tax 'death duties'. Taxes vary from country to country and tax laws can change. For example, there is no inheritance tax in Australia, whereas in the UK inheritance tax can be 40% of the value of assets above a specified threshold. The payment of inheritance tax has been argued to put the survival of family businesses at risk. It is for this reason that, in the UK, Business Property Relief was introduced in 1976, allowing the majority of business transfers on death to gain 100% Business Property Relief, which means they are exempt from 40% Inheritance Tax. However, this relief does not apply in every instance. The key point for succession planning is that legal advice and frequent review of succession plans are needed to empower families in business to understand the tax implications of their succession policy and actively manage their tax position as laws and circumstances change.

The succession process and learning

We have seen that succession is much more than handing over a baton at a particular point in time, but is, instead, a process of learning and development. The next generation, whether they be family or non-family members, need to learn to lead as the senior generation learns to let go. Next-generation owners and managers need to understand general principles of business, specific application of principles of family business, and the detail of their own business. The succession process is therefore as much about learning as it is about decision making.

As you will have realised from your own experience, we all learn through a variety of approaches and experiences. Learning can be experiential and situated, formal or informal. Learning is associated with how people make sense of their experiences, at work or in the family and social situations. Learning may emerge from social interactions as much, or more than, formal education. There are many theories of learning and we would recommend that you read specialist texts if this is your area of interest.

A lot of entrepreneurs learn from experience. Smilor (1997: 344) stated:

> Effective entrepreneurs are exceptional learners. They learn from everything. They learn from customers, suppliers, and especially competitors. They learn from employees and associates. They learn from other entrepreneurs. They learn from experience. They learn by doing. They learn from what works, and more importantly, from what doesn't work.

So, first generations might have gained a lot of their knowledge and understanding through experience. They may not be aware of the extent of tacit knowledge they hold and which the business draws on. The learning process of developing leaders as the business moves from one generation to the next is a dynamic, continual process, as family members share tacit knowledge, learn, and develop their skills from ongoing everyday practice (Hamilton, 2006). In many family businesses, learning the soft skills of leadership is like an informal apprenticeship, as knowledge and skills are passed from one generation to the next. It is difficult to transfer tacit knowledge, and leadership learning relies heavily on experience. Many family businesses are in a privileged position in that they can provide opportunities for younger family members to practice leadership and learn through experience.

Relationships with seniors can provide positive role models. Senior family members can be very influential even when they do not have a formal role in the business, influencing culture and expectations. Once-removed generations (e.g., grandparent to grandchild) can have very strong relationships, and the wisdom and friendship of grandparents is sometimes valued more than that of parents by younger generations. Whilst family relationships can provide an important context for junior family members to

> **Box 7.2 Engaging the next generation: Sir Michael Bibby.**
>
> Sir Michael Bibby, director of Bibby Group, stated:
>
>> The ability of a family firm to engage its young family members so they can become committed, educated, and responsible owners is a vital hallmark of successful family businesses ... The key to achieving engagement is by allowing the next generation sufficient space for them to set their own path ... creating space for the next generation to plan their own futures – not those set for them by their parents or by a sense of obligation. Space is required in which next generation family members are able to learn, communicate, and express their ideas ... They are all individuals whose needs, development, and capabilities will be different ... honest, open, and direct communication is critical in building inter-generational relationships. If seniors try too hard, talk down to younger family members, or pressure them, they may shy away. Next generation members must be engaged in planning their own future, and come to see the family business as a flexible and open environment in which they are invited to play a meaningful role.
>
> Source: Howorth et al., 2016a.

learn, they could be dominated by the older generation and younger members may become frustrated with expectations that they should defer to older members. Seniors can dominate, obstruct, and overshadow the business in a negative way, which may cause younger generations to disengage. Leadership is associated with status, hierarchy, and authority, and young adults might be reluctant to admit uncertainty. Marginalised or under-represented groups and individuals within an extended family may lack role models and consequently find it much more problematic to engage in the family business. Leadership learning needs a safe space divested of power dynamics, where learners feel comfortable enough to take psychological risks and expose vulnerabilities and frailties, seek support, and voice problems.

Succession process and education

After the founding generation, many family businesses engage later generations in an explicit educational programme. Families in business may believe that they have a responsibility to educate the next generation of owners to be responsible and understand their roles (see Box 7.2). Some invest considerably in the education and training of the next generation, in line with the mantra 'If you think learning is expensive, try ignorance' (Easterby-Smith, 2008: xxi). Specialist programmes are provided by leading business schools for members of the next generation, particularly aimed at wealthy family businesses, and many family business networks such as FBN-I and IFB have distinct next-generation programmes and networks.

The family may be aware of key areas where gaps exist in their knowledge. Younger family members may study a topic such as engineering or business or biotech because this is where the business has a need for knowledge. The family may decide that international experience would be helpful and thus target universities overseas or in specific target countries. Some families seek external business experience for their successor generation and they may have a policy that family members cannot be employed in the business unless they have a specified number of years employment elsewhere, sometimes in specified contexts at particular levels of management. On the plus side, such a policy means that gaps in knowledge may be filled and the firm's experience or skills expanded. However, on the downside, the next generation might be persuaded to undertake education in an area they would not otherwise have sought, and their motivation and interest may not be high; even worse, resentments could develop if they feel they have been persuaded or manipulated.

In the family business context, there is a danger that family and formal educational experiences are given greater credence than other forms of learning. However, it has been shown that young adults with a strong interest in business tend to experiment as entrepreneurs and find ways to learn, often informally, with their peer groups more than with other family members. Family businesses concerned with engaging younger generations in business need to recognise the importance and influence of peer networks outside the family context.

Next generation and gender

Leadership learning is influenced by the macro-environment and cultural and social norms, expectations, and behaviour, including those related to gender and ethnicity. Cultures vary in how gender influences entrepreneurs' development and leadership identity, but both men and women could be constrained and enabled by gendered power relations. There is still an assumption in many cultures that men are the natural successors for family businesses. Frequently, women have to perform additional work in order to fit in and gain acceptance. In family businesses, leadership power and authority often remain invested in male heirs. Where there are male and female heirs in a family business, women are frequently observed in the HR Director role, one which rarely leads to the top job (Stead, 2017).

Zellweger, Sieger and Englisch (2015) identified a 'gender gap' in the succession intentions of younger family business members, in that women were less likely to wish to take over leadership positions within the business.

Interestingly, this was even more pronounced where the leader of the business was their mother. Next-generation family members had more interest in joining the family business when both their parents were involved. Other studies have identified an association between gender, business sector, and variations in engagement with family businesses by next-generation family members (e.g., Howorth and Ali, 2001). Stereotypically, women appear less likely than men to engage in their family's businesses if the business is in heavy industry. These studies highlight once again that we need to consider the context of a particular family business and be careful not to over-generalise.

Next generation perspective

Studies of succession most often examine the perspective of the incumbent or the needs of the business; there is less understanding of the needs and aspirations of the next generation. Engagement of the next generation in the family business prior to them having a formal role is believed to be important in developing successors and has been associated with the long-term success of the business. The family business is also an excellent training ground for next generations to develop entrepreneurial and management skills that they could employ within the family business but that might equally help them succeed in other businesses. The next generation may face confusing and sometimes conflicting ideologies. Their preferences and plans may change as they grow through their teens to become young adults. They may feel pressure from other family members' perceived or voiced expectations that they will join the family business. On the other hand, they may be very keen to join the family business but feel excluded by senior or dominant family members or non-family managers. We have seen in earlier chapters that a younger generation can trigger innovation and regeneration of family businesses. In the previous chapter we considered the incumbent's perspective and we explained how their retirement style might impact on the business. Here, we examine studies of the next generation's perspective and their engagement with their family business prior to or as part of the succession process.

Engagement with family businesses may vary within a single family, as well as across business families and across time. There are many reasons why next-generation members might engage or not with their family's business. Where family members have a collective approach to their business/es and a shared vision, the next generation are more likely to engage positively in the business. Family members with a strong stewardship motivation are more likely to want to engage in their business to ensure its long-term viability and/or to protect the family's wealth rather than pursuing their own individual interests (Hamilton, 2013). However, as we saw in Chapter 2, family businesses are dynamic and constantly changing, as are the individuals involved in them. The case of Charlie Field (Case study 7.2) highlights that young people may change their mind about whether they want to join the family business or not. Their interests, ambitions, and circumstances change. Flexibility in succession planning allows for such dynamics.

In Chapter 5 we explained the theory of social capital. Family members who interact frequently will build bonding social capital and stronger ties with each other, and they are more likely to have a shared business vision. Socialisation into the family business helps to build cognitive social capital, i.e., shared understandings. Family social capital is likely to influence next generations to engage. In larger or later generation family businesses, the next generation may be widely dispersed and the ties less strong, making it more challenging to engage the next generation. Some family members who do not engage in the family business have had a negative experience of socialisation as a child or a young adult (Discua Cruz, Howorth and Hamilton, 2013), perhaps disliking the tasks or environment they were in, or, more likely, feeling they were forced to work in the family business while their peers were enjoying themselves. Within the same family, one sibling may experience socialisation as positive and another as negative. Psychological ownership will be lower among less engaged family members and will spiral, in that lack of engagement reduces psychological ownership, which reduces engagement, etc. Long established relationships between family members increase their knowledge of each other; this may increase trust and psychological safety, but where there are genuine beliefs that behaviours, the work ethic, or trustworthiness of other family members are negative, family members may disengage and factions could develop.

Key learning points

Succession is a process, not an event.

The succession process contains valuable learning opportunities for the junior and senior generations.

The succession planning process allows issues to be aired, considered, and addressed before succession is imminent and emotions are heightened.

Summary

If the long-term viability of the business is important to them, then family business leaders will want to ensure that their successors have the skills, motivation, and knowledge to enable the business to thrive. Succession is a critical juncture when the future of the business is at risk. A poorly managed succession process, the 'wrong' choice of successor, or conflict arising from opposing points of view can result in the failure of a family business.

Family businesses may avoid succession planning for a variety of reasons, including resistance to change, reluctance to allow negative emotions to surface, inability to address conflict, power games, lack of knowledge of what is required, and just being too busy to examine the long-term perspective.

Succession has been likened to a dance of mutual adjustment and also to a relay race. Both analogies provide helpful insights into successful succession processes. Relationships and communication are generally the most important factors for positive succession outcomes.

Succession may be judged in terms of its fairness. Procedural justice provides an explanation of why an outcome that appears unfair is more likely to be accepted if an agreed process and criteria are followed.

Succession is as much about learning as it is about criteria and processes. The next generation of owners and managers need to understand about business, about family business, and the specifics of their own business. Next generation learning occurs through formal and informal channels, it is often situated, and has been likened to an apprenticeship.

Whilst formal educational channels provide valuable learning, soft skills and leadership are more likely learned through experience. Family businesses can engage the next generation in many advantageous ways that provide valuable learning experiences that are of benefit within and outside the business.

Discussion questions

1. If you were a member of the next generation, what would influence your decision to join or not join your family in business?
2. How would you devise a succession process to reduce the risk of the 'Carnegie effect' (explained in Chapter 6)?

Case study 7.1: Fair shares and Gucci

As a symbol of style, luxury, and wealth, the Gucci brand is right up there with names like Versace, Hermes, and Louis Vuitton. Company founder Guccio Gucci began his firm in Florence in the early 1900s and rapidly developed a reputation for selling high quality goods made from Tuscan leather, which met with great approval from the cultured citizens of Florence, and the firm expanded quickly.

Gucci had five children and favoured an authoritarian style of parenting. His children had various degrees of enthusiasm for working in the family business. Aldo was the keenest, much more so than his brothers Vasco and Rodolfo (a fourth brother, Ugo, had no interest at all). Gradually, Aldo took on more senior roles until he was running the firm prior to his father's death. Gucci's daughter Grimalda worked in the shop with her husband, but was incensed to discover that, unlike her brothers, she had not inherited any shares. She took the issue to court but lost her case, and so began the Gucci family's battle for shares and power that would seethe for decades.

Aldo was successful in expanding the company around the world to 14 stores and 46 franchised boutiques. In 1974 Vasco died and his brothers bought his widow's shares, so that they each then owned an equal 50% stake of Gucci. However, Aldo privately resented Rodolfo's shareholding, believing it to be incommensurate with his input. Aldo had three sons – Giorgio, Paolo, and Roberto – and though he was as authoritarian a parent as his own father, he gave each of his sons a 3.3% shareholding in the company.

Gucci thrived in America and Aldo based himself in New York. Paolo, a talented designer, worked with Rodolfo in Florence, but their personalities clashed and he moved to the USA. However, he also failed to work harmoniously with his father and when he founded a rival fashion line, his father and uncle fired him.

The brothers were disunited on a separate arm of their business: Aldo had established Gucci Perfumes, which sold well, but Rodolfo had only a 20% stake. He wanted more and engaged his lawyers to contest the issue. As part of a strategy to combat Rodolfo at board level, Aldo approached Paolo and asked for his support. 'Why should I!?' responded Paolo, which prompted a row that ended with Aldo flinging a solid ashtray at him. Paolo became bent on revenge.

Three years later, Aldo tried to mend fences with his son: he offered his three sons 11% each in the company and Paolo was to head up a division and market his own line. However, Paolo felt undermined when his proposals for the new division were rejected at the next board meeting. He aired his grievances vociferously and father and son came to blows, with the son emerging bloodstained from the encounter. The media loved it, finding the saga every bit as entertaining as any TV soap opera. Paolo sued the company for $30million in damages.

A year later, Rodolfo died and his only son, Maurizio, inherited his shares. Following Paolo's lawsuits, Aldo's financial affairs were under investigation, threatening the company's stability. Maurizio made an alliance with Paolo and ultimately ousted Aldo from the company. Battles with the taxman in the USA and Italy followed, costing the family millions of dollars. External investors had little confidence in Maurizio and he ended up selling his shares. The Gucci family business was no longer owned by the Gucci family. Maurizio's wife Patrizia, whom he had left some years earlier, was outraged that her estranged husband had sold their children's birth right and paid a professional hitman to shoot him. Maurizio was murdered and Patrizia was sentenced to 29 years. Paolo died bankrupt.

The battles for fair shares had destroyed the family. Gordon and Nicholson (2008: 219) sum up: 'Failings in parenting and leadership abounded here … The abundance of money only acted as a turbocharger for people's greed … love, loyalty, forgiveness and charity were entirely absent, and needlessly so'.

Source: adapted from Grant Gordon and Nigel Nicholson (2008) *Family Wars*, pp. 208–219.

Case study 7.2: Socialisation and a change of heart

The Field family company had humble beginnings as the makers of coffins in the late 17th century but went on to become highly respected funeral directors, involved in the state funerals of royalty and the high ranking such as Queen Victoria, King Edward VII and the Duke of Wellington. In 2019 they were one of the ten oldest family businesses in the UK. Tenth generation family member Charlie Field was socialised into the C. P. J. Field family business from an early age.

He explains:

> From my earliest memories at school, I can remember teachers and parents of friends asking if I was going to join my family business and follow in the footsteps of my father. As the tenth generation of a family firm whose history stretches back over 300 years, it's easy to see why this may have seemed pre-ordained. School holidays often involved joining my father on branch visits or being dragged along to endless conferences in far-flung corners of the country. Without knowing it at the time, this was the start of a long induction and education process.
>
> (Howorth et al., 2016a)

Three hundred years of history could have weighed heavily on Charlie's shoulders but throughout his late teens and early twenties he was very clear that he did not want to join the family business. In total contrast to the Gucci case above, relationships were good in the Field family and Charlie was supported in his education and career choice.

Just before his 30th birthday, Charlie changed his mind and broached the possibility of him joining the family business. He explains:

> A few years earlier, my grandfather (the eighth generation) had told me how he had never felt any pressure to join, but like his father, after a few years in practice as an accountant he felt the magnetic draw back to the family company. My experience was very similar – no family pressure, just a personal desire to get a better understanding and contribute to something that has been such a large part of family life for so long.
>
> (Howorth et al., 2016a)

Charlie joined the business as Business Development and Marketing Director, becoming Chief Financial Officer in 2013 and Deputy Chair in 2016. He is one of five family directors, alongside his siblings and parents, with his father as Chair and significant shareholder. Succession has been a long process of the 10th generation stepping up as the 9th generation step back and pursue other interests. Charlie's brother, Jeremy Field, joined the family business in 2005 as Business Development Manager and was appointed as Managing Director in 2008. In 2016 Jeremy was appointed President of the National

Association of Funeral Directors, 29 years after his father had held the role. In his acceptance speech, Jeremy highlighted similar memories to those mentioned above by his brother, of following his father around the country attending NAFD conferences as a child. He also stated that he was immensely proud to be following in his father's footsteps. Jeremy and Charlie's sister, Emily Hendin, joined the family business in the same year as Charlie and is Marketing Director.

Charlie explains how the Field family manage to maintain good relationships:

> For me, the key to ensuring job satisfaction and sanity while working with my siblings and parents, has been in ensuring clear delineation of roles and responsibilities. We play to the strengths of the individuals and, where there are gaps in capability or knowledge, we are not afraid of looking outside of the family for support. Recognising the need for open and honest conversations with family members (often the hardest thing of all) is the key to success, ensuring that everyone understands each other's hopes, goals, and expectations. That way, we can ensure that we are all aligned in achieving the best for our company, our colleagues, and the family.
>
> (Howorth et al., 2016a)

All the Field family are involved in community initiatives and charity events, which give them a sense of personal satisfaction while contributing to the reputation of the business. C. P. J. Field have identified that not all their rival firms have successors willing or able to take over and they have pursued a strategy of expansion by acquiring other funeral directors, particularly where existing owners seek to retire.

Source: the Authors.

8 Finance, investment, and shareholding

Many of the issues that family businesses face in relation to finance are the same as those faced by other growing or owner-managed firms. It is important that we recognise whether an issue is related to the family's influence in a business or whether it is, for example, size-related. Other texts have provided extensive coverage of the issues that small firms face in relation to finance. In this chapter we will examine issues related to family-owned firms.

As they grow, family businesses must consider how far to extend ownership, whether to retain it within a group of family shareholders, stay private, or seek finance through listing shares. As family businesses move through generations, shareholdings become more dispersed and, for some families, dozens or even hundreds of family members may own shares. This chapter examines the implications of dispersed shareholding for the financial strategies that family owners might adopt, including the implications of pruning the family ownership tree.

It is often assumed that owners of family businesses have an aversion to debt, but, as with other assumptions or myths about family businesses, it is dangerous to generalise; some family businesses do appear to avoid debt but others use it extensively. Fewer family businesses use external equity. This can be explained by a difference in perspective. We have seen in previous chapters that, for many family businesses, their values hinge on a long-term perspective on business, whereas the stock markets are notoriously short term in their perspective. In this chapter we will see how financing decisions need to find a balance between satisfying the business need for resources whilst not compromising family owners' values.

This chapter examines the supply and demand of finance and provides an insight into some of the theories that help us to understand the issues and financial strategies for family businesses. The chapter assumes that the reader has a knowledge of common types of finance. We will examine family business use of debt and private equity. For some family firms, intergenerational succession may not be the way forward and therefore we will build on our introduction of alternative exit strategies in Chapter 6 to examine positive and negative aspects and issues in placing a value on the family business.

Learning objectives

Understand theories of supply and demand of finance and their applicability within a family business context.
Knowledge of financial strategies as they apply to family businesses.
Knowledge of issues surrounding exit strategies in family businesses.

Are finance issues different for family businesses?

The biggest difference in financing family firms is the family's influence on – and attitude towards – ownership. Gomez Mejia et al. (2011: 656) state that family firms 'are a distinct organisational form where non-economic factors play a pivotal role in (their) managerial choices'. Achieving financial wealth may be less important for some business-owning families than meeting their affective needs, such as identity, ability to exercise family influence, and perpetuation of the family dynasty, collectively termed 'socioemotional wealth' (Gomez-Mejia, Haynes and Nunez-Nickel, 2007). Maintaining or increasing socioemotional wealth is relevant to the financing of family firms because 'achieving this goal requires continued family control of the firm' (Gomez-Mejia, Haynes and Nunez-Nickel, 2007: 108). Business-owning families whose main aim is ensuring that their ownership continues through generations may therefore avoid financing strategies that will reduce the family's ownership share. Socioemotional wealth is a catch-all theory that has gained some traction because it captures the broad range of emotional and social motivations and objectives that family members may have in relation to their family business. There is evidence that many family-owned businesses avoid strategies that put their socioemotional wealth at risk.

Illiquid shares

A key difference for shareholders in family businesses as opposed to other types of businesses is that it is usually difficult to dispose of shares in family businesses because there is not a ready market; in other words, their shares lack liquidity. The lack of liquidity is often further exacerbated by specific restrictions that might be placed on the sale of family shares; for example, some family businesses restrict the sale of shares to only other family members, or shares might have to be offered back to the company, and therefore family business shares are more likely to be illiquid. Dividends can thus become more important for shareholders in family businesses than in other types of companies because family shareholders have less potential to obtain financial gains from selling their shares, so they look to dividends to give them a financial return on their investment.

Agency issues

In earlier chapters we have seen that the number of shareholders can increase significantly through the generations, so that some family businesses have hundreds of shareholders. Even when family businesses are not listed, they may still face agency issues associated with managing large numbers of shareholders, information asymmetries, and diverging objectives of owners and managers. Owner-managed family firms have no separation of ownership and control and agency theory is silent; in other words, the theory does not have any explanatory power. Where family firms have non-owning managers, there is more likely to be a misalignment of objectives, although this is not inevitable (see the earlier discussion on stewardship). Costs associated with attempts to align management's objectives with those of owners are termed 'agency costs'. Agency issues also arise between potential financiers and business owners. To understand the financing of firms, it is important to understand agency theory. Where there are external finance providers, owners, and non-owning managers, there may be a double agency issue because owners are principals in relation to managers but agents in relation to finance providers. Agency theory was explained earlier in the chapter on governance. We will look at it in more detail below under the supply of finance. As well as the classic owner-manager principal-agent configuration, and the finance-provider-owner-manager double agency problem, family businesses may face information asymmetries between major and minor shareholders, between family and non-family shareholders or between powerful and less powerful branches of the family, particularly where shares are dispersed.

Contextual factors

It is important to recognise these issues in order to understand the context for financing family businesses. Some of the other issues that family businesses face might be related to other aspects of the business rather than their family ownership *per se*. For example, women-owned businesses may face increased difficulties in obtaining finance in certain countries. Small businesses face issues associated with their size; fast-growing businesses face particularly extreme information asymmetries, making it difficult for finance providers to assess the business accurately; owner-managed businesses of all types may face issues relating to the entanglement of private and business assets. It is important in studying family businesses that distinctions are made between issues associated with family ownership and those associated with other factors that might similarly apply to non-family businesses.

Rights and responsibilities of family business shareholders

When family businesses are first founded they are often owner-managed, so that the rights and responsibilities of owners and managers are not distinguished from each other. As family businesses increase in size, ownership and management frequently become separate, and ownership becomes more dispersed. In the earlier chapter on governance, we highlighted the need to clarify the roles, rights, and responsibilities of various groups. The shareholders are the owners and primary investors of finance into the family business and therefore it is important to understand their rights and responsibilities in order to understand the financing of family businesses.

Family business owners can have significant power and influence in their firm. The relationship with management is often much closer than in non-family-owned, publicly listed firms. Family business owners often retain rights that in other firms might be delegated to the board of directors, such as having the right to veto investments over a certain value. The size of their shareholding gives them influence over directors' decision making, as they have the ultimate power to hire and fire directors. On a positive note, family business owners can provide expertise, wisdom, advice, social capital, and a presence that enhances the business. From a negative perspective, family business owners can undermine managers, interfere in strategies, favour promotion of family members, and foster their latest whim, making it difficult to recruit and retain high quality managers. In extreme cases, powerful family shareholders might put the business or family relationships at risk through forcing their personal wishes on the business. The Stronach case study at the end of this chapter provides an extreme example of the power of family business owners, which can be wielded for both good and bad.

Legally, shareholders' rights are to join and contribute to general meetings (usually held at least annually) and to vote on issues raised in those meetings, which include the appointment of directors. In practice, many family business owners own large blocks of shares and have considerable power to hold directors to account for their decisions. Majority owners in family businesses tend to have a much greater presence within the firm than shareholders in other types of businesses. The relationship between owners and managers therefore becomes key.

To fulfil their responsibility as shareholders, it is important to understand the business well enough to make informed decisions in shareholder meetings. As we explained in the earlier chapter on next generation learning, responsible shareholders need to understand business, they need to understand issues specific to family businesses, and they need to understand their own business in order to be able to hold management to account and have a positive influence on the family business. Some family businesses have developed effective learning processes to foster that understanding among their current and potential shareholders. Learning about family businesses should ensure that shareholders are aware of the bivalent nature of family involvement in the business – the capacity for positive and negative implications – highlighted throughout this book.

Family business shareholders will usually be involved in driving the values that underpin the business and the family and in converting those values into strategic goals for the business. The governance structures and processes that were explained in the earlier chapter might provide shareholders with additional rights and responsibilities. These will vary from business to business as their strategies and circumstances dictate. For example, shareholders may have varying voting rights or rights of veto on particular decisions. Such rights are specific to a business and are not statutory.

Supply of finance

Finance is supplied by a range of providers and through a variety of means. Traditional sources of finance can be separated into debt finance, where funds are loaned to the company and repaid, and equity finance, where the investor takes an ownership stake in the business in return for providing funds. In addition, businesses can sometimes access grant funding or support through crowdfunding for specific initiatives.

Finance is only a means to obtain resources and many family businesses bypass the need for finance by obtaining resources directly. It is fairly common for family members to share resources, providing free or cheap labour and expertise as well as physical resources. This is called bootstrapping, after the phrase to 'pull yourself up by your bootstraps', which refers to old-style boots that had straps enabling them to be pulled on easily but also involved lifting the foot (or feet) off the ground. Bootstrapping in this context is any type of informal or personal arrangement to provide finance or resources to help the business. Often, bootstrapping is used by entrepreneurs when founding their businesses. Family businesses, however, tend to continue to draw on other family members throughout their existence. Examples might include family members providing free consultancy or advice, cheap labour at peak periods, lending assets, and sharing assets between different family businesses. Family businesses that are embedded in a community may also benefit from resources provided by other community members. Bootstrapping thus reduces the need for actual finance.

The supply of finance is subject to enduring academic research, particularly focussing on the efficiency of financial markets and whether credit rationing or finance gaps persist. Although here we look at supply and demand of finance separately in order to understand them, it is important to recognise that in practice they are interdependent, with the conditions of supply affecting demand and vice versa (Howorth, 2001).

Information asymmetries and agency theory

Earlier, in the chapter on corporate governance, we explained agency theory in relation to owners and managers. Agency theory can also help us to understand the supply of finance. Here, the supplier of funding is the principal and the receiver of funding is an agent. The principal, or funder, provides finance, trusting that the firm's owners and managers (agents) will act to achieve expected returns.

The supply of finance is typically associated with information asymmetries, wherein the funding provider will have less information about the firm and its prospects than the firm will have. However, finance providers usually have extensive knowledge about typical firms and average returns in a particular set of circumstances. Financing decisions at their most fundamental level are based on an assessment of expectations with regard to risk and return: what is the expected return and what is the risk of not achieving that return. Higher risks are usually associated with higher returns and vice versa. Finance is about forecasting the future. Finance providers will apply an interest rate based on the average risk for a typical firm in a particular set of circumstances. However, while providers may have a good understanding of the context and average returns, the business managers will have a better understanding of their individual circumstances. Those firms who believe they are a lower-than-average risk, based on their more complete inside knowledge, may refuse to accept the terms and look for alternative sources of financing. Those that believe they are a higher-than-average risk may, however, be very happy to accept average terms. This results in the portfolio of firms in that particular finance provider's portfolio being higher than the average risk. This scenario is termed 'adverse selection'. In order to reduce potential adverse selection, finance providers may require, or firms can offer, signals of lower risk. Signalling typically involves business owners demonstrating that they are willing to share the risk by, for example, providing collateral in the form of personal assets or contributing a percentage of the funding requirement. Collateral and guarantees are therefore very common in debt finance. An important signal for equity providers is how the risks and returns are shared: entrepreneurs can signal their confidence in their business by showing that they are sharing in the risk, e.g., investing a significant proportion themselves.

A further agency issue faced by finance providers is 'moral hazard', which is the risk or 'hazard' that business owners may request funding for a particular business plan but, once funding is obtained, and because someone else is taking the risk, they may use such funds for higher risk projects. Moral hazard is typically controlled in the same way by requiring collateral and/or a significant proportion of funds from business owners, and by monitoring the business. Monitoring may take the form of requiring regular updates and, in higher risk investments, may also involve visits to the business or meetings with managers.

Personal and business finances and assets thus become intertwined. Family business owners may be required to provide collateral in the form of personal assets, typically property such as the family home. Directors may be asked to personally guarantee a loan.

Demand for finance

Demand for finance refers to a firm or market's requirements and preference for particular types or levels of finance. Theories and explanations might examine overall demand within a particular group or sector, such as family firms, or they might consider individual demand at the level of the firm.

The pecking order hypothesis

The pecking order hypothesis (POH) is a theory about the demand for finance. The theory suggests that firms will seek finance according to a pecking order of internal sources (retained profit), then debt, and finally external equity. The pecking order hypothesis is based on information asymmetries and suggests that firms will prefer sources of finance where information asymmetries are lower. An information asymmetry occurs when one party in a relationship or transaction has more information than the other. When you are buying a car, the person you are buying it from is likely to have more information about how reliable the car is than you have – this is an information asymmetry. You would probably pay more for a reliable car than an unreliable one but, because you do not know the reliability of the car you are buying (i.e., there is an information asymmetry), you will want to pay less to compensate you for the risk of it being unreliable. In the same way, a finance provider with less information about the firm than insiders is likely to require compensation for the risk of default (in the case of debt finance) or not meeting required returns (in the case of equity finance). Information asymmetries are greater for providers of equity than for debt because debt providers are only looking at the likelihood of repayments being honoured, whereas equity providers need the firm to meet growth expectations, which rely on a wider range of factors. It has been argued that debt and equity providers have better information about markets and factors associated with business success than the firms they are assessing and therefore information asymmetry explanations may be less simple than portrayed in theories such as POH.

Howorth (2001) highlighted that for some firms the pecking order was truncated, in that such firms would only employ internal sources of finance, or internal sources and debt finance. Family firms are frequently assumed to be debt-averse, and it has been suggested that the lack of willingness to take on debt constrains their growth. This is rarely the case as most firms operate with some short-term debt, either trade credit, credit cards, or a bank overdraft (line of credit). However, a small percentage of family firms do indeed avoid taking on long-term debt, and it has been suggested that this might make them more resilient during financial or market crises (Wilson, Wright and Scholes, 2013). Poutziouris (2001) provided evidence that family firms compared with non-family firms retained more profit, used less debt, and were less likely to use private equity capital. However, in contrast, family-owned business groups in Thailand have been criticised for being excessive risk takers, using debt finance to expand aggressively (Suehiro and Wailerdsak, 2004).

Empirical tests of the pecking order hypothesis have provided inconclusive and sometimes conflicting results: observations suggest that there may be a pecking order, but it does not hold in all circumstances. Family business researchers recognise the importance of 'soft' variables, but these are often not easy to measure or access. Many financial models and tests use secondary data and are restricted in the variables that they can examine, often resorting to 'proxy' variables, which are the best available but often weak approximations of the variables they represent. For example, it is difficult to measure the value of 'smart' money, which contributes expertise as well as finance but might vary from one provider to another. It is unsurprising, then, that results are contradictory or inconclusive.

Financial strategies

Determination of a financial strategy for family firms involves balancing business growth and profitability expectations with owners' requirements for returns and the risks for both owners and businesses. If owners expect or require high returns in the form of dividends, this reduces the amount of profits available to reinvest in the growth of the business. If the family's wealth is undiversified and all tied up in the business, then they may be risk-averse and less willing to invest in innovation or growth projects. We have previously highlighted that family business shareholders may have an increased demand for dividends than shareholders in non-family firms because their shares are less liquid and they have less opportunity to gain returns from increases in share prices. In the USA, a study of publicly listed firms found that family firms on average invested less in R&D than non-family firms and they had less long-term debt, which would support the risk-averse hypothesis. The same study reported that family firms had higher dividend payouts than non-family firms (Anderson, Duru and Reeb, 2012). In the following sections we will look in more detail at aspects of financial strategy that are especially pertinent to family firms.

Private equity

Private equity is invested mostly in established firms. As we have seen in earlier chapters, family-owned businesses are the dominant form of established private firms and therefore we might expect that they would be the target of private equity. However, private family firms may avoid private equity because they do not want anyone outside the family to own shares in their businesses. The pecking order hypothesis, outlined above, indicates that private equity could be a finance of last resort. Under that hypothesis, some family business owners might willingly accept reduced growth of their firms rather than seek external finance. Aversion towards external capital has been shown to be higher when family firm owners place increased importance on the pursuit of independence (Poutziouris, 2001). Tappeiner et al. (2012) set out to examine the use of private equity by family businesses in a sample of German firms. They suggested that the pecking order had not considered family effects and therefore was incomplete, meaning it might apply differently in a family firm context or even not be valid in that context.

At its best, private equity provides needed finance to enable the growth of firms along with valuable managerial expertise, increased rigour from an external perspective, and skills in growing businesses. Benefits arise from growth that could not be achieved without significant investment. Family businesses may be more likely to benefit from the managerial resources that private equity investors can provide, particularly if they have been dependent on an internal or family pool of managerial resources. External control mechanisms required by investors may help mitigate any negative effects of altruism and nepotism in the family firm.

However, private equity investors expect a return on their investment and will usually be aiming for an exit within five to seven years, typically through a sale or flotation, and they will usually require control rights, often a seat on the board, and rights of veto. As we have seen, some family businesses are wary of sharing ownership and ceding control rights. Family firm owners from the founding generations may be reluctant to share control because they see the firm as their 'baby' (Howorth, 2001). However, others have suggested that aversion to private equity appears to increase over generations and with more dispersed ownership (Blanco-Mazagatos, Quevedo-Puente and Castrillo, 2007). If family owners are concerned that investors have a relatively short-term perspective and are worried about funding the private equity investors' exit strategy, they might avoid equity finance and access the benefits of external perspectives through directly employing non-executive directors and non-family managers and engaging in industry benchmarking. Tappeiner et al. (2012) describe evidence that minority private equity investments might provide family business owners with the funding and expertise of private equity providers, whilst allowing the family owners to retain control.

In 2019 the founding family of defence company Cobham asked the UK government to intervene to block an American private equity firm from taking over the company. Cobham, a FTSE 250 company, was founded by Sir Alan Cobham in 1934, who was succeeded by his son Sir Michael Cobham in 1969. From 1992, the company was run by a non-family CEO and grew through acquisitions. Total revenues in 2018 were £1.8 billion. By 2019 the family's shareholding was 1.5% of the total, which was substantial in monetary terms but not sufficient to give them any power in decision making. Lady Cobham wrote to the UK government in August 2019 stating that the private equity firm was 'opportunist' and that assurances by private equity firms were 'not worth the paper they are written on'. Lady Cobham's letter highlights a mistrust of private equity companies. David Lockwood, the CEO, stated that he had 'personal sympathy with a shareholder who has an emotional link as well as an economic link' to a company, but he believed the deal was in the shareholders' best interests.[1]

The Cobham example shows differences in attitudes towards the ownership of a company. Members of founding families often have a particularly strong emotional attachment, even when they are no longer majority owners or involved in the management of the company. The case also demonstrates that the founding family's shareholding and power can dwindle through a public listing and through introducing new shareholders via acquisitions. For some, the family's shareholding is reduced to the point where they can no longer be defined as family-controlled businesses, although the business might still carry their family name.

Public listing of family businesses

As we have seen, for many family businesses the idea of selling shares to anyone outside the family is anathema. However, we must not assume that this is the case for all family businesses. A small percentage of the largest family businesses list their shares on a stock exchange, making them publicly available. For example, in the UK, 12.5% of the largest listed companies are family controlled (Kotlar et al., 2019). In order to meet the EU definition of a family firm, 25% of the shares of a publicly listed firm must remain in the control of members of the same family (for definitions see Chapter 2). Many of the advantages of a public listing (IPO or initial public offering) are the same for family and non-family firms, including the financial investment itself providing cash to invest in further growth and an increased profile for the business. For some family shareholders, the opportunity of selling some shares or an exit strategy may be particularly appealing. The cost of an IPO is prohibitive to all but the largest businesses. The key reason why many large family businesses do not opt for a public listing relates to loss of control.

Classes of shares

As we have seen throughout this book, a significant proportion of family businesses are very sophisticated and not the naïve unprofessional business owners that are sometimes assumed. Variations in the class or voting rights of shares is one tool that can be used to expand equity whilst retaining control within a smaller, family group. However, private equity providers are reluctant to invest in equity without significant control rights to manage their investment.

Some family firms have introduced variation in classes of shares to manage succession and the issues associated with ever-expanding numbers of family shareholders. Younger family members might be provided with a number of shares with restricted voting rights in order to introduce them to the rights and responsibilities of ownership and allow them to gain experience without the senior generation ceding control. For example, a block of particular shares might only have one vote that is shared among a number of shareholders.

Pruning the family tree

Pruning the family tree refers to reducing the number of family shareholders in order to reduce complexity and improve the 'fruitfulness' of the business (Lambrecht and Lievens, 2008). Pruning the family tree might also include reducing the number of family managers but most often refers to a reduction in shareholders. Large numbers of disengaged family shareholders are a cost to the business and they can be a distraction or even a blockage to the main purpose of the business. More distant family shareholders may have a weaker commitment to the business and more interest in financial returns from their shares. An increased number of shareholders provides greater likelihood of differences in opinion, personal interests clashing with business interests, and increased conflict. Higher dividends mean less money available for reinvestment in the business. Pruning the family tree might therefore be a win–win situation for the business and the distant shareholders.

The actual mechanics of pruning the family tree are very straightforward. Shares are bought from less engaged or distant family members to reduce the number of family shareholders. Shares can either be bought back by the business or bought up by other family shareholders. The valuation of shares, however, is less straightforward. Share values are based on expected returns, but there may be huge variations in the expectations of sellers and buyers, especially when shares are not publicly traded. (Valuing the family business is examined in a later section of this chapter.) There is no absolutely correct value of shares and they are only ever worth what someone will pay for them. In some cases, exiting shareholders may accept a lower value for their shares to ensure the future of the business. In other cases, shares may need to be bought at a much higher value to ensure that the buyout goes through, to protect family relationships and to avoid protracted negotiations.

The emotional aspects are not so straightforward and the buyout process has the potential to threaten family relationships. Procedural justice has been shown to be important in perceptions of fairness when negotiating buyout values (Howorth, Westhead and Wright, 2004). Fairness is more likely to be perceived, and good relationships maintained, when the process is believed to be fair, which requires involvement in the process, agreement of decision criteria and clear explanations. Disagreements are more likely where family owners perceive that a decision or process is out of line with their interpretation of family values and norms. Exits and buyouts in a family business context have the potential to lead to conflict and disagreements that can cause longstanding rifts between family members (Howorth, Westhead and Wright, 2004).

Exit strategies

Research rarely considers exit strategies in relation to family businesses as there is an assumption that family businesses will wish to continue across many generations. We saw in the chapter on succession that individual family owners may need to liquidate their investment to fund their retirement plans. Sometimes there is no successor for a family business, or little interest in continuing the family business, and family owners may decide to sell the firm. For family owners, the decision to harvest their investment may be a positive one. For the firm, a new ownership regime may be a boost and bring innovation, efficiencies, and regeneration.

Family owners can exit through a trade sale, where the business is sold to a third party. The advantages of a trade sale are that it provides a clear transfer of ownership and former family owners can move on to new adventures. The disadvantages are that there is little time for knowledge transfer and key information, contacts, customers, and suppliers may be lost. Many family firms are highly dependent on the tacit knowledge of key individuals, particularly family owner-managers who have been involved in the firm for a long time. IPOs are an alternative exit strategy but, as we saw above, they are out of reach for the majority of family businesses.

Management buyouts (MBOs) or management buyins (MBIs) are an alternative means of realising the owners' investment while allowing continued independent ownership of the firm. MBO/MBIs provide increased continuity, as some of the management team become owners of the business. The firm's identity and ethos are more likely to remain similar and, often, former family owners continue to be involved in the firm as advisers or in a non-executive capacity for a period of time after the buyout. A well-planned and executed MBO reduces the risk of loss of knowledge from exiting owner-managers. Most MBOs and MBIs will be funded through a combination of private equity and debt. Post MBO/I, firms can have very high levels of debt, the increased cost and risk of which can undermine firm performance. Where family members are involved in the MBO team, there is potential for conflict, particularly if negotiations become competitive (Howorth, Westhead and Wright, 2004).

Exit strategies require a valuation of the business in order that a value can be placed on any shares that are being bought or sold, whether it is through trade sale, IPO, buyback, or MBO/I.

Negotiating a value for the family business

Family business owners who are contemplating exit strategies will wish to understand how much their share of the business is worth. Successors who are buying shares, whether as the next generation of family owners or through MBO/I, IPO, or trade sale, will want to ensure that they are paying a fair price. However, values are not absolute and in many circumstances some negotiation may be involved. The true value of a firm may only become apparent after a deal has been completed (Howorth, Westhead and Wright, 2004). The private, even secretive, nature of some business-owning families may result in very low levels of transparency and higher information asymmetries between potential external investors and the family firm. Higher information asymmetries are associated with greater potential for undervaluation of a firm by external investors.

Howorth, Westhead and Wright (2004) highlighted that valuing the family business can be an emotional, competitive process that in some cases leads to a total breakdown of family relationships. Family owners, particularly the founding generation, may place a higher value on their firm because they have invested effort into its development and their emotional attachment is high; this is known as the 'endowment effect'. An example of the endowment effect can be seen when valuing items that are precious to us, but not necessarily precious to anyone else. Perhaps the antiques dealer values the necklace that your grandmother gave you at £100 but for you it is priceless and you would never sell it for that amount. It would probably be different if you had bought the necklace at a flea market. Imagine how it might feel if your grandmother left you a business that she founded 50 years ago and you know it cost her dearly to make it successful. Could you sell it? If so, how would you value it?

Putting the two together – undervaluation by investors due to information asymmetries and overvaluation by investees (family firm owners) due to the endowment effect – it is easy to see why the two parties might not agree, and it further explains why some family firm owners are unwilling to seek external equity (Poutziouris, 2001).

Business valuation is not an exact science and a sale will include negotiation of price. Dabholkar, Johnston and Cathey (1994) theorise that negotiation behaviour will depend on whether there is an expected continuation of the relationship with the other party and whether negotiators focus on their own individual or joint gains. When vendors and purchasers wish to maximise their own gains and have no intention of continuing the relationship post-sale, negotiation behaviour is likely to be competitive, with each trying to secure the best deal at the expense of the other. Family firm vendors who expect a continuing commitment to the firm post-sale, but aim to maximise their own gains, are more likely to engage in command behaviour, stressing that what they want is best for 'their' firm. In both competitive and command negotiation behaviour, there will be an unwillingness to share information, and negotiators might engage in threats, promises, positional commitments, and persuasion to get their own way. Where family firm vendors and purchasers focus on maximising gains for both parties, there will be increased information sharing. If long-term relationships are important, behaviour will be 'co-ordinative' and feature flexibility and effective communication. Howorth, Westhead and Wright (2004) identified that this type of behaviour was expected in MBOs of family firms if relationships were good, there was a commitment to the long-term future of the firm and the relationship between owners and managers was perceived to be more important than immediate individual gains. The fourth permutation is where there is no relationship between the parties but both aim to cooperate to secure the best deal for both vendor and purchaser.

Understanding future expectations with regard to family owners' relationship with their firm provides an insight into their position when they are attempting to value the business. We have seen previously that emotional attachments are prevalent in family businesses. Valuation is not an exact science and values can be affected by source dependence and investments of time and emotions. Finance theory indicates that sunk costs should be ignored in valuing an investment. However, the emotions tied up in family firms often lead to family owners over-valuing their firm because they 'have invested so much into it'.

Key learning point

Finance for family firms, like so many other areas of family business, is an arena for the intertwining of emotional and rational behaviours. A major assumption of finance theory is economic rationality, but we have seen that this assumption does not hold for family businesses. Non-economic factors play a pivotal role in finance for family businesses. Family businesses are characterised by difficulties in separating family and business aspects and this is particularly visible in the intertwining of family and business resources, which includes finance, but bootstrapping of resources can also reduce the need for actual finance. As family businesses grow, dispersion of shareholdings can lead to increased emphasis on financial returns and weaker emotional attachment to the business. Financial strategies for some family businesses include pruning the family tree to reduce the number of shareholders.

Summary

This chapter examined financing of family businesses and highlighted again that it is important not to make sweeping generalisations. A key question for family business owners is how far to extend ownership to support the investment needs of the business. Although some family firms are averse to debt, most family businesses use some form of debt. Many avoid introducing external (non-family) equity into the firm, mainly due to concerns about losing control. In this case, a truncated pecking order may exist. For a minority of family businesses, their investment strategy will include a public listing or the introduction of private equity. This chapter highlighted the positive and negative aspects of different financing strategies and explained some of the issues pertinent to family businesses.

Many of the financial issues that family businesses face are the same as other firms and relate more to their context, size, industry, or growth trajectories. Issues specific to family businesses arise from the intertwining of family and business. Determination of a financial strategy for family firms thus involves balancing the business' growth and profitability expectations with the owners' requirements for returns and the risks for both owners and business. The illiquid nature of many family business shares means that returns for shareholders are mostly through dividends. However, high dividend payouts reduce the funds available to invest in the business. For many families in business, all their wealth is tied up in their business, and because they do not have a diversified portfolio of assets, they may prefer a lower risk business strategy. The interdependence of supply and demand was highlighted, and we noted that information asymmetries may exist between various groups, leading to agency issues and costs. Family business owners aiming to signal their lower risk may have increased intertwining of family and business resources.

Throughout the book we have emphasised the influence of non-economic factors on family businesses and these continue to be important in family business finance. Emotional attachments can influence decision making. Powerful family shareholders can have positive and negative influences on management, strategies, and investment decisions. Endowment effects can lead to excessively high valuations of the business' worth, constraining exit options or undermining attempts to prune the family tree. Valuation of the business is not a science but a negotiation between interested parties. We noted that family business owners often over-value their businesses because of the emotional investment by themselves and preceding generations, in contrast to investment theory, which purports the irrelevance of sunk costs.

Discussion questions

1. Imagine that on your next birthday you will be gifted a minority (less than 1%) of the shares in your family's business. What would your concerns be? Are there any theories that provide insights into your new role as a shareholder? In the future it is likely that you will inherit a majority (more than 50%) of the shares of the family business, which is managed by a non-family CEO. What involvement would you expect to have in the firm and how does this align with your legal rights?
2. Why might a family business prune the family tree? What alternative options are available to them? If you were the one being pruned, what would you be concerned about?

Case study 8.1: The Stronach succession

Creating and growing a business that generates millions of dollars and employs hundreds of staff is a great achievement, but with power comes social and financial responsibility to many interconnected stakeholders.

Frank Stronach, an Austrian émigré, set up a tool and die business in Canada in 1957, three years after settling there. Rapid expansion followed and by the late 1960s Stronach had merged his firm with industrial parts manufacturer Magna. Within a decade, Magna was one of the world's leading names in auto parts manufacturing. Frank Stronach was labelled by some as autocratic and irascible, but the success of his enterprise was undeniable.

The stock market crash of 1987 did not do Stronach's firm any permanent damage, but the scare led Stronach to institute a 'no debt' policy to mitigate any recurrence. The avoidance of debt is believed to have helped Magna shrug off the 2008 financial tsunami like it was no more than a wave. Feted as a shining example of Canada's enterprise culture, Stronach sought to apply his skill to other businesses, developing a series of passion projects – building theme parks, buying racetracks, starting an airline.

However, the new initiatives were less successful. The theme park never got off the ground, neither did the airline. Stronach had a lot of success with racehorses but his passion for racing was not shared by some Magna investors, who were angered that the profits of the auto parts business were invested in buying a racetrack. Stronach quelled their disquiet by agreeing not to invest in any further non-automotive businesses for at least eight years and beginning a succession plan by establishing a family trust and appointing his daughter Belinda as CEO.

Belinda was interested in the family firm from an early age and quit her university degree at age 20 because she wanted to work for her father. She briefly left the company to go into politics but returned to take back the reins a few years later. Frank continued with diversification attempts into unconnected ventures like energy drinks and electric bikes, while Belinda developed a gift for boosting the racing and racetrack business. Frank decided to go into politics in his birth nation of Austria, founding the 'Team Stronach' political party. To operate in Austria without paying large amounts of tax he had to relinquish his position as super-trustee of the family trust.

Frank's close friend Alon Ossip, a former tax lawyer, was vice-president of the company and Belinda tried to get him to persuade Frank to curtail spending. However, Frank carried on as before; his biggest 'passion project' was commissioning a gigantic sculpture at his Florida racetrack of the mythical Pegasus fighting a dragon. Standing well over 100 feet high, the cost rose from an initial estimate of $6 million to $30 million. Seeing money haemorrhage out of the company, Belinda eventually used her executive power to halt her father's activities. The fall-out meant that one side of the family began suing the other, with *Toronto Life* magazine labelling it as a $500million family feud. Frank alleged that his resignation as super-trustee was nothing more than an expedient and short-term action, but Belinda's lawyers refuted that, saying he had no decision-making power.

Consider how you might feel from each perspective. If you had founded a successful company like Frank Stronach, how would you feel about your entitlement to decide on investments? How would you feel if you were

Belinda and had joined the company to work with a father you admired but were now embroiled in a legal battle with him? What were the advantages and disadvantages of setting up a family trust?

Source: the Authors.

Note

1 Quotes are from *The Financial Times*, 4 August 2019. Available at www.ft.com/content/d60f30b0-b69c-11e9-8a88-aa6628ac896c.

9 Community, philanthropy, and social responsibility

The wealthiest families in the world contribute billions to charitable causes, manage large family foundations, and have powerful roles in advocating for causes close to their hearts. In addition, there are millions of small family businesses actively contributing to local causes and undertaking leadership roles in their local communities. Both family and non-family businesses engage in charitable activities, often under the banner of corporate social responsibility. In this chapter we go beyond corporate social responsibility to explore the community, philanthropic, and charitable activities of business families.

Throughout the book we have emphasised the importance of understanding family businesses within a specific context. In this chapter we will drill down into the community context to examine how family businesses engage with the communities around them. Although some businesses may see this as an aspect of corporate social responsibility or CSR, this chapter shows that for many families in business the roots of community engagement are deep and the engagement is personal. Concepts introduced in earlier chapters arise to illuminate our understanding. Paternalism might extend beyond family and employee boundaries to encompass employees' families, local communities, and industry colleagues. Stewardship might extend to protecting the environment beyond the family business. The intertwining of family and business values comes to the fore as we consider how different generations become involved in philanthropic and community endeavours.

Family businesses are often well-known within the communities in which they trade and many of them support their local community, financially and through community-strengthening initiatives. In Chapter 5 we examined the importance of social capital, noting that family relationships tend to endure. Social capital was defined as the goodwill available to individuals and groups. In this chapter we will build our understanding of social capital by examining embeddedness. We will study how embeddedness captures the deep and entwined bonds and connections that some business-owning families have with a community, inspiring beneficial community initiatives, philanthropy, and reciprocity. In Chapter 7 we saw how the succession process might instil shared values in the next generation, but we noted that some next generation family members might not undertake an executive role. For them, there may be greater fulfilment in community initiatives and the philanthropic aspects of their family's business than in the business itself.

Over 80% of the world's family businesses are believed to practise philanthropy at some level (*Forbes*, 2015). Philanthropy is defined as actions, ideas, and events that further the welfare of others, including gifts, fund-raising, and volunteering. Philanthropy has been described as an essential dimension of family entrepreneurship (Rey-Garcia and Puig-Raposo, 2013), helping to strengthen bonds within the family and between the firm and the communities within which it operates. Throughout the world, the names of family business leaders have endured for generations through their philanthropic legacy. The biggest philanthropic foundations in the USA are household names: Rockefeller, Carnegie, and Ford, and more recently the Bill and Melinda Gates Foundation. In Britain, organisations such as the Joseph Rowntree Foundation, Leverhulme Trust, and Garfield Weston Foundation continue to undertake charitable work many years after their eponymous founders have passed. Libraries, museums, and learning institutions frequently bear the names of local businessmen and women who invested their wealth in improving the lives of the places they cared about – Carnegie Libraries, John Moores University in the UK, Johns Hopkins University in the USA, Annamalai University and Birla Institutes of Technology in India, McGill University in Canada, Federico Santa Maria Technical University in Chile – the list is huge. However, 'naming' is not always viewed positively. In 2019 the University of Pennsylvania announced a name change of their law school to the University of Pennsylvania Carey Law School in honour of a historic $125 million gift from the W. P. Carey Foundation, but the renaming caused consternation among some alumni, who said they would no longer support their alma mater.

The philanthropist Andrew Carnegie has been variously attributed as stating that wealth is not here to feed our egos but to feed the hungry and to help people help themselves. Carnegie is also famous for saying that wealthy people should spend the final third of their life giving away their wealth, and to die rich was a disgrace.

In this chapter we examine wealthy and not so wealthy family businesses to identify the ways they engage with communities and philanthropy. Explanations are explored, introducing the concept of embeddedness, social and contextual influences on behaviour, as well as more mundane business considerations like tax benefits and marketing potential.

Learning objectives

Understand influences on family businesses' engagement in their community, including embeddedness, faith, and reciprocity.
Knowledge and understanding of how families in business perceive and enact their social responsibilities.
Knowledge of motivations and patterns of family business philanthropy.

Distinguishing between different concepts

The concept of giving something back to the community in which a business operates goes back as long as business itself. Paternalistic companies of the past (and present) have taken a strong interest in the welfare of their employees, providing housing, social programmes, and welfare initiatives. As societies have evolved, though, the control exercised by paternalistic employers has become less acceptable and the emphasis has shifted to companies being socially responsible. The concept of corporate social responsibility (CSR) has expanded to reflect that.

Whilst recognising that there is a great deal of overlap between philanthropy, corporate social responsibility, and community engagement, it is important that we understand how they differ. We start therefore by establishing some definitions.

Philanthropy

Etymologically, philanthropy derives from the Greek meaning 'love of mankind'. In business terms, philanthropic companies might distribute some of their profits to people or organisations less fortunate or successful than themselves, or they might instigate initiatives that can be of benefit to their immediate community or society at large. Philanthropy is understood as voluntary behaviours and actions resulting from a commitment to the well-being of others (Feliu and Botero, 2016).

Philanthropy can be directed through a business, undertaken by individuals connected with the family business, e.g., owners, or managed through formal channels such as family foundations or trusts. In general use, philanthropy refers to financial giving. Many universities have a development office whose role is to seek and attract philanthropic donations, frequently in association with the alumni office. American university alumni have a long tradition of financially endowing their place of learning, bestowing huge sums on the institutions that awarded them their degrees and the scale of gifts is something that universities in many other countries can only dream of. Even comparatively minor learning institutions in the USA regularly receive six-figure donations; for example, Macalester College in Minnesota has an endowment worth over $650 million (Hannah Fearn in *Times HE*, 2009). Throughout the world, entrance portals to university buildings, hospitals, and other institutions are adorned with the names of business leaders, companies, and other philanthropists that have provided gifts to fund them.

The Tata case study at the end of this chapter (9.1) highlights that members of the Tata family have founded several individual trusts, collectively known as the Tata Trusts, and are a powerful driver of social action and change in India. One Tata trust has established institutions such as the National Centre for the Performing Arts, while another is working to equip every medical college with a dedicated cancer care facility. Child labour is still prevalent in some areas in India, so the trusts are working to ensure that all children receive a proper education and are not forced into labouring jobs while they are still children. Tata Trusts focus on institutional endowments and programme support rather than charitable giving.

The key point in defining philanthropy is that it is voluntary and not a requirement for businesses or family business owners. However, there may be expectations and norms that govern behaviour, which we will examine below.

Corporate social responsibility

Corporate social responsibility (CSR) refers only to the activities of a business, whether family or non-family owned, large or small. Philanthropic efforts of family business owners such as foundations set up by individuals or groups of family members would not be included under a strict definition of CSR. Two theories have become fundamental to understanding CSR. Stakeholder theory highlights that businesses have responsibilities to all those who are affected by their actions, known as stakeholders. Stakeholders can be separated into groups of customers, suppliers, communities, employees, and financiers (Freeman, 1984). Family-owned businesses would also include groups of family members, for example owners and next generation members, as specific types of stakeholders. By including next generation members as a group of stakeholders, the long-term perspective of family businesses is captured, frequently expressed as a responsibility towards future generations.

The second theory that has become fundamental to studies of corporate social responsibility is Archie Carroll's CSR pyramid (Carroll, 1991). The CSR pyramid indicates that businesses' basic responsibility is economic, to be profitable; at the same time, businesses also have a legal responsibility to follow applicable laws; on top of that they have an ethical responsibility, to do what is fair, right, and just, ensuring their actions cause no harm; finally, businesses are expected to be good corporate citizens, this is captured at the top of Carroll's pyramid as a philanthropic responsibility. More specifically, philanthropic responsibility is about contributing financial and human resources to the community and improving quality of life (Carroll, 1991: 42). The key point to recognise about Carroll's corporate social responsibility pyramid is that responsibilities are concurrent, not sequential; in other words, the social responsibilities of a business are expected to include all these areas at the same time.

In Carroll's pyramid, philanthropy is one element of corporate social responsibility. However, in practice, the terms can sometimes be used interchangeably. In India, the Companies Act (2013) mandates a minimum level of CSR activities for large Indian companies, requiring them to spend at least 2% of their average net profits on CSR activities (Kumar, 2018). The India Companies Act defines CSR as activities that promote poverty reduction, education, health, environmental sustainability, gender equality, and vocational skills development. This is more closely aligned with just the philanthropic and ethical elements of Carroll's model of CSR.

Many countries require companies to report on their CSR activities, usually as part of the annual reporting system. However, the requirements for reporting on CSR are believed to have led, in some cases, to what is called 'greenwashing', where the reported CSR activities are not perceived to be coherent with observed business practices. ISO 26000 was developed in 2010 to provide an international guidance standard. Note that ISO 26000 is voluntary and can be applied to most types of organisations, but it is guidance and cannot be certificated.

Charitable giving

Charitable giving is one aspect of philanthropy and includes any gift of financial or other resources to charities or worthy causes. Charitable giving can be from individuals or from the business itself. In many countries charitable giving attracts tax benefits that might include offsetting donations against business profits to reduce tax, or top-ups that increase the charitable donation. For example, in the UK, higher rate taxpayers can personally claim back the difference between basic rate and higher rate tax on all charitable donations through the UK government's Gift Aid scheme.

Both family and non-family owned businesses engage in charitable giving. A 2005 survey by Coutts found that as many as 87% of family businesses support charitable causes, compared with 80% of non-family firms (Evans, 2005). The reasons that the survey gives for high levels of giving by family firms centre around the importance that family firms attach to values and principles, particularly with regard to the community in which they operate. However, it should be noted that charitable giving is not the domain of just family firms, as a very high percentage of both family and non-family firms engage in charitable giving. Differences tend to be more notable between countries or cultures, rather than between family and non-family owned businesses. In 2016 a report by Ernst and Young, in conjunction with the University of St Gallen, disclosed that $67 billion was donated by American firms. Family businesses in the UK gave away over £900 million in 2016, which was almost twice as much as the £490 million donated by German family firms. Overall, UK family and non-family businesses give away around £10 billion per annum in charitable or philanthropic donations.

The largest reported charitable givers are from the USA. Bill Gates is currently top of the list, having given away well over $30 billion in his lifetime. Financier Warren Buffet – he who uttered the quote that has been cited numerous times about winning the ovarian lottery by being born in the United States – is just a few million behind, and has stated that his entire $60 billion fortune will be given away either within his lifetime or on his death. In the UK, Scottish entrepreneur turned philanthropist Tom Hunter has already donated £100 million to worthy causes, Lord Sainsbury,

£200 million plus and counting, including a massive £82 million to fund a Cambridge University research facility (how many Nectar points did he get for that?), while George Weston, whose family have a controlling interest in Associated British Foods, gives vast sums away to housing corporations, youth groups, and churches via the Garfield Weston Foundation, a charity that was started by his grandfather back in 1958. In 2018 the Garfield Weston Foundation distributed £69.5 million to its beneficiaries.

However, we should note that for many cultures and faiths, charitable giving is something that is done in secret and therefore reported amounts of giving are not necessarily reliable.

Community engagement

Community engagement includes the charitable and philanthropic activities of a family business but, in addition, all the activities that family business members become involved with in their community, whether paid or unpaid, such as running sports clubs, governing schools, serving in local government and business associations, and acting as charity trustees. As we see in the Tata Sons (Case Study 9.1) and Wilsden Equestrian Centre (Case Study 9.2) cases, family members can have multiple connections and undertake a variety of roles. The association of some family business names with specific places is so strong that it may continue long after the business itself has moved or been taken over: Rockefellers in New York, Rowntrees in York, Cadburys in Birmingham. Business families that have operated for generations in a town may be regarded affectionately or otherwise by the townsfolk, who sometimes refer to them by a nickname.

Family business members may strategically choose to take on specific community roles that enhance their business; for example, serving on the local council might help ensure that planning regulations are not detrimental to their business; chairing a business association might give influence and early warning of changes in their industry. Some roles are selected out of personal interest, including sporting or charitable passions. Others may be a deliberate decision to enhance particular skills, knowledge, or connections, especially among next generation family members. Sometimes it is traditional to have a representative from the dominant local family business occupy particular roles in the community.

Sports clubs frequently receive support from family businesses, based on the personal interests of family members. Loyalty to a specific club can extend across generations and ranges from sponsoring the local team (as in our case study 9.2) to investing millions into a leading European football club. Juventus in Italy, funded by the Agnelli family, or Manchester United in England, backed for a long time by the Edwards family, are examples of clubs where successive generations of a business family have supported a club financially.

Mostly the financial return on investment in a football club is negative. Investment in sports clubs appears to be linked to strong identification with a town or city, alongside owners' passion for the particular sport, rather than to financial returns. Unusually in business, association with an unsuccessful team does not appear to affect business branding detrimentally. Bet365, for example, an online betting business run by the Coates family, with their headquarters in Stoke-on-Trent, allied themselves with Stoke-on-Trent's football team, Stoke City, by having the club's stadium renamed as the Bet365 stadium. Stadium naming is not a low-profile association. The name of a club's stadium is mentioned in every single match report, which in the case of the English Premier League means that the stadium's name is mentioned every week in the 100-plus countries that regularly receive broadcasts. Not long afterwards, the club was relegated from the Premier League, but Bet365 continued to thrive, with profits rising by 31% in 2018, the year that Stoke City were relegated.

The concept of community engagement may be more significant in smaller towns and rural areas, especially for smaller family businesses who might be insignificant in a large city. Rural communities may be less diverse and more likely to contain people who share 'similar values, norms, meanings, history, and identity' (Shepherd and Patzelt, 2011: 139). Farming is more often than not a family affair and psychological ownership of the countryside is strong. Rural villages may have local plans, councils, and community facilities that provide opportunities for community engagement. Local parks, sports grounds, and community centres may owe their continued existence to the philanthropic efforts of their community.

Whatever the reasons, community engagement can have benefits for the family business as well as the community, enhancing social capital, building reputation and commitment. The combination of roles of various family members can make some family businesses extremely influential within a community. The dark side of community engagement is that it can be used for political purposes, from influencing local planning decisions to uprooting political systems. Allegations have been made of undue political influence against some of the most powerful family foundations in the world, including the Rockefeller and Ford foundations, Charles Stewart Mott Foundation and George Soros' Open Society Institute.

Theoretical insights

In the following sections we look at some of the theories that help to explain aspects of business families' involvement in philanthropy and community engagement activities. The key concepts are embeddedness, altruism, and reciprocity. We will then look at some of the cultural and contextual drivers of philanthropy, including values, norms, and business (specifically marketing) drivers.

Embeddedness

Family businesses operate within a specific context, as we have noted previously. The context includes the networks, ties, and relationships of members of the family business, including social networks, business relationships, and all those connections arising from family members, owners, and employees' involvement in various organisations, leisure, sporting, and faith activities. Where a family business has multiple connections within a specific community it is likely to be 'embedded' within that community.

Embeddedness refers to being deeply tied into a place or context. The term was first adopted by Karl Polanyi in the 1960s to explain the difference between capitalist and non-capitalist economies; Polanyi argued that economies were strongly embedded in social, religious, and cultural institutions, and that they cannot be understood without taking account of their socio-cultural and political contexts. Mark Granovetter and others developed the concept further to explain its influence on choices and decisions. Embeddedness emphasises the obligations, norms, and values arising from social, religious, and political institutions. For businesses, embeddedness relates to the degree to which their economic activity is influenced by non-economic institutions. Embeddedness is a multi-layered concept in that individuals, families, and family businesses are simultaneously embedded in multiple social, spatial, and institutional communities. For example, an immigrant family may be embedded within their place of origin as well as their current place, they may be embedded within a religious community and also within a family (social) group. The choices that the family make will likely be influenced by obligations, norms, and values from all four (and other) communities. Their family business might engage in philanthropic and community activities relating to one or all of these spheres of influence. Embeddedness engenders perceived responsibilities towards a community and helps to explain reciprocity observed within communities.

Altruism, reciprocity, and giving

In earlier chapters we explained the prevalence of altruism within family businesses. Altruism is an unconditional act of giving, with no expectation of reward. Reciprocity is the social norm of reciprocal giving, or having received something positive, you provide something positive in return. Reciprocity can also be negative, wherein someone who has been treated badly might respond similarly or even worse.

There are many reasons why people give of their time or their resources for others. We are not just concerned with financial giving, although that is the area that receives greater emphasis in family businesses. Serge-Christophe Kolm (2006: 18) suggests that:

> One may give for eliciting self-satisfaction, praise, gratitude, esteem, admiration, liking, or love …; for gaining an aura of generosity in one's

own eyes and in the eyes of other persons whose judgment one values ... One may give for showing and proving one's friendship, affection, liking or love .... People also often give in given circumstances simply because they feel they have to do it, possibly because it is a tradition, in considering more or less the judgment of their conscience or of other people, but also sometimes by pure habit and inertia.

Giving that is motivated by some intrinsic reward is non-altruistic. Altruistic giving, on the other hand, is motivated purely by a wish to improve another's lot and can be divided into hedonistic altruism, which is based on compassion, pity, and empathy, and normative altruism, which is based on morals and believing it to be the 'right thing to do'.

Many major religions adhere to the 'Golden Rule' of treating others as you would like them to treat you. This is an example of generalised reciprocity. Generalised reciprocity is the act of giving without any immediate expectation of reward but the general expectation that a reciprocal act will occur in the future; a simple example would be if you buy your friends a coffee, you might expect that at some point in the future one of them will buy you one. Balanced reciprocity occurs where there is equal exchange, for example in the giving of Christmas gifts. Balanced reciprocity is direct in that the giver and recipient exchange something of similar value. Generalised reciprocity might be indirect in that the giver gives to one or more of a group and may receive a reward from elsewhere in the group. Rewards include intangible gifts such as praise, recognition, and prestige as well as tangible awards.

Reciprocity and embeddedness help to explain philanthropy. For example, family business owners might think 'this community has been good to our family, so we want to give something back'.

The Cigar Family Charitable Foundation was founded by the Fuente and Newman families in 2001 to give back to the people of the Dominican Republic where their factory is based (Severino Bueno, Rodriguez Polanci and Perez Estrella, 2019). The main aim is to support the development of the population, focussing on children and young people and projects include education, healthcare, vocational training, and clean water. The Foundation works closely with government ministries and raises funds through high profile funding events, drawing on the families' social and business connections. For example, a Cars and Cigars event in Detroit raised over $800,000. In 2005 Carlito Fuente was shocked to learn that the children they were supporting through primary education were stymied in their dreams because there was no affordable high school. Carlito took out a personal loan for hundreds of thousands of dollars to provide a speedy response for the children he had met and went on to expand the Foundation's activities to include high school education. This example illustrates the intertwining of business and individual finances, motivations, and passions within family business philanthropy.

Cultural, contextual, and business drivers of philanthropy

Several authors, scholars, and business people have attempted to capture what makes a business philanthropic. A report for the Institute for Family Business (Breeze, 2009) suggests that family businesses are 'Natural Philanthropists'. In the Foreword, Stephen Rubin, chair of Pentland Group, family owners of Berghaus, Speedo, and many other brands that are household names, emphasises the importance of values and a long-term stewardship perspective:

> The presence of family values in a business setting, the commitment to stewardship through the generations and the balancing of long-term objectives against the requirement to generate short-term profit, are features that predispose family businesses towards being philanthropic and socially responsible.
>
> (Rubin, 2009: 5)

The drivers for CSR and philanthropy can be divided into three areas: values, social norms, and marketing. Values and an ethos of 'giving something back' is the most obvious motivation. Additionally, family business owners may be influenced by peer pressure or what they perceive to be social norms. From a business point of view, philanthropy and CSR provide marketing benefits in terms of building social and reputational capital, contributing to a positive brand image, that also influences recruitment and retention of talented employees. From a family point of view, philanthropy and community engagement can help educate the next generation and other family members about responsibilities, family legacy, and wealth management, as well as enabling them to develop practical and social skills. Working together with senior generations on philanthropic or community projects can help transfer social capital, values, and learning between generations (Breeze, 2009).

The different drivers have potential to create sites of tension for families in business. The reputations of family owners are tied into the brands of their businesses, for both positive and negative effect. Individuals' values and norms might include not boasting about philanthropy and charitable giving, but the marketing department might perceive it as a positive contribution to their brand-building efforts and push individuals to publicise their charitable giving. Criticisms of companies' CSR efforts contradicting other business practices or amounting to 'green washing' might make family owners wary of having genuine charitable efforts subject to scrutiny in the public domain. The tension between business imperatives and family or owner values, highlighted early in this book, is at play here.

Rubin (2009) goes on to argue that philanthropy creates benefits for the business and its shareholders as well as the wider community:

A philanthropic and socially responsible company generates benefits not only for its shareholders but for all its stakeholders, which includes employees, suppliers, customers, and their wider communities.
Stephen Rubin OBE, chairman of the Pentland Group (2009)

Faith and family business philanthropy

A key driver of values and norms might be religious affiliation, and religious faith is a major driver of philanthropic initiatives. Business people from all faiths are motivated by their beliefs to share their wealth. We observed earlier that most major religions subscribe to the Golden Rule of treating others as you would have them treat you. The command to 'love your neighbour as (you love) yourself' is at the heart of the Torah in Judaism and is the major commandment of Christianity. It underpins Islam's five pillars, one of which is 'sharing of wealth with the less fortunate'. The stated aim of the World Congress of Muslim Philanthropists is to 'advance effective and accountable giving' and to 'mobilize financial and human resources to confront social needs and advance strategic philanthropy' through their global network of individuals, corporations, and foundations. Muslim boxer Muhammad Ali is widely quoted as saying 'Service to others is the rent you pay for your room here on earth'. In the Hindu religion, the act of giving is 'dāna' and the charitable are believed to receive good things in life and in the afterlife: the Hindu religion distinguishes between pure, enlightened charity (sāttvikam), charity that is ego driven (rajas), and charity that is ignorant or destructive (tamas) given to an unworthy person at the wrong time or place. Confucius was an early proponent of the Golden Rule. When asked was there one word to guide a person throughout life, Confucius replied 'shu', which means reciprocity, and he continued 'never impose on others what you would not choose for yourself' (Confucius, Analects 15: 24).

Parents and grandparents tend to bring up children in the same faith as their own and, across generations, family businesses may hold strongly to particular values and traditions based on the faith of the family owners. The Joseph Rowntree Foundation, for example, was started in York over 100 years ago by the eponymous founder, who sought to alleviate housing shortage and simultaneously tackle social problems in the city where Rowntree established and developed the confectionery business. Rowntree's principles were shaped by the Quaker faith that he practised, and were influenced by observing the consequences of events like Ireland's potato famine. Like the Cadbury family, to whom the Rowntrees were related, the tenets and practises of Quakerism were passed from generation to generation and the children, grandchildren, and great-grandchildren of Joseph Rowntree displayed great enthusiasm for adopting these principles into the working practises of the business. Arnold Stephenson Rowntree, son of John Stephenson Rowntree, was a vociferous defender of the right to conscientious objection during the First World War, while Joseph's son Benjamin was a champion of workers' rights, writing extensively on the subject. Their work is carried on through the Joseph Rowntree Foundation, which researches social policy and campaigns for human rights, while its sister organisation, the Joseph Rowntree Housing Trust, provides and manages over 2,000 homes.

As religions and societies have progressed, philanthropy has expanded from the initial concept of charitable giving to promoting social justice or addressing the underpinning causes of poverty. Many family business foundations are actively involved in such causes. The Maadi Community Foundation of Cairo promotes religious pluralism, with the goal of avoiding strife between different religions (Fausia, 2010), while there are a number of programmes pioneered by Dompet Dhuafa, Indonesia's leading philanthropic institution, to achieve environmental objectives or encourage healthy eating.

In addition to prescribing how their followers are expected to act towards others, religions might prescribe specifically about expected levels of giving, for example tithing 10% of your income. This can lead to norms and obligations, but also to feelings of shame or guilt for non-conformers. The social norm that wealthy religious families should engage in philanthropy has led to criticism of religious CEOs of some family businesses who are perceived to not conform to expectations. Sam Walton, founder of Walmart, was a Presbyterian Christian, much criticised for Walmart's low level of charitable giving (e.g., Ortega, 1999), which is mainly distributed through the Walmart Foundation and Walton Family Foundation. Walton wrote in his autobiography:

> We feel very strongly that Walmart really is not, and should not be, in the charity business. We don't believe in taking a lot of money out of Walmart's cash registers and giving it to charity for the simple reason that any debit has to be passed along to somebody – either our shareholders or our customers.
>
> (Walton, 1993)

More recently, significant increases in the level of philanthropy by the Walton family and Walmart have been noted, but criticism has continued with some saying it is self-interested, supporting political agendas, or focussed on localities where Walmart wishes to improve its public image (see, e.g., Hopgood, 2008). The Walton family are reputed to be worth over $160 billion (according to Bloomberg, 2018) and their shares in Walmart can generate millions of dollars in dividends each quarter. According to their annual report, the Walton Family Foundation donated $595 million in grants in 2018. However, Walmart has also been criticised for making charitable donations instead of paying higher wages to staff. When a family business is a significant employer or embedded in a locality, the activities of the family as well as the business are the subject of scrutiny and comment.

Practicalities of philanthropy

The practicalities of philanthropy entail decisions about what, where, and how giving is operationalised. Decisions on levels of giving may examine criteria for determining how much to give, for example a set percentage of pre-tax profits or of income. For some businesses it is important to make giving tax-effective. Criteria need to be agreed on for which causes will be supported or excluded. Family members may have particular values, beliefs, or interests that influence the focus of philanthropy in the business. Families in business have choices in how they manage their philanthropic and community activities. Vehicles include foundations, charitable trusts, and management through a family office or family council (see Chapter 4). A key decision is in differentiating between corporate and family activities. Foundations may be purely family or corporate, or they may be hybrid and include funding from both sources (Feliu and Botero, 2016). In reality, family business owners may engage in philanthropy at the individual, family, and corporate levels simultaneously.

Determination of focus and beneficiaries is key. An Ernst and Young (2016) survey on family business philanthropy indicated that the mechanism by which beneficiaries were chosen varied with company size. Owners of firms with 100 employees or less tended to personally oversee their philanthropic projects, as did owners of very large companies of 5,000 employees and above. In the latter case, owners of very large operations might step back from day-to-day business involvement and assume a more supervisory and/or advisory role, which includes philanthropic projects. The family has therefore more control over such initiatives. Medium-sized family firms are different, though; as their business grows and running their companies becomes more complex, they often outsource philanthropy to a third party, a non-family specialist agency. The relationship between business size and family control of philanthropy is therefore somewhat U-shaped.

Key learning point

For many business families, philanthropy and community engagement are an essential element of family entrepreneurship, providing business and family benefits. Drivers and patterns of philanthropic behaviours vary between families, businesses, and individuals.

Summary

Business families throughout the world contribute billions in charitable donations, engaging with local, national, and international causes and communities. Throughout the world, the names of family business leaders have endured for generations through their philanthropic legacies.

Derived from the Greek meaning 'love of mankind', philanthropy represents voluntary behaviours and actions resulting from a commitment to the well-being of others. CSR is distinct from philanthropy as CSR refers to the activities of a business, whereas philanthropy can be at the individual, family, or business level. Philanthropy usually refers to financial giving, whereas CSR encompasses a range of corporate responsibilities.

The drivers for CSR, philanthropy, and community engagement can be divided into three areas: values, social norms, and marketing. Values may arise from a particular faith, many of which adhere to the Golden Rule. Community engagement can have benefits for the family business as well as the community, enhancing social capital, building reputation and commitment.

Where a family business has multiple connections within a specific community, it is likely 'embedded', and its actions will be influenced by expectations and norms arising from institutions within that community. Reciprocity is a social norm that can drive giving.

The dark side of community engagement and philanthropy is that it can introduce significant power that can be used to influence or manipulate for business and political purposes, from influencing local planning decisions to uprooting political systems.

Discussion questions

1. How would you explain the engagement with their communities of families in business?
2. What do you think motivates philanthropy by families in business?
3. Investigate the philanthropic and community activities of a family business known to you. How are they influenced by expectations arising from their specific cultural context?

Case study 9.1: Tata Sons philanthropy in India

People often ask 'Why is Ratan Tata not listed as the wealthiest man in India?' The simple answer is because the large majority of shares in Tata Sons is owned by charitable trusts set up by members of the Tata family. Individual members of the Tata family only own a tiny percentage of shares in Tata Sons, which is the holding company of the Tata Group. Nevertheless, Ratan Tata's less than 1% share of Tata Sons is estimated to be worth just under $1billion. The combined shareholdings of the various Tata trusts is believed to be about 66% of the total holdings in Tata Sons.

The Tata philanthropic tradition began in 1892 with the founding of the J. N. Tata Endowment Fund, named after its founder and founder of Tata Group, Jamsetji Nusserwanji Tata. This first Tata trust provided financial support for Indians to gain higher education. Endowing philanthropic trusts named after themselves has become the norm in the Tata family. Two major trusts, the Sir Ratan Tata Trust and the Sir Dorabji Tata Trust, operate alongside a number of minor trusts. Both the major trusts resulted from the wills of the founder's sons, who each bequeathed their wealth to the founding of a new trust, the Sir Ratan Tata Trust in 1919 and the Sir Dorabji Tata Trust in 1932.

Minor trusts include: JRD Tata Trust (1944), named after Jehangir Ratan Dadabhoy Tata, Chairman of Tata Group from 1938; Navajbi Ratan Tata Trust (1974), allied with the Sir Ratan Tata Trust; Jamsetji Tata Trust (1974); JRD and Thelma J Tata Trust (1991), supporting oppressed women and children; Lady Tata Memorial Trust (1932), specifically for leukaemia research and fundamental science research; Lady Meherbai Dorabji Tata Trust (1932), supporting Indian women in higher education abroad; Tata Education Trust, Tata Social Welfare Trust, and RD Tata Trust, all founded in 1990.

The Tata family includes an array of siblings, cousins, and overlapping generations. Notwithstanding any individual charitable efforts, the philanthropy of Tata Sons is highly formalised and systematic. To make the most of the significant amount of funds at their disposal, the Tata Trusts tend to invest in institutional endowments and programme support rather than traditional charitable aid. Support for individuals focusses on higher education.

Tata's founder, Jamsetji Nusserwanji Tata (JNT), is quoted as saying: '[w]hat advances a nation is not so much to prop up its weakest and most helpless members, as to lift up the best and most gifted so as to make them of the greatest service to the country' (Lala, 2004, cited in Kumar, 2018). JNT's philosophy of investing in institutions, programmes, and individuals who are most likely to solve issues underpinning India's problems has continued to be a mainstay of the Tata Trusts. Such 'constructive philanthropy' is based on the belief that a single scientific discovery could benefit millions of people and have much greater impact than providing aid to individuals. Tata Trusts thus focus on the prevention of social distress rather than relief. Themes include rural livelihoods, natural resource management, urban poverty, education and healthcare, building civil society, human rights, and arts and culture (Kumar, 2018).

Tata philanthropy is secular, with a distinctive national drive, and while originally giving preference to the Parsi community of the Tata family, it is open to all Indian nationals. It is believed that, compared with other 20th-century philanthropists in India, they were unique in their 'extensive and sustained commitment to scientific development' and their 'systematic and organized philanthropy supporting science, social science, humanities, and industry' (Kumar, 2018: 1430).

What is your opinion of the Tata family's approach to philanthropy in India? What alternative strategies might they have considered? Consider the positive and negative implications of different strategies for family members, the business, and beneficiaries at the individual, community, and societal levels.

Source: adapted from Arun Kumar (2018) 'Pragmatic and paradoxical philanthropy: Tatas' gift giving and scientific development in India'. *Development and Change* 49(6): 1422–1446.

Case study 9.2: Wilsden Equestrian Centre

Jeannette Wheeler founded a riding school with her sister and her mother in 1980. It was one of the first in the region to gain approval by the British Horse Society and quickly established a reputation for high quality and expertise. Following her sister's exit and the retirement of her mother, the family business is now owned and managed by Jeannette, her husband, and her daughter Abigail. Jeannette and her husband live on the premises, along with her father and her adult son in separate houses. Jeannette's husband and son are keen football fans; her son voluntarily manages a local team, which he named after the business, and the business regularly sponsors their city's team in the English football league.

The riding school is deeply embedded within the local community. In some families, three generations have learned to ride there. The business depends on a local catchment area for its customers and Jeannette places a strong emphasis on maintaining a good reputation in the region and nationally. The business frequently appears in the local press with good news stories and pictures of horses; national recognition has included a number of awards and two visits by the Princess Royal.

In 1999 Jeannette founded a separate charity, Throstle Nest RDA, under the auspices of the national Riding for the Disabled Association. A raft of volunteers work alongside the riding school's staff to provide disabled children and adults with the support they need to learn to ride and look after horses. Volunteers include retirees looking for social interaction and exercise, students and unemployed people requiring work experience, and members of the local community seeking meaningful volunteering opportunities. The charity requires funds to pay for lessons, equipment, and activities. This comes from a range of sources: the business resources staff and ponies to provide pony rides at local events, profits from refreshments sold at the business go to the charity, and every year Jeannette's daughter Abigail organises a dance in aid of the charity. Other family members not involved in the business support the charity by serving as volunteers, trustees, and helping at fundraising events. Local businesses also support the charity financially, including the village co-operative store and local branches of national companies.

Wilsden Equestrian Centre also hosts the local branch of the Pony Club, focussing specifically on children who do not have their own ponies. More recently, the business has joined a national initiative – 'Changing Lives Through Horses' – which provides youngsters who struggle with formal education with an opportunity to spend time at the riding school and learn about horses, building their self-confidence and skills. In addition, like many riding schools, Wilsden Equestrian Centre provides opportunities for teenagers to spend time helping look after horses on a voluntary basis. Volunteer helpers receive valuable training and benefit the business by reducing the need for additional paid staff at busy times. Parents appreciate the social and technical skills their teenagers develop and the riding school has close relationships with their families.

Although they are separate entities, the charity is strongly dependent on the family business for its premises, organisation of volunteers, and fundraising efforts. Consider how this case exemplifies embeddedness. Which stakeholders in the community might have an influence on the family business activities and how might the family business influence the community?

In addition, consider any issues that you foresee for Wilsden Equestrian Centre in the near future.

Source: the Authors. Further information at wilsdenequestriancentre.co.uk.

10 Longevity and the future for family firms

In Chapter 1 we presented the question of whether family businesses are a more efficient model of business or whether they are an anachronism, best replaced by 'professionally-run' businesses. We introduced the controversial Chandlerian viewpoint that family-controlled businesses might be a barrier to innovation and highlighted that there was much disagreement with this viewpoint. In later chapters we have seen that, in general, family businesses are survivors and appear to outlast their non-family business rivals.

In this final chapter we will pick up some of the threads alluded to earlier and examine what contributes to the success of longstanding family firms. We will draw on historical perspectives because an understanding of the past provides us with valuable insights into the present and some indication of the future. Theories of innovation will be considered and we will look at how important innovation is to the survival of different types of family businesses.

Finally, we will consider what the future might hold for family businesses. When the 'silicon chip revolution' began in the 1970s, many assumed that jobs would be destroyed: production line workers, typists, even sales personnel were variously predicted to be superfluous in the new computer age. However, new jobs emerged as old ones disappeared. In the 21st century, artificial intelligence, or AI, is considered to be the big threat to jobs as sophisticated robots are developed to undertake service and manufacturing jobs. If family business owners take a patriarchal approach to their business and employees, will they look to safeguard jobs that technology threatens to make obsolete? Or will they embrace innovation? How do the values that family owners bring to their firms influence the future direction of the business? As we wrote this book, one of the UK's oldest family businesses, R. Durtnell and Sons, announced that they were facing collapse after more than 400 years in business. They were saved from the brink by a restructuring deal and some tolerant creditors. Are we likely to see a reduction in family companies as traditional industries decline? What this and other future trends will mean for the family firm will be discussed in this chapter.

Learning objectives

Understand influences on family business longevity and the tension between continuity and change.
Understand insights from historical perspectives, including path dependency.
Understand how theories of innovation and long-term orientation apply to family businesses.

Looking back to look forward

Longevity is a balancing act between continuity and change. History examines continuity and change in relation to context, and business historians can provide us with useful insights into family business longevity. Historical analysis may not be able to predict the future but it shows us how a business has come to be as it is. Many family businesses exist in their current form because of a particular event or series of events in their history. To understand why a family business is as it is, we need to examine their past.

Historians help us to appreciate the significance of context. Future opportunities make sense only within a specific context (Roscoe, Discua Cruz and Howorth, 2013). Legal and regulatory frameworks, institutions, and even the climate can influence the opportunities, strategies, and future direction of a family business. Business historians have also examined why family firms persist in some countries more than others, by examining the cultural, structural, and legal determinants of family ownership over other forms of organisations. Consider family business in China, where private enterprise was taboo from the 1950s to the 1990s, the one-child policy constrains opportunities for family succession, and the Communist Party continues to have a powerful influence on business activities (Li et al., 2015). Expansion of the Chinese economy and rapid internationalisation have created immense opportunities for Chinese businesses. The future of family business in China will, however, be influenced by this social, economic, and political history.

The oldest family businesses in the world

Whatever the future may hold, family firms have certainly been around for a long, long time – a venerably long time in some cases. The award for the world's longest-lived family business used to belong to construction company Kongo Gumi, of Osaka, Japan. They built their first temple in 578 AD, and continued erecting temples, castles, and other structures for over 1,400 years. In 2006 the company succumbed to excessive debt and an unfavourable business climate to become a subsidiary of Takamatsu Construction, and ceased being an independent family business. Now the oldest family business award belongs to Hoshi Ryokan, a spa hotel in the Awazu Onsen area of Japan, founded in 718 AD, and owned and managed by the same family for

46 generations. The demise of the independent Kongo Gumi highlights that longevity is not guaranteed, even for ancient family businesses such as these.

A few family businesses are over one thousand years old but many others can trace their family ownership back for hundreds of years. The exact foundation date is often educated guesswork, as businesses may have started out informally and records might not have been kept. Nevertheless, we are able to identify many anciently founded family enterprises still operating today, as shown in Box 10.1. Logically, the oldest family businesses in the world are in traditional industries. We are unlikely to find anyone making apps or video games in the 17th century! However, as industries decline we see that some of the oldest family businesses have adapted and moved into different areas of activity.

An inspection of the businesses highlighted in Box 10.1 shows some family businesses with continuous ownership, some where the business has continued but ownership has moved to a different family, and others that have changed the business completely while maintaining the same identity and continuing family ownership. The key point about longevity is that it is a balance between continuity and change, not preserving the past to the detriment of the business, but not losing sight of it either; instead, longevity is about building on knowledge, experience, and resources built up over time to innovate and create new opportunities. These longstanding firms have survived world wars, revolutions, and plagues. In the next section we will look at what insights into longevity are provided by historical perspectives.

A historical perspective on longevity

When we examine family businesses from a historical perspective, we gain a contextualised insight into their development and a rounded understanding of aids, barriers, and hindrances to their longevity. Historians highlight the importance of analysing family firms within context, including their national histories, environmental and cultural developments, in order to understand their strategies, successes, and failures. Each family firm is embedded within a society that has a particular array of values, attitudes, laws, and business practises.

An important concept that historians emphasise is 'path dependence'. The most basic interpretation of path dependence is that what happened in the past affects the future, a concept that is sometimes articulated as 'history matters'. For family businesses, the decisions and events that have occurred in the past provide a particular set of resources, attitudes, and strategies that influence the future direction of the business. Historians looking at path dependence emphasise events as sequences within a political, environmental, economic, legal, societal, and industry context. The path of a family business might be influenced by, for example, war, natural disasters, changes in legislation, society or technology, and many other externalities, which could be interdependent or concurrent. For

Box 10.1 Some of the oldest family businesses in the world.

CHATEAU DE GOULAINE, the famous vineyard in Haute Goulaine, France, can trace commercial wine production back to at least 1000 AD. The chateau is famous for production of le Petit Beurre biscuits and the invention of 'beurre blanc' white sauce, a staple component in the dishes of chefs throughout the world.

FONDERIA PONTIFICIA MARINELLI, a bell foundry in Agnone, Italy, can trace their roots back to at least 1040 AD, but the exact date of founding is unknown. The Marinelli family became involved from 1339. In 2000 their Jubilee bell was hung in St Peter's Square, Rome, and in 2004 a new bell was installed in the Leaning Tower of Pisa. They still employ the same method of wax casting that was used 1000 years ago.

HOTEL PILGRIM HAUS is an inn that first opened its doors to guests in Soest, Germany, in 1304 AD. It is on the Way of St James and was built to house pilgrims on their way to Santiago de Compostela.

WHITECHAPEL BELL FOUNDRY, in London, is Britain's oldest family business, having first traded in 1420, but its family ownership is not continuous, having been owned by two different families in that time.

R. J. BALSON & SONS, a butcher's shop in Dorset, England, was founded in 1515, when Henry VIII was king of England, and has been owned by 26 generations of the Balson family.

JOHN BROOKE & SONS ran a woollen mill in Huddersfield, UK, from 1541. Brookes manufactured uniforms for the British, French, and Russian armies over hundreds of years. The decline of the UK woollen industry led to a change of direction in the 1990s, when the mill was transformed into an office park, which is still controlled by the Brookes family.

BERENBERG BANK, founded in 1590 in Hamburg, Germany, is believed to be the world's oldest merchant bank. The Berenberg family started out as cloth merchants in the 16th century. They continue to control 25% of the company. A predominance of female offspring means that descendants carry a variety of names, including Gossler and Seyler.

R. DURTNELL & SONS, construction, Kent, UK. Brothers John and Brian Durtnell built their first house in 1593, and the firm was involved in the construction of several landmark British buildings, including Buckingham Palace. By 2019 13 generations of the Durtnell family had been involved in the company.

TORAYA is a Japanese confectionery company in Tokyo who have made the much-loved Japanese delicacy wagashi since before 1600 AD. The firm has passed from father to son through 18 generations.

ZILDJIAN translates literally as cymbal maker. The Zildjian Cymbal Company originates from the Ottoman Empire (Turkey). In 1618 Avedis I discovered a metal alloy that was perfect for making cymbals and was given the name 'Zildjian' by the Sultan. The family emigrated to the USA in 1909 and found their cymbals in great demand by jazz musicians. The firm is run by 14th generation members Craigie and Debbie, the first women to lead the firm. Their daughters are 15th generation shareholders.

(Information correct in 2019.)

example, William Grant and Sons (Wm Grants), one of the world's leading whisky distillers, faced a significant decline in sales during the 1920s when prohibition in the USA, Canada, Scandinavia, Belgium, and Russia devastated their export business. In 1923 William Grant died, leaving his sons, son-in-law, and grandchildren to manage the business. His grandson, William Grant Gordon, persuaded the company to increase production despite declining sales. When prohibition in the USA and Canada ended, Wm Grants were ready with a high quality, longer-aged whisky. However, World War Two followed shortly after and could have been the end of the company, as production of whisky was halted in the UK because barley was only available for food production and coal was in short supply. As the War ended, the Grant Gordon family demonstrated their commitment to the longevity of their business by re-opening their distilleries using peat instead of coal, which gave their whisky a flavour that was distinct from their rivals.

The example of Wm Grants demonstrates that family businesses do not operate in a vacuum. Historians remind us that outcomes are usually due to sequences of contingent events, which can be examined using 'path analysis'. Along a path of events, critical junctures occur that can influence the future of the business or family. The easiest way to imagine a critical juncture is as a crossroads in the progress of the business that requires a decision in terms of which direction to choose. If William Grant Gordon had not pushed for increased production or the switch from coal to peat had not been made, the business might be very different or not exist at all. As families create narratives about their past it is tempting to assume a particular event in history is key to who or what they are. Family members from successive generations may persist in assumptions that 'it's all because … ' or 'if only … '. However, a critical juncture is nearly always part of a path or sequence of connected events, and whilst a particular decision or happening may be very significant, we need to recognise that it will have occurred in and been influenced by a specific context.

History is about avoiding excessive simplification and recognising variety. It helps us to understand that, in reality, multi-causality and contextualisation are important in understanding the longevity of family businesses and their variation in structures, strategies, and outcomes. Many management and economic models are simplifications highlighting specific relationships and influences in our attempts to make sense of reality, but historians would warn us to be keenly aware of all the externalities that might be driving our findings. Had prohibition continued in their key markets or even expanded, or if the outcome of World War Two had been different, then Wm Grants might have failed and not become one of the largest whisky distillers in the world, and the Grant Gordon family would not be one of the wealthiest families in the UK.

Continuity and change: an insight into innovation

The interplay between the continuities of past experiences and the discontinuity of new events lies at the heart of family business. Families are a natural site of change: as people are born, age and die, relationships change, family structures vary, and responsibilities shift. However, some elements of families remain constant: for example, your parents will always be your parents. We have seen in some of the case studies in earlier chapters that a parent's influence can continue, for good or bad, even after their death.

For family businesses to achieve longevity, it might be assumed that innovation is crucial. However, looking at the oldest family businesses in the world (Box 10.1) reveals a strong element of continuity. Fonderia Pontificia Marinelli continue to cast bells using the same method they used 1000 years ago. Toraya have continued making wagashi through 18 generations of family ownership. Hoshi Ryokan and Pilgrim Haus have always been hotelkeepers. Does this suggest that longevity does not require innovation? Tracing the history of any longstanding business reveals variations in the extent to which they might be viewed as innovative businesses.

Innovation is not about total change but about balancing continuity and change to provide new combinations of knowledge, sometimes combining old and new knowledge, sometimes crossing boundaries between distinct areas. Innovation can be in relation to products, services, processes, or business methods. Some family firms produce traditional products but are innovative in their marketing and branding. For example, the McIlhenny family produce a hot pepper sauce, a product that is quite common in the southern states of the USA, but there is only one Tabasco, which the McIlhennys' company markets very successfully. Since 1868 different generations of the McIlhenny family have used their social, political, and military connections very effectively to spread their brand and gain commitment to Tabasco, so that it has become synonymous with hot pepper sauce.

One of the oldest family businesses in the USA, Zildjian (2019), has roots going hundreds of years further back into the Ottoman Empire. The company's claim is that, 'blending old world concepts with new world techniques, Zildjian has evolved with both music and technology, continuing to innovate the process of cymbal making'. The cymbals produced in 1623 were used for calls to prayer, religious feasts, and in the army. Their use is very different in the 21st century, when they are in many of the world's leading orchestras and are part of the drum-kit for jazz, rock, and pop drummers, including the Beatles' Ringo Starr. Zildjian have expanded their product range into other percussion instruments and accessories but they have kept secret their process for treating alloys and turning them into cymbals of 'extraordinary clarity and sustain' (zildjian.com). The Zildjian family claim the process is the same as that developed by Avedis I for the Ottoman Sultan in 1618, when metals arrived on camel trains and machines were powered by donkeys.

Theories of innovation

The examples provided above indicate that innovation is not just about high technology products. Innovation occurs at different levels, helpfully captured as the 4Ps – process, product, position, and paradigm innovation (Tidd and Bessant, 2015). Paradigm innovation involves a shift in how we think about something – for example, the switch from landlines to cell phones that changed the way we thought about communication. One family-controlled business that has taken advantage of innovation in this specific paradigm shift is one of the world's largest technology companies, Samsung. In 1938 Lee Byung-chull used his inheritance to set up a trading company that he named Samsung, which means three stars. Samsung first entered the electronics industry in 1969, producing black and white televisions. During the 1970s and 1980s, Samsung developed expertise in electronics and semi-conductors that in the 2000s led to the Samsung Galaxy smartphone, which frequently tops the lists of the world's best-selling cell phones.

The paradigm, position, product, process distinction of innovations is a simple model that helps us realise the various types of innovation.

A complementary distinction is made between radical and incremental innovations. Radical innovations are game-changers that represent a major shift in what we do. Incremental innovations are smaller changes to existing products and processes. In reality, what we observe is that innovations are most often a series of incremental changes that build into a radical innovation or paradigm shift. Samsung's development of the Galaxy smartphone was the result of series of innovations in electronics, programming, semi-conductors, batteries, and component parts. One good idea is not usually sufficient for long-term survival and success – entrepreneurs need constant creativity and innovation. Longstanding family businesses most often experience innovation as incremental changes to processes, products, and services, and only rarely as radical changes.

Studies of innovation emphasise the importance of looking outside the business and industry, discontinuous thinking and creativity, as well as investing in R&D, structures, and processes that enable innovation (Tidd and Bessant, 2015). Crises can generate innovation by forcing alternatives to be considered, as in the case of Wm Grants when the shortage of coal led them to use peat and create the distinctive flavour of their whisky. Within the organisation, innovations need championing and support by senior management to ensure that they proceed. In the following section we will look specifically at how family-controlled businesses might help or hinder innovation.

How might family businesses help or hinder innovation?

The phrase 'clogs to clogs in three generations' assumes that founding generations are the innovators and succeeding generations contribute to the demise of family businesses. Chandler and others have argued that family businesses stifle innovation. However, these views are sweeping generalisations. Throughout this book we have emphasised that the attributes family ownership brings to business are bivalent, in that they can have positive and negative effects. In Chapter 3 we highlighted that there are different types of family firms. Some family businesses are highly innovative and some are not very innovative at all. Some survive for many generations and others last only a few years. The important thing here is to understand how various aspects of family ownership might help or hinder innovation.

In Chapter 3 we explained that family businesses with entrenched family objectives are likely to have worse performance. Emphasising short-term family socio-economic wealth can erode resources and stifle innovation (Miller et al., 2015). Nepotism and cronyism restrict the talent pool and reduce diversity, constraining innovation by reducing the breadth of knowledge, experience, and networks. Network theory tells us that weak ties are especially important for generating new ideas. Parental altruism can lead to younger generations shirking their responsibilities, creating disquiet with non-family employees, lowering trust, and making employees less likely to come forward with new ideas. Chapter 8 highlighted that family owners might be especially risk-averse if all their family's wealth is invested in the business and they may be less inclined to support innovations through external debt or equity funding.

On the other hand, family ownership can bring heightened commitment to the family business. Steier and Muethel (2014) contend that families are 'high trust' organisations, enabling the firm to pursue its objectives without worrying whether other people in the enterprise might undermine them. High trust is associated with psychological safety. Where psychological safety is high, people are more willing to share innovative ideas or take personal risks. Family and other employees may be willing to 'go the extra mile' to ensure the success of their family business, particularly where there is a strong sense of purpose or stewardship. Family businesses can draw on the human capital and networks of family members who have no formal role in the firm. This can provide access to skills, knowledge, markets, and resources that generate innovation. Family businesses with longstanding ties with stakeholders often have close, high-trust relationships that facilitate new combinations of knowledge, testing of ideas, and support for innovation. Closely aligned stewardship motivations among family owners, managers, and employees increase trust within the business and can provide quicker decision making, less bureaucratic processes, and enable the family business to be more nimble in taking advantage of opportunities.

In Chapters 6 and 7 we examined succession and noted that, ideally, succession should be prepared and planned for. Whether succession is a crisis or a smooth handover, the transfer of ownership and management provides a disruption that can stimulate innovation. New generations of owners and managers bring new knowledge, skills, and ideas. Many business families educate the next generation overseas, extending the ideas, knowledge, and networks available to the business. However, generations in waiting can be frustrated if dominant incumbent senior generations dismiss their ideas, thus stifling innovation. Some might assume that founding generations are the innovators, but there are many examples of longstanding family businesses where a later generation were the key innovators: for example, it was the second generation of the Cadbury family who developed eating chocolate, which became the foundation of their iconic chocolate business. George Cadbury Jr brought expertise learned on his chemistry degree at University College London and continued experimenting, the result of which was Cadbury's Dairy Milk, one of the world's most enduring confectionery brands, first produced in 1906.

For innovations to be implemented they usually need support at the highest level in the organisation. In family-controlled businesses, innovation often needs a senior family member to champion ideas. Senior family members have a lot of power to overtly or inadvertently encourage or stifle innovation. Paternalistic senior managers might dismiss the ideas of younger or junior family members. Founders can become stuck in the groove of what has worked for them in the past.

The shadow of a preceding generation can stifle innovation long after the person has gone. Family members and employees can defer to the previous generation with statements such as 'the old man wouldn't have done it that way' or 'Mum never wanted us to … '. Styles of management can also linger and impact behaviour in successive generations. Mary Rose provides a poignant example in her study of the multi-generational 19th-century cotton giant Samuel Greg and Co. Samuel Greg was a dominant character who failed to allow his son Robert any responsibility, thus ill-equipping him to take over the business. Robert himself repeated the domineering pattern of behaviour, stifling innovation in his own son. Rose (1986) provides samples from letters between father and son where Robert states: 'In the first place, I don't think your turn of mind and general character suitable for business, either for comfort or success'. For two generations there was little innovation in the company due to the stifling shadow of parents.

Family culture and the upbringing of children can generate attitudes that either facilitate or discourage the creativity needed for innovation, as shown in Box 10.2. Successful long-standing family businesses tend to have different generations innovating together in high-trust collaborative relationships. If parental styles that stifle creativity pertain in the business-owning family, innovation could be constrained.

At various points in this book we have mentioned the commitment to future generations that can give family owners a long-term perspective on business. Innovation requires deep financial commitment. Many innovations will fail, cost more, or take longer to generate revenues than forecast.

Box 10.2 Elements of family culture that can stifle creativity.

Emphasis on being right or having the 'correct' answer
Focus on being logical
Following rules
Constantly being practical
Viewing play as frivolous – being told not to be childish or to 'act your age'
Being punished for mistakes, leading to fear of failure
Being made to feel foolish
Being told that you are not creative
Heavy discipline and criticism
Emphasising self-reliance and not engaging with others

Family owners with a long-term perspective are more likely to be willing to provide the patient financial capital needed to support the ups and downs of innovation. Mapping the progress of family businesses over generations shows cycles of innovation, periods of low and high innovation in various generations, not just, or indeed not always, the founding generation. In the following section we look at a conceptualisation of long-term orientation.

Long-term orientation

Long-term orientation (LTO) captures a firm's tendency to prioritise key aspects of their business that emerge after a firm has been in existence for a long time (Lumpkin and Brigham, 2011). Lumpkin and Brigham identified three elements of long-term orientation – futurity, continuity, and perseverance. Futurity is about looking to and planning for the long-term impacts that company decisions and actions might have. Futurity causes firms to make plans and strive to achieve them rather than react to events. Family businesses display this attitude when they consider what the business will look like for future generations and undertake long-term succession planning. Continuity is about a commitment to the continuation and survival of the business. Continuity emphasises sticking to the purpose and guiding principles of the business, as well as securing a reputation that endures. For family businesses, continuity includes the commitment to continuing family ownership of the business. Perseverance is the practice of continuing to make efforts in the present day, especially through adversity, because they will yield benefits in the future (Brigham et al., 2014). Perseverance enables family businesses to endure economic cycles, disasters, and the vagaries of business.

Long-term orientation is a combination of these three elements. Futurity is linked to innovation because innovation can improve long-term prospects; continuity can inspire managers and proprietors to embrace innovation, because it can beget longevity, and perseverance can help leaders to keep pursuing long-term innovation initiatives because they may be the best chances of long-term survival.

Danny Miller and Isabelle Le Breton-Miller (2005) examined the histories of 24 old and 'great' family-controlled businesses who were 'managing for the long run'. Four priorities were identified that were key to these businesses' enduring success: Command (giving senior leaders considerable authority in decision-making); Continuity (adherence to a long-term mission); Community (developing a strong culture with concern for all employees), and Connection (long established relationships with stakeholders and suppliers). Commitment was also shown to be important.

Miller and Le Breton-Miller (2005) observe that family-controlled businesses who are 'managing for the long run' concentrate on honing their products and skills rather than chasing short-term profits. They cite H.H. Timken, the second-generation leader of the Timken Company, a world-renowned manufacturer of tapered roller bearings: 'If there was any one thing that fixed in my mind, it was that we must continue to make our products better; it was the thought that it carried the family name'. Timken is typical of family business owners whose commitment to the long-term success of their business is tied in with a pride and responsibility because the business carries their family name. Many family business leaders feel a heavy responsibility for ensuring that a business that has been around for generations should not fail 'on their watch'.

Andrew Wates, former Chair of family-controlled construction firm the Wates Group, explained their long-term orientation as follows:

> Families instinctively focus on intergenerational transition. Contemplating what shape of business you want to pass on comes quite naturally. This makes you think about risk, competencies, and markets. Sustainability is not an added extra, but an integral part of how families do business. There are practical aspects of long-termism around financial gearing, risk analysis, and people and team development that rise to the top of the agenda when you break away from chasing short-term results.
>
> (Ernst and Young, 2012)

Clinton et al. (2018) found that long-term orientation was associated with incorporating the values of the founder in the future direction of the company, as well as considering the social responsibilities of the company, the continuation of tradition and legacy, and caring about the other family members who were involved in the business.

Industry and technology

All businesses need to be aware of changes in their environment that might impact their business. Students of business will be aware of the widely used PEST analysis and its many derivatives (PESTLE, etc.). As the historians reminded us earlier, a family business does not operate in isolation and PESTLE provides a helpful acronym to remind us to consider Political, Economic, Social, Technological, Legal, and Environmental trends and changes in examining family businesses and in considering strategies for particular family businesses. The resources and capabilities needed for innovation will be different in high and low velocity markets (Miller et al., 2015).

Lee was assisted in the development of Samsung by protectionist policies of the South Korean government that shielded Samsung from competition and provided financing. South Korea's economic development policy included allowing power to be concentrated in the hands of family-run conglomerates called chaebol. The top ten chaebol own more than 27% of all business assets in South Korea and Samsung is believed to generate 20% of the country's revenue (Pae, 2019). However, the close relationship between chaebol and government has led to a number of scandals and bribery allegations, including, in 2017, third-generation family member and Samsung vice-chairman Lee Jae-yong being sentenced to five years for bribery, a sentence that was reduced and suspended in 2018. Lee Jae-yong followed in the footsteps of his father, Samsung chairman Lee Kun-hee, who was also previously convicted of corruption but later acquitted.

The photographic industry is a prime example of an area of life and business that is full of invention and innovation. Camera manufacturers were always looking to improve their products, making ever-more sophisticated models. High-end cameras contained a multitude of high-tech features – focussing systems that followed the movement of the user's eye, motor drives that could take nine frames a second, image-stabilising lenses that borrowed from helicopter technology. Film and photographic paper companies were also always striving to make their products sharper, richer, more responsive, employing highly qualified scientists. Then, at the turn of the 21st century, digital images created a new turn in the road and film was diverted down a cul-de-sac from which there was no escape.

Dale Photographic Services is a small family-run business, established in Leeds, UK, in 1984 by Allan, Stephen, and Paul Ridsdale. The business was established to provide 'same day' colour processing of photographic film and to sell photographic equipment, specialising in 'medium format' equipment, used by professional and keen amateur photographers. In the 30-plus years since the Ridsdale family launched their business, the demand for their printing process has all but disappeared, the equipment they were selling has become almost obsolete, only of interest to history buffs, and the method of purchase has changed beyond recognition from the high street shop format their business was founded on. Dale Photographic are only in existence because they made major changes to their products, marketing, sales processes, and business model. They developed a national presence through advertising in photographic magazines, which established a mail order customer base and provided the first followers for their website launched in 1998. Buying habits shifted to greater emphasis on purchasing online and Dale Photographic launched an online sales site in 2003. In line with our earlier explanation of path dependence, we can see how each development or innovation led from earlier ones. Some aspects of Dale Photographic have continued: family ownership, location, industry, and type of customers. Their long-term orientation and commitment to continuing as a family business has required change and innovation.

What does the future hold for family businesses?

To return to our questions from the introduction of this chapter: if family business owners take a patriarchal approach to their business and employees, will they look to safeguard jobs that technology threatens to make obsolete? Or will they embrace innovation? How do the values that family owners bring to their firms influence the future direction of the business? Are we likely to see a reduction in family companies as traditional industries decline?

Kongo Gumi, Wm Durtnell, and indeed Thomas Cook provide warnings that longstanding businesses are not guaranteed survival. At a meeting in Amazon's spiritual home in Seattle, their founder, Jeff Bezos, replied to an employee's question with an answer that astonished media commentators. The employee asked what Bezos had learned from the failure of big retailers like Sears. With a frankness rarely seen in big-company CEOs, Bezos answered, 'Amazon is not too big to fail. In fact, I predict one day Amazon *will* fail. Amazon will go bankrupt. If you look at large companies, their lifespans tend to be 30-plus years, not a hundred-plus years'.

Bezos was not criticising his own company, but suggesting that all large companies had a limited lifespan. This statement illustrates a key difference between family businesses with a long-term orientation and non-family firms. It is highly unlikely that the head of a family firm would forecast their firm's obsolescence; the long-term orientation associated with family businesses emphasises continuity, handing the baton on to the next generation, and the generation after that. Family business owners take personal and collective pride in their company, an attitude that is often not shared by non-family firms, whose interest can be transient and opportunistic. The suggestion that patriarchal approaches will avoid innovation is rather short-sighted: family business owners' commitments to the continuity of their businesses, and responsibility towards employees and other stakeholders, necessitate innovation and adaptation to change.

So if Bezos' prophecy were to come true, and Amazon were to sink beneath the waves, what would be the last things they hear? Would it be the latest tech phenomenon, banging their drums to tell everyone how fantastic they are? Or would it be the crashing cymbals of Zildjian and the bells of Whitechapel Bell Foundry, still ringing for their family businesses after hundreds of years?

Key learning points

Longevity requires a combination of continuity and discontinuity. Longstanding family businesses demonstrate a commitment to continuing family ownership and a long-term perspective, captured in the concept of long-term orientation, which encompasses futurity, continuity, and perseverance.

There is no evidence to suggest overall that family-owned businesses are less innovative than their non-family counterparts. Family businesses tend to survive longer than non-family businesses. Family business survivors show good business sense and a keen awareness of potential constraints and opportunities in their wider context.

Innovation is most often incremental and occurs in cycles, including periods of low innovation. Innovation in family businesses can be stifled by aspects of family upbringing, dominant senior family leaders, inability to involve external talent, and entrenched family objectives.

Summary

A significant number of individual family businesses have survived for many hundreds of years. Longstanding family businesses have survived through wars, revolutions, and plagues, as well as step-changes in markets, industries, technology, and demand for their products and services.

It is important to examine family businesses within their context. History shows us that the longevity of businesses is a combination of continuity and discontinuity. Innovation is sometimes radical but more often a series of incremental innovations occurring at different levels – product, process, position, and paradigm. Longstanding family businesses might not have been innovative in the start-up stage but demonstrate periods of higher and lower innovation, with the emphasis on incremental innovations in processes, business models, and marketing, as well as products and services.

Family members bring a commitment to the business that is captured in the concept of long-term orientation. High trust within family businesses and good family relationships increase psychological safety, generating creativity and innovation. Success for family businesses can be calculated against many measures: financial gains and wealth, market position, invention, innovation, generosity, longevity, reputation, and survival.

Discussion questions

1. Which aspects of a family business could help and which aspects could hinder innovation?
2. If you had to advise a family business on its approach to developing the next generation, what would you recommend?
3. What do you think the future holds for family businesses in your country?

Case study 10.1: J. W. Lees continuity and discontinuity

For William Lees-Jones, managing director of Manchester brewer JW Lees, businesses find the road to longevity by keeping their eyes and ears open, looking at how other businesses develop, listening to what competitors say, as well as what their own customers say and think. Longevity is not achieved by looking to a firm's history, however long and distinguished that history may be, it is the future that will ensure ongoing longevity.

'The thing that keeps me awake at night is how we can continue to build a really great business', says William Lees-Jones.

> The family firms who are really good at that are in markets like Germany – there's a lot we can learn from their approach in terms of building long-term businesses and attracting talent. In the family business sector, there's always going to be a challenge attracting talent and there's always going to be a challenge in terms of innovation. You can't afford to be too paternalistic.

JW Lees has been in business for 190 years, but the road has been bumpy at several times in its history. William's grandfather and his brother struggled to work in harmony for 50 years, with no little detriment to the business. It was only when his grandfather bought out the other family members that the business began to prosper again. The firm then diversified from its core business of brewing and pubs into wholesalers, hotels, and off-licences. When William became managing director, he considered some of the diversification a distraction and turned the focus back onto core activities.

Three sixth-generation family members currently work in the business, but JW Lees has a rule that family members have to work elsewhere for five years to gain experience and be acquainted with different ideas. As an example, one of William's sons is studying for a degree in hospitality and hotel management, and William thinks he will go to work for an international hotel group for a few years to expose him to outside influences. To be progressive, William says, means

> finding a way to balance the experience of older family members with the enthusiasm of the younger generation, as well as listening to and engaging with the professional managers that are working in the business. We have to exploit all the resources technology now gives us. We just doubled our digital marketing budget, and that's just the start.

Source: adapted from *UK Family Business Survey*, 2017, PWC, pp. 35–36.

References

Anderson, R. and Reeb, D. (2003) 'Founding-family ownership and firm performance: evidence from S&P 500.' *Journal of Finance* 58: 653–684.

Anderson, R.C., Duru, A. and Reeb, D.M. (2012) 'Investment policy in family controlled firms.' *Journal of Banking and Finance* 36 (6): 1744–1758.

Astrachan, J.H., Klein, S.B. and Smyrnios, K.X. (2002) 'The F-PEC scale of family influence: a proposal for solving the family business definition problem.' *Family Business Review* 15: 45–58.

Berle, A. and Means, G. (1932) *The Modern Corporation and Private Property*. New York: Palgrave MacMillan.

Bettys. (2018) Bettys and Taylors website – www.bettysandtaylors.co.uk/about-us/our-board-and-executives/our-collaborative-ceo.

Blanco-Mazagatos, V., Quevedo-Puente, E. and Castrillo, L.A. (2007) 'The trade-off between financial resources and agency costs in the family business: an exploratory study.' *Family Business Review* 20 (3): 199–213.

Bloom, N. and Van Reenen, J. (2007) 'Measuring and explaining management practices across firms and countries.' *Quarterly Journal of Economics* 122: 1351–1408.

Boyd, B., Goto, T. and Hollensen, S. (2010) 'Dunfoss: internationalization of the family business and formation of Asian joint ventures.' In J. Astrachan, et al. (eds) *Family Business Casebook 2008–2009*. Kennesaw, GA: Cox Family Enterprise Center, pp. 1–24.

Breeze, B. (2009) *Natural Philanthropists: Findings of the Family Business Philanthropy and Social Responsibility Inquiry*. London: Institute for Family Business (UK).

Cadbury, A. (2000) *Family Firms and Their Governance: Creating Tomorrow's Company from Today's*. London: Egon Zehnder International.

Carney, M. and Gedajlovic, E. (2002) 'The co-evolution of institutional environments and organizational strategies: the rise of family business groups in the ASEAN region.' *Organization Studies* 23 (1): 1–29.

Carroll, A.B. (1991) 'The pyramid of corporate social responsibility: toward the moral management of organizational stakeholders.' *Business Horizons* 34 (4): 39–48.

Chandler Jr., A.D. (1990) *Scale and Scope*. Cambridge, MA: Harvard University Press.

Colli, A., Howorth, C. and Rose, M. (2013) 'Long term perspectives on family business.' *Business History* 55 (6): 841–854.

Corbetta, G. and Salvato, C. (2012) *Strategies for Longevity in Family Firms: A European Perspective*. Bocconi on Management Series. Basingstoke: Palgrave MacMillan.

Craig, J. and Moores, K. (2004) 'The professionalization process in family business: the Dennis Family Corporation case.' In J. Astrachan, P. Poutziouris and K. Soufani (eds)

Family Business Casebook Annual 2004. Kennesaw, GA: Cox Family Enterprise Center, pp. 91–122.

Dabholkar, P.A., Johnston, W.A. and Cathey, A.S. (1994) 'The dynamics of long term business-to-business exchange relationships.' *Journal of Academy of Marketing Science* 22 (2): 130–145.

Daily, C.M. and Dalton, D.R. (1992) 'Financial performance of founder-managed versus professionally managed small corporations.' *Journal of Small Business Management* 30 (2): 25–34.

Davis, J. (2019) John A. Davis website, https://johndavis.com/three-circle-model-family-business-system.

Davis, J., Schoorman, F.D. and Donaldson, L. (1997) 'Toward a stewardship theory of management.' *Academy of Management Review* 22 (1): 20–47.

Dekker, J., Lybaert, N., Steijvers, T. and Depaire, B. (2015) 'The effect of family business professionalization as a multidimensional construct on firm performance.' *Journal of Small Business Management* 53 (2): 516–538.

DiMaggio, P. and Powell, W. (1983) 'The iron cage revisited: institutional isomorphism and collective reality in organizational fields.' *American Sociological Review* 48 (2): 147–160.

Discua Cruz, A., Hadjielias, E. and Howorth, C. (2016) 'Family entrepreneurial teams.' In C. Ben-Hafaiedh and T. Cooney (eds) *Research Handbook on Entrepreneurial Teams Theory and Practice*. Cheltenham: Edward Elgar.

Discua Cruz, A., Howorth, C. and Hamilton, E. (2013) 'Intrafamily entrepreneurship: the formation and membership of family entrepreneurial teams.' *Entrepreneurship Theory and Practice* 37 (1): 17–46.

Donaldson, L. (1990) 'The ethereal hand: organizational economics and management theory.' *Academy of Management Review* 15: 369–381.

Donaldson, L. and Davis, J.H. (1991) 'Stewardship theory or agency theory: CEO governance and shareholder returns.' *Australian Journal of Management* 16 (1): 49–64.

Dutch Centre of Expertise in Family Business. (2019) University of Applied Sciences, Windesheim, NL, www.windesheim.com/research/strategic-entrepreneurship/dutch-centre-of-expertise-in-family-business.

Dyck, B., Mauws, M., Starke, F.A. and Mischke, G.A. (2002) 'Passing the baton. The importance of sequence, timing, technique and communication in executive succession.' *Journal of Business Venturing* 17 (2): 143–162.

Easterby-Smith, M. (2008) 'A conversation between entrepreneurship and organizational learning.' In Preface to R.T. Harrison and C.M. Leitch (eds) *Entrepreneurial Learning: Conceptual Frameworks and Applications*. Abingdon: Routledge, pp. xix–xxii.

Eckrich, C.J. and McClure, S.L. (2012) *The Family Council Handbook*. New York: Palgrave MacMillan.

Eisenhardt, K.M., Kahwajy, J.L. and Bourgeois, L.J. (1997) 'How management teams can have a good fight.' *Harvard Business Review* July–August 1997: 77–85.

Ernst & Young with FBN International. (2012) *Built to Last: Family Businesses Lead the Way to Sustainable Growth*. London: EYGM Limited, p. 28.

Feliu, N. and Botero, I.C. (2016) 'Philanthropy in family enterprises: a review of literature.' *Family Business Review* 29 (1): 121–141.

File, K.M. and Prince, R.A. (1996) 'Attributions for family business failure: the heir's perspective.' *Family Business Review* 9 (2): 171–184.

Fitzgerald, M.A. and Muske, G. (2002) 'Copreneurs: an exploration and comparison to other family businesses.' *Family Business Review* XV 1: 1–16.

Freeman, R.E. (1984) *Strategic Management: A Stakeholder Approach*. Boston, MA: Pitman Publishing.

Gedajlovic, E. and Carney, M. (2010) 'Markets hierarchies and families: toward a transactions cost theory of the family firm.' *Entrepreneurship Theory and Practice* 34 (6): 1145–1171.

Gersick, K.E., Davis, J., Hampton, M.M. and Lansberg, I. (1997) *Generation to Generation: Life Cycles of the Family Business*. Boston, MA: Harvard Business School Press.

Gomez Mejia, L., Cruz, C., Berrone, P. and De Castro, J. (2011) 'The bind that ties: socioemotional wealth preservation in family firms.' *The Academy of Management Annals* 5 (1): 653–707.

Gomez-Mejia, L.R., Haynes, K., Nunez-Nickel, M., et al. (2007) 'Socioemotional wealth and business risk in family controlled firms: evidence from Spanish olive oil mills.' *Administrative Science Quarterly* 52: 106–137.

Gordon, G. and Nicholson, N. (2008) *Family Wars: Stories and Insights from Famous Family Business Feuds*. London: Kogan Page.

Granovetter, M. (1973) 'The strength of weak ties.' *American Journal of Sociology* 78: 1360–1380.

Habberson, T.G. (2006) 'Commentary: a framework for managing the familiness and agency advantages in family firms.' *Entrepreneurship: Theory and Practice* 30 (6): 879–886.

Hall, A. and Nordqvist, M. (2008) 'Professional management in family businesses: toward an extended understanding.' *Family Business Review* 21 (1): 51–69.

Hamilton, E. (2006) 'Whose story is it anyway? Narrative accounts of the role of women in founding and establishing family businesses.' *International Small Business Journal* 24: 253–271.

Hamilton, E. (2013) *Entrepreneurship across Generations: Narrative, Gender and Learning in Family Business*. Cheltenham: Edward Elgar.

Handler, W. (1990) 'Succession in family firms: a mutual role adjustment between entrepreneur and next-generation family members.' *Entrepreneurship Theory and Practice* 15: 37–51.

Hiebl, M.R.W. (2013) 'Risk aversion in family firms: what do we really know?' *Journal of Risk Finance* 14 (1): 49–70.

Höhmann, -H.-H. and Welter, F. (2005) *Trust and Entrepreneurship: A West-East Perspective*. Cheltenham: Edward Elgar.

Hopgood, S. (2008) 'Saying "No" to Wal-Mart? Money and morality in professional humanitarianism.' In M. Barnett and T.G. Weiss (eds) *Humanitarianism in Question: Politics, Power, Ethics*. Ithaca, NY: Cornell University Press, pp. 98–123.

Howorth, C. and Ali, Z.A. (2001) 'Family business succession in Portugal.' *Family Business Review* 14 (3): 231–244.

Howorth, C., Parkinson, C., Leitch, C. and Stead, V. (2016a) *Next Generation Engagement in Family Businesses*. London: IFB Research Foundation.

Howorth, C., Westhead, P. and Wright, M. (2004) 'Buyouts, information asymmetry and the family management dyad.' *Journal of Business Venturing* 19 (4): 509–534.

Howorth, C., Wright, M., Westhead, P. and Allcock, D. (2016b) 'Company metamorphosis: professionalization waves, family firms and management buyouts.' *Small Business Economics* 47 (3): 803–817.

Howorth, C.A. (2001) 'Small firms' demand for finance: a research note.' *International Small Business Journal* 19 (4): 78–86.

References

Jensen, M.C. and Meckling, W.H. (1976) 'Theory of the firm: managerial behavior, agency costs and ownership structure.' *Journal of Financial Economics* 3: 305–360.

Kidwell, R., Eddleston, K., Cater III, J.J. and Kellermanns, F. (2013) 'How one bad family member can undermine the family firm: preventing the Fredo effect.' *Business Horizons* 56: 5–12.

Kolm, S.-C. (2006) 'Introduction to the economics of giving, altruism and reciprocity.' In S.-C. Kolm and J.M. Ythier (eds) *Handbook of the Economics of Giving, Altruism and Reciprocity* (Vol. 1). Elsevier, pp. 1–114.

Kotlar, J., Cuomo, F., Gaia, S. and Zattoni, A. (2019) *Corporate Governance in Large UK Family Firms: An IFB Research Foundation Report*. London: IFB Research Foundation.

KPMG. (2018) Female family business CEOs' tips for success. KPMG Australia March 2018, https://home.kpmg/xx/en/home/insights/2018/03/female-family-business-ceo-tips-for-success.html.

Lambrecht, J. and Lievens, J. (2008) 'Pruning the family tree: an unexplored path to family business continuity and family harmony.' *Family Business Review* 21 (4): 295–313.

LeCouvie, K. (2016) *Co-CEO Structure: Are Two Heads Better than One in a Family Business?* Chicago, IL: Family Business Consulting Group Publications.

Lewin, K. (1943) 'Psychology and the process of group living.' *Journal of Social Psychology* 17: 113–131.

Mandl, I. (2008) Overview of family business relevant issues: Contract No. 30-CE-0164021/00–51 final report. Vienna: Austrian Institute for SME Research.

Mayer, R.C., Davis, J.H. and Schoorman, F.D. (1995) 'An integrative model of organizational trust.' *Academy of Management Review* 20 (3): 709–734.

Melin, L. and Nordqvist, M. (2007) 'The reflexive dynamics of institutionalization: the case of the family business.' *Strategic Organization* 5 (3): 321–333.

Meyer, J.P. and Allen, N.J. (1997) *Commitment in the Workplace: Theory Research and Application*. London: Sage.

Miller, D. and Le Breton-Miller, I. (2005) *Managing for the Long Run: Lessons in Competitive Advantage from Great Family Businesses*. Boston, MA: Harvard Business School Press.

Morris, M.H., Williams, R.O., Allen, J.A. and Avila, R.A. (1997) 'Correlates of success in family business transitions.' *Journal of Business Venturing* 12 (5): 341–422.

Nahapiet, J. and Ghoshal, S. (1998) 'Social capital, intellectual capital, and the organizational advantage.' *Academy of Management Review* 23: 242–266.

Ortega, B. (1999) *Sam We Trust: The Untold Story of Sam Walton and How Wal-mart Is Devouring the World*. London: Kogan Page.

Pae, P. (2019) 'South Korea's Chaebol' on Bloomberg.com, www.bloomberg.com/quicktake/republic-samsung, updated 29 August 2019.

Parada, M.J., Nordqvist, M. and Gimeno, A. (2010) 'Institutionalizing the family business: the role of professional associations in fostering a change of values.' *Family Business Review* 23 (4): 355–372.

Pearson, A.W., Carr, J.C. and Shaw, J.C. (2008) 'Toward a theory of familiness: a social capital perspective.' *Entrepreneurship Theory and Practice* 32 (6): 949–969.

Pendergast, J., Ward, J. and De Pontet, S.B. (2011) *Building A Successful Family Business Board: A Guide for Leaders, Directors and Families*. New York: Palgrave MacMillan.

Pieper, T.M., Klein, S.B. and Jaskiewicz, P. (2008) 'The impact of goal alignment on board existence and top management team composition: evidence from family-influenced businesses.' *Journal of Small Business Management* 46 (3): 372–394.

Poutziouris, P., Sitorus, S. and Chittenden, F. (2002) *The Financial Affairs of Family Companies*. London: Sand Aire Private Equity and Grant Thornton.

Poutziouris, P.Z. (2001) 'The views of family companies on venture capital: empirical evidence from the UK small to medium-size enterprising economy.' *Family Business Review* 14 (3): 277–291.

Reay, T. and Steier, L. (2004) 'The case of the prodigal daughter.' In J. Astrachan, P. Poutziouris and K. Soufani (eds) *Family Business Casebook Annual 2004*. Kennesaw, GA: Cox Family Enterprise Center, pp. 77–90.

Rey-Garcia, M. and Puig-Raposo, N. (2013) 'Globalization and the organization of family philanthropy: a case of isomorphism?' *Business History* 55: 1019–1046.

Rosa, P., Howorth, C. and Discua Cruz, A. (2014) 'Habitual and portfolio entrepreneurship and the family in business.' In L. Melin, M. Nordqvist and P. Sharma (eds) *The SAGE Handbook of Family Business*. London: Sage, pp. 364–382.

Roscoe, P., Discua Cruz, A. and Howorth, C. (2013) 'How does an old firm learn new tricks? A material account of entrepreneurial opportunity.' *Business History* 55: 53–72.

Rose, M.B. (1986) *The Gregs of Quarry Bank Mill: The Rise and Decline of a Family Firm (1750–1914)*. Cambridge, MA: Cambridge University Press.

Rubin, S. (2009) *Foreword in B. Breeze, Natural Philanthropists: Findings of the Family Business Philanthropy and Social Responsibility Inquiry*. London: IFB Research Foundation, p. 5.

Salvato, C. and Corbetta, G. (2014) 'Strategic content and process in family business.' In L. Melin, M. Nordqvist and P. Sharma (eds) *The Sage Handbook of Family Business*. London: Sage, pp. 295–320.

Sarasvathy, S.D. (2001) 'Causation and effectuation: toward a theoretical shift from economic inevitability to entrepreneurial contingency.' *Academy of Management Review* 26 (2): 243–263.

Severino Bueno, I., Rodriguez Polanci, B. and Perez Estrella, C. (2019) 'Cigar family charitable foundation: the birthplace of so many dreams, from emotions to strategy.' In C.G. Muller, I.C. Botero, A. Discua Cruz and R. Subramanian (eds) *Family Firms in Latin America*. New York: Routledge.

Shane, S. and Venkataraman, S. (2000) 'The promise of entrepreneurship as a field of research.' *Academy of Management Review* 25 (1): 217–226.

Shanker, M.C. and Astrachan, J.H. (1996) 'Myths and realities: family businesses contribution to the US economy – a framework for assessing family business statistics.' *Family Business Review* 9 (2): 107–124.

Sharma, P. (2004) 'An overview of the field of family business studies: current status and directions for the future.' *Family Business Review* 17 (1): 1–36.

Smilor, R.W. (1997) 'Entrepreneurship: reflections on a subversive activity.' *Journal of Business Venturing* 12 (5): 341–421.

Sonnenfeld, J. (1988) *The Hero's Farewell: What Happens When CEOs Retire*. Oxford: Oxford University Press.

Stead, V. (2017) 'Belonging and women entrepreneurs: women's navigation of gendered assumptions in entrepreneurial practice.' *International Small Business Journal* 35 (1): 61–77.

Steier, L. and Muethel, M. (2014) 'Trust and family businesses.' In L. Melin, M. Nordqvist and P. Sharma (eds) *The Sage Handbook of Family Business*. London: Sage, pp. 498–513.

Stewart, A. and Hitt, M.A. (2012) 'Why can't a family business be more like a nonfamily business? Modes of professionalization in family firms.' *Family Business Review* 25 (1): 58–86.

Suehiro, A. and Wailerdsak, N. (2004) 'Family business in Thailand: its management, governance, and future challenges.' *ASEAN Economic Bulletin* 21 (1): 81–93.

Sutherland, J.W. (1975) *Systems: Analysis, Administration, and Architecture.* New York: Van Nostrand.

Tagiuri, R. and Davis, J.A. (1982) 'Bivalent attributes of the family firm.' *Family Business Review* 9 (2): 199–208. Working Paper, Harvard Business School, Cambridge. Reprinted 1996.

Tappeiner, F., Howorth, C., Achleitner, A.K. and Schraml, S. (2012) 'Demand for private equity minority investments: a study of large family firms.' *Journal of Family Business Strategy* 3 (1): 38–51.

Tidd, J. and Bessant, J.R. (2015) *Innovation and Entrepreneurship.* Wiley.

Ucbasaran, D., Wright, M. and Westhead, P. (2003) 'A longitudinal study of habitual entrepreneurs: starters and acquirers.' *Entrepreneurship & Regional Development* 15 (3): 207–228.

Van de Ven, A. (1989) 'Nothing is quite so practical as a good theory.' *Academy of Management Review* 14 (4): 486–489.

Villalonga, B. and Amit, R. (2006) 'How do family ownership, control and management affect firm value?' *Journal of Financial Economics* 80: 385–417.

Walton, S. with Huey, J. (1993) *Made in America: My Story.* New York: Bantam Doubleday Books.

Weick, K.E. (1989) 'Theory construction as disciplined imagination.' *Academy of Management Review* 14 (4): 516–531.

Westhead, P. and Cowling, M. (1997) 'Performance contrasts between family and non-family unquoted companies in the UK.' *International Journal of Entrepreneurial Behaviour & Research* 3: 30–52.

Westhead, P. and Cowling, M. (1998) 'Family firm research: the need for a methodological rethink.' *Entrepreneurship Theory and Practice* 23 (1): 31–56.

Westhead, P. and Howorth, C. (2006) 'Ownership and management issues associated with family firm performance and company objectives.' *Family Business Review* 19 (4): 301–316.

Westhead, P. and Howorth, C. (2007) '"Types" of private family firms: an exploratory conceptual and empirical analysis.' *Entrepreneurship and Regional Development* 19 (5): 405–431.

Wilson, N., Wright, M. and Scholes, L. (2013) 'Family business survival and the role of boards.' *Entrepreneurship Theory and Practice* 37 (6): 1369–1389.

Wright, M. and Vanaelst, I. (2009) 'Introduction.' In M. Wright and I. Vanaelst (eds) *Entrepreneurial Teams and New Business Creation* (Vol. 13). Cheltenham: Edward Elgar, pp. iix–xli.

Zellweger, T., Sieger, P. and Englisch, P. (2015) *Coming Home or Breaking Free: Reloaded.* GUESSS Report. EY Family Business Center of Excellence, EYGM Ltd.

Zildjian. (2019) Zildjian website, https://zildjian.com, accessed 3 September 2019.

Index

advisory board 16, 56, 89, 100
agency theory 13–14, 36–37, 58, 59, 93, 123, 125–126
altruism 45, 145–146, 162

Bettys and Taylors 2, 7, 94–95
Bibby Line 67–68: Sir Michael Bibby 113
board of directors 54–57, 60, 62, 90, 92, 94, 118, 124
Brown Brothers 100–101
Brown, Eliza 91, 100–101

Carnegie, Andrew 88, 139
Carnegie effect 88, 117
Carroll, Archie 141
Chandler, Alfred 4, 155, 162
charitable giving 7–8, 94, 139, 142–143, 147, 148, 149, 151–152, 153
charitable trusts 150, 151–152
Cigar Family Charitable Foundation 146
Clarks Shoes 47–48, 66–67, 92
Cobham 129–130
Columbia Sportswear 46–47
community engagement 120, 143–144, 145, 148–149, 153
constructive philanthropy 152
corporate social responsibility 141–142, 147
CSR *see* corporate social responsibility
CSR Pyramid 141

Dale Photographic 167
Danfoss 79–80
death 19, 42, 46, 84, 91, 100, 111
definition of family business 30–33
dividends 16, 47, 55, 122, 128, 131, 135
divorce 18, 19, 20, 86–87
Dennis Family 61–62

E and J Gallo 41–43
effectuation 73
embeddedness 7, 66, 68, 125, 138, 145, 153
exit strategies 96–98, 129, 130, 131, 132–134

faith: religious 148–149
familiness 33–34, 64, 65, 67–69
family agreement, *see* family charter
family assembly 51
family business groups 69, 73, 74–75, 77
family charter 49–51, 90
family conflict 45, 49, 69, 104, 110, 131
family constitution *see* family charter
family council 51–52, 60, 61
family entrepreneurial teams 69, 73, 75–77
family meetings 51
family office 52–53
Fiat 31
Field C P J 119–120: Charlie Field 115–116
finance: demand for 127; supply of 125–126
finance – strategy 128
football clubs 33, 94, 143–144, 153
foundations 139, 140, 143, 144, 146, 148–149, 150
F-PEC scale 34
Fredo effect 69

genogram 20–22
giving 139, 140, 142–143, 145–146
The Golden Rule 146, 148
governance – corporate 53–57
governance – family 48–53
Gucci 117–118
Guinness 60–61, 99

habitual entrepreneurs 72
heterogeneity of family firms 33–39
historical perspective 4, 156–160, 164, 167

information asymmetry 125–126, 127
inheritance tax 95, 111
innovation 109, 110, 115, 128, 160–165

joint CEOs 93–95
Joseph Rowntree Foundation 8, 139, 148–149
Juventus FC 31, 143
JW Lees 169–170

liquidity of shares 16, 122, 128, 135
long-term orientation 165–166
longevity 157–160
LVMH 84, 85, 87, 99–100

McIlhenny family – *see* Tabasco
management buyouts (MBO) 58, 97, 132
management succession 90–95
Mars 3, 30

nepotism 47, 162
next generation 96, 106, 109, 112–116
non-executive directors 55, 56, 129

oldest family business 156–157, 158–159
ownership succession 83–89, 95–98

path dependence 157, 167
pecking order hypothesis 127
Pentland Group 3: Stephen Rubin 147, 148
philanthropy – definition 140
political influence 144, 166
portfolio entrepreneurship 72–77
power 80–81, 84, 104–105, 151
private equity 127–130
procedural justice 85, 110–111, 131
primogeniture 85, 86, 91, 111
professionalization 57–58
pruning the family tree 70, 131
psychological ownership 16, 86, 116
public listing 130

reciprocity 145–146, 148
retirement styles 47, 83–84, 88–90

Samsung 161, 162, 166–167
selling the family business 96, 132–133
share buyback – *see* pruning the family tree
shareholders, minor and majority 23–25, 30–33, 47, 77, 92, 122, 123
shareholders, rights and responsibilities 123–125
Sharma's four types of family firms 35
sibling rivalry 41, 104
social capital 63, 65–69
socialisation 116, 119–120
socio-emotional wealth 13, 122
stakeholders 17, 54, 141, 148
stewardship 36–37, 52, 69–70, 138, 147
stop-gap manager 93
Stronach 135–137
succession planning 19, 86, 88, 103–107, 107–110
succession process 107–110, 112–114
successor selection 85–86, 111
survival 111, 157, 162, 165

Tabasco 161
Tata Sons 30, 33, 75, 140, 151–153
tax 84, 111, 150
Three-Circle Model 14–18
Three-Dimensional Development Model 18–20
transgenerational entrepreneurship 65
trust and trustworthiness 45, 48, 68–69, 70–72, 110
trusts – ownership 24, 25, 75, 87, 136–137, 151–153
types of family firms 34–39

valuation of business 131, 132–134

Walmart 3, 31, 149
Westhead and Howorth types of family firms 37–39
Wilsden Equestrian Centre 153–154
Wm Grant and Sons 159–160

Zildjian cymbals 159, 161